Piotr Idczak, Ida Musiałkowska
Financial Engineering in Sustainable Funding of Urban Development in the EU

Piotr Idczak, Ida Musiałkowska

Financial Engineering in Sustainable Funding of Urban Development in the EU

—

Reflections on the JESSICA Initiative

DE GRUYTER

ISBN 978-3-11-153073-4
e-ISBN (PDF) 978-3-11-076219-8
e-ISBN (EPUB) 978-3-11-076223-5

Library of Congress Control Number: 2022935815

Bibliographic information published by the Deutsche Nationalbibliothek
The Deutsche Nationalbibliothek lists this publication in the Deutsche Nationalbibliografie; detailed bibliographic data are available on the internet at http://dnb.dnb.de.

© 2024 Walter de Gruyter GmbH, Berlin/Boston
This volume is text- and page-identical with the hardback published in 2022.
Cover image: Piotr Idczak; EU flag: shaadjutt / iStock / Getty Images Plus

www.degruyter.com

Contents

List of figures —— VII

List of tables —— IX

List of abbreviations —— XI

Introduction —— 1

1 Background – urban economics —— 11
1.1 The economic dimension of urbanisation —— 11
1.2 Agglomeration economies and diseconomies —— 18
1.3 The importance of "place" —— 26
1.4 Market failures in urban growth —— 34
1.5 The intra-urban effects of agglomeration economies on cities —— 41

2 The theoretical underpinning of a place-based perspective on sustainable urban development —— 49
2.1 Urban policy as a response to urban needs —— 49
2.1.1 Urban land use planning and policy-making —— 49
2.1.2 Strategic approach and urban policy fundamental for effective interventions —— 51
2.1.3 Territorial integrated approach —— 53
2.2 Urban regeneration —— 56
2.2.1 Purpose and concept of urban regeneration —— 56
2.2.2 Urban regeneration policy framework —— 63
2.2.3 Urban regeneration themes —— 72
2.3 Model of integrated approach to urban regeneration —— 87

3 Urban policy as a part of cohesion policy – towards repayable assistance —— 99
3.1 Cohesion policy objectives and framework —— 99
3.2 Cohesion policy support for sustainable urban development —— 102
3.3 Rationale for the revolving mechanism in urban policy —— 107
3.4 Principles of repayable financial instruments used for urban development —— 111

4 JESSICA initiative — 115
4.1   Legal foundations — 115
4.2   Institutional system of JESSICA funding — 118
4.3   Rules on the eligibility of project expenditure — 122
4.4   Ex-ante analyses of the implementation of JESSICA in Poland — 124
4.5   Implementation of JESSICA funding in Poland — 127

5 JESSICA initiative and sustainable urban development – empirical evidence from Poland — 135
5.1   Rationale of the research and objectives — 135
5.2   Data collection and preparation — 140
5.3   Methods and research design — 141
5.4   Results, analysis and discussions — 153
5.5   Synthesis and assessment: lessons and added value — 194

6 Overall assessment and policy recommendations — 199
6.1   Added value and challenges — 199
6.2   Policy recommendations — 203

Conclusions — 211

References — 219

Index — 239

List of figures

Figure 1: External economies of urbanisation
Figure 2: The spatially hierarchical organisation of the urban system
Figure 3: The formation process for deprived urban areas
Figure 4: Different options for area-based regeneration at the local level
Figure 5: The model of the integrated approach to urban regeneration applicable at the European level
Figure 6: The prism of urban sustainability
Figure 7: The JESSICA institutional system in the years 2007–2013
Figure 8: The institutional system of JESSICA in Poland in the years 2007–2013
Figure 9: JESSICA regions and the location of JESSICA projects in Poland
Figure 10: Operationalisation of the assessment of the JESSICA projects
Figure 11: Mutual dependencies of the involved variables
Figure 12: Effect display for the predictors of the project capacity to generate revenues
Figure 13: Interaction effect of the company status on the project capacity to generate revenues
Figure 14: Interaction effect of the project capacity to generate revenues on positive market effects
Figure 15: Effect display for the predictors of the project capacity to create social impacts
Figure 16: Assessment of the JESSICA dimensions by projects implemented in Poland in 2007–2015 (results of the survey)
Figure 17: Histogram of the composite indicator
Figure 18: Composite indicator in Polish regions by type of project and type of beneficiary
Figure 19: Dendrogram for the Genie linkage algorithm of the composite indicator
Figure 20: Clusters by the composite indicator
Figure 21: Clusters by the value of the JESSICA projects
Figure 22: Distribution of clusters of projects in regions
Figure 23: Distribution of clusters of projects according to type of beneficary
Figure 24: Location of the JESSICA project in Poznań
Figure 25: Sub-indicators in the territorial impact assessment of JESSICA projects implemented in Poznań
Figure 26: Indicators in the assessment of the territorial impact of JESSICA projects implemented in Poznań
Figure 27: SDE for the spatial spread of JESSICA projects in Poland
Figure 28: Location of JESSICA projects in Mazowieckie in the context of MA
Figure 29: Location of JESSICA projects in Pomorskie in the context of MA
Figure 30: Location of JESSICA projects in Śląskie in the context of MA
Figure 31: Location of JESSICA projects in Wielkopolskie in the context of MA
Figure 32: Location of JESSICA projects in Zachodniopomorskie in the context of MA
Figure 33: Distribution of JESSICA funding across Polish cities
Figure 34: Mutual dependencies of the city's size and the value of the JESSICA loan
Figure 35: Proposal for a new JESSICA institutional system

https://doi.org/10.1515/9783110762198-001

List of tables

Table 1: Forces affecting geographical concentration
Table 2: Dimensions and initiatives of urban regeneration
Table 3: JESSICA in the Polish regional operational programmes for the years 2007–2013
Table 4: Properties of an ellipse for the purpose of the overall interpretations
Table 5: Number of JESSICA projects implemented in 2007–2015 according to their capacity to generate revenues
Table 6: Identification of differences based on the Wilcoxon rank sum test
Table 7: Coefficients of logistic regression for JESSICA projects implemented in Poland
Table 8: Results of ANOVA for JESSICA projects implemented in Poland
Table 9: Characteristics of clusters of projects by JESSICA support areas
Table 10: SDE parameters of JESSICA projects in five regions
Table 11: Distribution of JESSICA projects and funding among Polish cities

List of abbreviations

BGK	Bank Gospodarstwa Krajowego (Polish development bank)
BOŚ	Bank Ochrony Środowiska S.A. (Polish development bank focused on ecology)
BZWBK	Bank Zachodni WBK S.A. (Polish private bank)
CEB	Council of Europe Development Bank
COCOF	European Commission's Coordinating Committee of the Funds
CP	EU Cohesion Policy
CPT	Central Place Theory
DG Regio	European Commission's Directorate General for Regional and Urban Policy
EIB	European Investment Bank
EIF	European Investment Fund
ERDF	European Regional Development Fund
ESIF	European Structural and Investment Funds
EU	European Union
FEIs	Financial engineering instruments
FUAW	Urban Functional Area of the City of Warsaw in the Mazowieckie region
HF	Holding fund
IPSUD	Integrated plan for sustainable urban development
IURP	Integrated urban regeneration programme
JESSICA	Joint European Support for Investments in City Areas
LUP	Land use planning
MAs	Metropolitan areas of the regional capital cities
MUSV	Metropolis of the Upper Silesian Valley in the Śląskie region
MVA	Multivariate analysis
OP(s)	Operational Programme(s)
PIP	Potential impact of a project
PI	Policy intensity
PMA	Poznań Metropolitan Area in the Wielkopolskie region
PPPs	Public–private partnerships
ROP(s)	Regional Operational Programme(s)
SDE	Standard deviational ellipse
SMA	Szczecin Metropolitan Area in the Zachodniopomorskie region
TCMA	Tri-City Metropolitan Area (Gdańsk-Gdynia-Sopot) in the Pomorskie region
TIA	Territorial impact assessment
TIM	Territorial impacts indicator
UDF	Urban development fund
US	Urban sensibility

Introduction

> To plan for the improvement of the urban scene
> whilst ignoring economic considerations would be to invite disaster.
> (Goodall, 1972)

Cities and urban agglomerations have often been described as engines of economic growth and development for regions and countries. On the one hand, they offer access to a number of jobs, cultural activities and personal development opportunities that make the city a nice place to live. On the other hand, they provide a labour force as well as a wealth of talent and expertise within the local workforce, and a sales market which undoubtedly make them great places to do business. The result of this is that they undergo changes over time, which is reflected in the continuous modifications of their visual appearance as well as in the relatively quick customisation of various urban functions to inhabitants' needs (Mikrut-Majeranek, 2015). Cities are places of permanent transformation in which the dominant discourse is about growth understood both in terms of wealth and urban expansion (Thorns, 2002). The continuous impact of agglomeration economies implies that consumers, workers and businesses tend to accumulate in a place or area, since they can benefit, together with various institutions, from positive externalities and increasing returns to scale. However, the concentration of these resources in a location with a high density of different activities may also lead to negative externalities such as traffic congestion, pollution, price increases and a lack of affordable housing, urban sprawl, rising costs of urban infrastructure, social tensions and higher crime rates, a degraded environment, health problems and as a consequence a reduced quality of life (Capello & Faggian, 2002; Duranton & Kerr, 2018; Glaeser, 2010; Hołuj, 2018; Krugman & Wells, 2012; Paradowska, 2006; Regnier & Legras, 2018; Stiglitz, 2013; van den Bergh, 2010; Verhoef & Nijkamp, 2008). In what follows, it is argued that the same market forces that makes a city "thick", cohesive and well performing may also result in the occurrence of inequalities inside the urban settlements. This view, among other things, is substantiated by the findings in the literature on segregation in European cities. Musterd and colleagues (2017) and Fainstein and Fainstein (2018) found that in some places situated in inner-city areas local populations suffer from a concentration of inequalities: poor hous-

---

Piotr Idczak, Ida Musiałkowska, Poznań University of Economics and Business, Department of European Studies. Address: Al. Niepodległości 10, 61-875 Poznań. E-mail: piotr.idczak@ue.poznan.pl; ida.musialkowska@ue.poznan.pl

ing, unemployment, low-quality education, difficulties or even the inability to access some public services. Their findings also strongly suggest that the concentration of inequalities results in social and spatial polarisation. The unequal distribution of wealth in the urban space leads to a territorial division of residential areas into those inhabited by the richer or poorer groups of society. Thus, what clearly emerges are two separate and contradictive zones existing alongside one another, namely on the one hand, areas of stability and affluence and on the other, deprived areas experiencing a poor quality of life. A typical pattern of urban deprivation demonstrates that the most deprived areas are generally located in the older districts of the cities – i.e. zones with declining industry, riddled with poor housing, blighted by unemployment and socially excluded from more prosperous districts.

Accordingly, although cities are generally considered a driving force of the modern socio-economic development of regions and countries, as the European Commission (2011a) reported, they do not grow uniformly, especially when one takes into account the spatial dimension of their development. Not only does this concern the significant differences noticeable in the level of their growth rates in the last decades but may also result in the occurrence of intra-urban inequalities and the interlinked deprivations related to spatial variations among urban settlements. It is indeed important to acknowledge that cities also face the serious threat of economic stagnation or even decline (European Commission, 2011a; OECD, 2018). Alongside the unprecedented growth in recent decades, cities are considered the main locus of acute problems such as ageing, unemployment, exclusion, segregation etc. A comparison of European cities' situations indicates that they suffer, to varying degrees, from an increasing share of the population at risk of poverty, low work-intensity households and post-industrial areas resulting from the challenges of increased global competitiveness (Budde et al., 2010; Colini et al., 2013). The progressive degradation of urban infrastructure and adverse demographic changes have not only had a negative impact on the local labour market but also discourage businesses from investing.

A similar picture of intra-urban disparities also emerges when looking at the situation of Polish towns and cities. Generally speaking, a remarkable feature of the development trends of Polish cities is that despite a significant increase in average living standards over time, there is evidence not only of growing social disparities but also of the poor getting poorer. Existing inequalities, arising from the progressive degradation of the material substance, such as buildings and urban infrastructure, as well as adverse demographic changes, have a negative impact on the local labour market and discourage businesses from investing (Jarczewski & Ziobrowski, 2010; OECD, 2011; Węcławowicz, Łotocka, & Baucz,

2010). Moreover, cities are characterised in particular by a decline in their population coupled with an intense process of suburbanisation (Heffner, 2016; Stryjakiewicz, Ciesiółka, & Jaroszewska, 2012). Some city districts, including city centres and even entire cities, have lost their original economic functions which, as a consequence of fewer labour market opportunities, has affected the polarisation between urban inhabitants. An observable sign of urban transition is also the relatively large share of post-industrial, post-railway and post-military areas in the urban space. In fact, these manifold urban changes concern various areas of public life, and their underlying causes are undoubtedly of a structural nature. Most importantly, however, these urban changes, reflected in increasing inequalities, become highly visible primarily at the spatially concentrated levels of cities and their surroundings.

Based on the above it can be concluded that urban areas are the places where most social and economic challenges play out. Existing inequalities call for multidimensional measures to combat those development difficulties. However, only such remedial measures should be taken that, in response to the prior identified overriding reasons, ensure proper handling of the conflicts of interest expressed by the stakeholders concerned. In order to tackle a wide range of problems encountered in deprived urban areas, regeneration projects are promoted to support the sustainable urban development and growth of cities.[1] To address weakening links between economic growth and social progress – and the resulting growth in income disparities and socio-spatial segregation – and at the same time give due consideration to cities' great potential to contribute to the creation of jobs and sustainable economic growth, it was decided at the beginning of the 2010s to incorporate formally the urban dimension into the framework of EU cohesion policy. Nevertheless, there were specific objectives and possibilities to delegate to cities funds dealing with urban issues within the programmes of the cohesion policy between 2007 and 2013. Furthermore, fiscal turbulences caused by the financial crisis of the late 2000s, which greatly weakened public finances, led to the European Commission's decision to estab-

---

[1] Sustainable urban development sets the way forward for the safeguarding of welfare and safety of the residents of cities in the face of continuous structural transformation and climate change. It integrates various policy actions aimed at achieving a balance between the growth of urban areas and protection of the environment, while taking into account citizens' needs and expectations with regard to living, employment, income, social services, public spaces and transportation in the urban areas. This concept stands for a major set of planning principles and objectives for cities that needs to be capable of providing positive environmental outcomes accompanied at the same time by advantages related to human health and well-being. Sustainable urban development focuses on people. For more see Taylor (2021).

lish the JESSICA initiative (Joint European Support for Investments in City Areas). It was put forward in order to implement regeneration projects within an innovative framework of a revolving financing system. The underpinning aim of JESSICA was to support investments that need to generate profit, while contributing to sustainable urban development. In other words, the assumption here was to create sustainable funding – i.e. a process of investment decisions that take into account the environmental, social and governance factors of a project or series of activities. Thus, the rationale was to propose an different approach offering a more sustainable alternative to the assistance traditionally provided through grants. Further, expected benefits included the possibility of leveraging additional private sector funding and stimulating collaboration between the territorial authorities, financial institutions and private investors, which would allow the pooling of expertise and the building of new kinds of partnerships. Thus, overall, the rationale behind JESSICA was to use financial engineering instruments[2] to promote more effective and efficient urban regeneration initiatives.

The key challenge for the JESSICA initiative was to make optimal use of the synergies between the revolving investment funds and the integrated urban planning objectives. Such an approach was expected to result in many possible benefits for all stakeholders of the urban development process. First, structural funds provided in the form of the repayable model would recycle financial resources and thus enhance and accelerate investments in disadvantaged urban areas. A further benefit would be a catalytic effect to intensify both the public and private sectors and their financial and managerial capabilities to cooperate effectively and to develop joint urban development projects. Finally, the financial engineering instruments would not only support and promote sustainable urban development but also provide incentives that lower the risk to capital investments and consequently allow overcoming existing market failures. In general, the JESSICA initiative was supposed to deliver on the sustainable outcomes sought by cities. By improving the availability of capital and its risk–return profile in combination with an integrated approach, multi-level governance and partnership, this initiative would bring real added value to urban communities.

---

[2] The term financial engineering refers to the variety of strategies aimed at designing, developing and implementing new financial instruments or innovative financial products to address specific financial issues. It consists in using financial expertise and knowledge which, in combination with analytical techniques and empirical methods, should facilitate taking advantage of new financial opportunities and solving various economic problems. Financial engineering is quite often applied to leverage funds from different sources of financing (both private and public) to promote particular types of investment.

However, some studies of JESSICA that were carried out at the end of the implementation period of 2007–2013 clearly reported both shortcomings and achievements that were far from the expected goals. These included: weaknesses in the project assessment procedure that could result in a lack of addressing actual market needs, little real impact on the ground and a relatively low real leverage rate vis-à-vis the private sector and a disappointing multiplier effect (Bode, 2015, pp. 174–178); the novelty of JESSICA, combined with a lack of expertise and an existing "grant-framework culture" which led to uncertainty, especially in the public sector with regard to the use of financial revolving instruments and the creation of public–private partnerships (Fotino, 2014, pp. 245–251); cooperation problems between the public authorities and private entities that could cause tensions, misunderstandings and clashes of interest (Dąbrowski, 2014, 2015). Other studies pointed out that key decisions on project selection were made by financial institutions, whose operating objectives could differ from the objectives of the EU cohesion policy. As a consequence, the benefits assumed by JESSICA's designers at the EU level could be only partially achieved (Musiałkowska & Idczak, 2016). In a later paper (Nadler & Nadler, 2018), the authors identified a few other weak elements, such as the incapacity of private financial institutions to risk sharing, the relatively high implementation and administrative costs, and low financing at the project level. Overall, it was quickly apparent that significant bottlenecks and obstacles were hindering the effective and efficient realisation of JESSICA (EIB, 2012b).

The pace of the implementation of projects within the framework of JESSICA has proved to be insufficient in Poland, too. In an exploratory study, Musiałkowska and Idczak (2016) found that the scope of projects was very often limited to the infrastructural investments and did not consider the regeneration process in a comprehensive manner. As a result, the projects implemented could improve the physical urban structures, but did not tackle social and spatial problems. However, at the preliminary stage of research, understanding of the socio-economic dimension of sustainable urban regeneration policy remained limited, especially concerning the assessment and measurement of impacts of the JESSICA projects. There was therefore a clear need for further research in this field. In-depth analysis of the positive and negative socio-economic results of projects implemented within the JESSICA framework would clearly be worthwhile. Moreover, there was a need to answer whether it would be possible to apply financial engineering instruments within the framework of EU cohesion policy in a way that would take into consideration the comprehensive character of the regeneration process of deprived urban areas.

Therefore, the overall objective of this research is to determine whether the JESSICA initiative as a revolving funding instrument is an effective tool for supporting urban regeneration activities and contributes to achieving sustainable urban development. A well-functioning urban regeneration process requires an integrated approach comprehensively encompassing all components of the spatial, social and economic dimensions of urban development. Such an approach requires strategic planning, good cooperation and effective coordination between all the actors involved and at each phase of the regeneration process (from diagnosing to implementing). Incorporating a spatial dimension into the process of socio-economic transformation is one of the key elements of a successful regeneration of deprived urban areas. Thus, due to the complexity of the JESSICA initiative, with regard to both the functioning of the institutional funding model (financial engineering mechanisms) and the expected urban effects of the JESSICA projects, the main objective was broken down into two groups of detailed objectives: first, the specific objectives related to the policy level at which JESSICA aims to promote urban regeneration and sustainable urban development;[3] and second, the operational objectives related to the implementation level at which the JESSICA projects should be both financially sustainable (during the investment and operational stages) and socio-economically desirable (by contributing to the creation of social well-being). The first group of specific research objectives included:

1. to define the initiatives that, through an integrated approach, contribute to improving people's living conditions and business environment in deprived urban areas, including spatial, economic, social, environmental and governance aspects of urban regeneration;
2. to identify the successful regeneration measures applied so far in selected European cities in the context of the integrated approach to urban regeneration (integrated urban regeneration) and construct a model of integrated urban regeneration applicable at the European level;
3. to determine the position of urban regeneration against the so-called integrated approach aimed at achieving territorial cohesion;
4. to investigate and assess the rules and institutional system used as part of JESSICA and compare them to the model approach to integrated urban regeneration;
5. to verify the effectiveness of the JESSICA initiative as an instrument to improve the situation in deprived urban areas and reduce urban inequalities, thus contributing to achieving the goals of urban policy at the national and European levels;

---

3 The differences between these two terms are explained in section 2.2.1.

6. to draw lessons for decision-makers and for the ongoing policy debates on the ways to improve regeneration initiatives in deprived urban areas with the use of financial engineering instruments.

The second group covered operational objectives that aimed at investigating the implementation level of the JESSICA initiative on the subject of the realisation of the JESSICA project and the effects these projects generated in urban areas are presented in Chapter 5. These objectives further supplement and specify the particular objective no. 5.

The spatial scope of this study in reference to the descriptive research encompasses European countries. As far as the empirical examination is concerned, the scope covers the five Polish regions – i.e. those which implemented the JESSICA initiative. The main reason for the choice of regions for the purpose of this study was simple – among European countries Poland was the biggest beneficiary, and the amount of funds earmarked by the five Polish regions for JESSICA support was the third largest contribution among all the EU Member States that decided to launch JESSICA. The empirical analysis builds on a dataset containing details on all the projects implemented within the framework of the JESSICA initiative in Poland during the 2007–2015 period. This dataset was created personally by the authors on the basis of information made available by the Marshal Offices of all regions implementing the JESSICA initiative and institutions acting as managers of the urban development funds. In addition, data regarding projects were supplemented by the results of the examination of other sources such as project descriptions, policy reports, official websites and field studies etc.

Investigation of the implementation of the various intervention initiatives in terms of their efficiency and effectiveness in achieving the objectives set out at the policy level covers many aspects and requires the use of an approach based on the positivism paradigm. A main goal of positivist inquiry is to generate explanatory associations or causal relationships that finally contribute to ultimately lead to an explanation of the phenomena in question. In this case, it consists in examining causal relationships existing between the public intervention actions (projects) undertaken and their effects in the form of achieved (previously intended) states (objectives) or stimulation of processes permanently triggering the achievement of these states. Such recognition of the research process boils down to confrontation of the adopted intervention mechanism and its outcome with the theoretical model of its operation. As a result, it is possible to demonstrate the success or failure of an intervention and, in the case of failure, to indicate remedial action. To this end, it was reasonable to use a research approach applicable to the process of evaluation of public programmes. This, in turn, requires the use of elements of realistic evaluation (Chen, 2012; Olejniczak, 2008, pp. 32–33; Pawson & Tilley, 1997). The approach based on a realistic evaluation has one more advantage which is essential to the study. This approach does not impose any specific methods. Moreover, it requires the use of multiple methods and multiple data sources that should be suitable and properly chosen to fit the needs and to take into account the existing opportunities (Pawson & Tilley, 2001, p. 323). It is assumed that both qualitative and quantitative methods can be used. In the theoretical part of the study, based on the descriptive research, an extensive literature survey of concepts and theories as well as previous research findings was carried out, followed by logical (epistemological) reasoning, a systemic approach and modelling. The empirical part of the study included many methods and techniques that were used depending on the particular objectives to be achieved – e.g. for binary variables (non-parametric statistical hypothesis tests, logistic regression and ANOVA analysis), for research based on experts' judgements (principal component analysis, Genie linkage algorithm and modified TARGET_TIA as a territorial impact assessment technique), and for assessing spatial distribution (the directional distribution method [standard deviational ellipse – SDE] and aesthetic mappings). Other methods were used in order to supplement the reasoning possibilities and meet specific needs of the study, including, among others: geocoding, field studies, the observation participatory method and interviews.

The book comprises six chapters. Each chapter takes a broad theme and considers issues that represent particular stages of the reasoning leading to the final conclusions. Chapter 1 discusses the various theoretical ways to understand urban economics and how market forces affect the development of cities. Chapter 2 provides the background to urban policy and urban regeneration, explaining the theoretical and conceptual underpinning of the integrated place-based approaches. It also extends the knowledge of urban regeneration by elaborating the set of activities that under the umbrella of urban regeneration should be helpful in reversing the deprivation of inner-city areas, and by providing a model of integrated urban regeneration applicable at the European level. Chapter 3 describes the urban dimension in EU cohesion policy and details the regulatory provisions and rationale for repayable financial instruments in urban policy. Chapter 4 presents the legislative framework and institutional system of the JESSICA initiative, and shows in detail the implementation of JESSICA support in Poland. Chapter 5 relates the operational objectives of the study and provides the methodology applied in the research, with an overview of the source collection and data-gathering process. It also examines empirically the JESSICA mechanism from the perspective of the JESSICA projects and provides evidence of the positive impacts of JESSICA on urban areas. This chapter makes use of the previous studies conducted by the authors on JESSICA (Idczak & Mrozik, 2021; Idczak, Mrozik, & Musiałkowska, 2021; Idczak, Musiałkowska, & Mrozik, 2019b; Idczak & Musiałkowska, 2019; Musiałkowska & Idczak, 2020) – it includes, to some extent, repetition but extends and supplements the previous work. Chapter 6 provides a synthesis and assessment of the key challenges, added value and lessons, proposing a change in the JESSICA institutional system.

This study summarises most of the work and investigations carried out under the research project "Regeneration Process of Degraded Urban Areas within the Framework of the JESSICA Initiative" funded by the National Science Centre, Poland. This book has greatly benefited from the discussions held at the following events: three conferences of the Regional Studies Association in Santiago de Compostela, Lugano and Lublin, two workshops organised by the RSA Research Network on EU Cohesion Policy (CPnet), the conference organised by ILPES CEPAL in Santiago de Chile and at the Cracow University of Economics, a workshop with Professor Peter Nijkamp, and seminars organised by colleagues from the Department of European Studies at the Poznań University of Economics and Business.

Acknowledgements

The study is supported by the National Science Centre, Poland (2015/19/D/HS5/01561).

We wish to thank Professor Ewa Małuszyńska for her helpful comments and outstanding support on an earlier draft of this study and Professor Małgorzata Dziembała for their insightful advice on this final version.

1 Background – urban economics

1.1 The economic dimension of urbanisation

Cities are organic systems. The ongoing organisation of society is especially reliant on an urban way of life. The development of urban systems is the result of interdependent and never-ending streams of decisions. Some of them are more formal, while others less so; some are conscious decisions and others not; a great quantity of them are private decisions, whereas other are public ones. This complex of decisions taken by individuals, firms, public institutions etc. is solely responsible for forming and directing urban development by igniting it at certain times and particular places. These decisions relate distinctly to the maintenance of the general equilibrium, in the long run, between the needs of the population and the availability and allocation of resources. Since the economic resources are limited in quantity and vary in quality, decisions to allocate them among competing uses are taken to achieve the highest possible level of economic efficiency. This is the natural consequence of economic forces which, through market mechanisms, are capable of providing the most efficient economic outcomes. Moreover, economic forces are seen as the most powerful of urbanising forces that strengthen the tendency for both individuals and firms to favour urban concentration (Goodall, 1972, pp. 1–5). To individuals, cities offer a wide range of products, services and amenities which would be unobtainable elsewhere. Firms, in turn, locate in or close to urban areas to reap the benefits of internal production efficiency gains, access to a large pool of workers and suppliers, and the existence of a favourable business environment. Hence, both households and firms look for spatial proximity as they need to interact for a variety of socio-economic reasons. With a viable economic base, the city has the necessary capacity to develop cultural, social and aesthetic values, and interpersonal activities that provide meaning for human beings. Without a supportive economic foundation, all of these component aspects of human development (in public and private, economic and social matters etc.) cannot be realised. It follows that the city must ensure an effective economic organisation to have "a viable cultural and social base". Therefore, it can be argued, as suggested by Henderson and Ledebur (1972, p. 5), that the city should be understood as an economic organisation. If so, the understanding of the fundamental economic processes governing the complex urban system and determining its development

Piotr Idczak

https://doi.org/10.1515/9783110762198-005

calls for the application of economic theory to urbanisation processes. As the functioning of the urban system is driven largely by economic forces due to their productive, distributive and balance-oriented properties, the claim made in the opening sentence of this chapter, that cities are organic systems, seems reasonable.

Cities are commonly seen as productive engines of growth. There is a large consensus in the literature that urban areas are more efficient at generating economic product than rural ones. The spatially uneven growth is explained as the result of different factor productivity levels which are mostly influenced by city size, and more precisely, by the size of the market (Capello, 2001). This happens as cities bring economies of scale, boost markets, create jobs and provide fertile conditions for new economic activities to flourish. In fact, people tend to move to the cities because they offer real opportunities for a better and more prosperous life. According to Glaeser (2011), the main reason for the existence of cities is to *connect people*. Humans possess an innate tendency to be close to one another and to seek connections with the different forms of lifestyle offered by urban areas. Otherwise, it would be difficult to explain the permanently increasing and tough competition for land and buildings, as reported by the rising share of housing costs in consumers' expenditure. Individuals and firms search for spatial proximity because they want to interact for numerous of economic and social reasons. The so-called "pull motives" grouping people in cities are highlighted, *inter alia* by Florida (2002), as crucial factors that actually boost individuals' and organisational economic productivity. Cities harness their common social and cultural preferences as well as professional skills and creative abilities and turn them into economic value, thus increasing the quality of life.

It is absolutely clear that the decisions and operations of the individuals and firms (along with state-owned enterprises) depend on the spatial arrangement of the urban system. But, as mentioned by Proost and Thisse (2019, p. 579), natural (geographical) factors cannot be used exclusively to explain the reasons for which some cities exist. Geographical factors are helpful for providing the understanding of where cities are rather than *why they exist and how they grow*. In fact, advantages and disadvantages, and historical attributes associated with a geographical location likely interact in specific ways. City formation entails the increase of urban population but it also stimulated by the horizontal expansion of urban areas. This is so because the process of urbanisation, although it is stimulated by economic forces, has a spatial dimension in which factors of production, firms and localities become gradually specialised and more differentiated from each other. This process organises economic and social spheres placing absolute emphasis on spatial reconfigurations, matching market response to market needs and *vice versa*.[1] However, economic interactions occur in different markets, therefore a city (urban area) can be seen as an interrelated network of economic markets: housing, labour, land, transport, capital market and so on, situated in a limited spatial area. The spatial extent of each of these markets does not inevitably coincide, yet they overlap and interlock in such a way as to mould an urban economy which can be regarded as a principal unit of employment and income generation (Goodall, 1972). Consequently, this unit (city) constituting any larger geographical concentration of economic agents is of major interest for urban economics (Button, 1976). Or, to put it another way, drawing on McDonald (1997, p. 1), urban economics is *the study of economies that are organised as urban areas.*

It seems that economic factors have been a prime stimulus of urban development and formation of cities. Notwithstanding this, cities as complex, dynamic social organisations cannot be understood separately from the economic, social and political factors that ensure their existence and functioning. To provide better understanding of the line of argument set out here, it is necessary to give a brief overview of why cities exist and how present-day cities fit into the long-term urbanisation process.

Most literature considers that cities owe their existence to a combination of an accumulated agricultural surplus and the various kinds of socio-economic activities that people engage in. As noted by Evans (1985, pp. 9–10), although there are many reasons for the growth of cities – such as economies of scale in production, the spatially uneven distribution of resources and the needs of government centres – agricultural marketable surplus is one necessary condition for the emergence of urban centres. Put simply, if the agricultural output exceeds the subsistence requirements of the rural population, then the unutilised amount of goods is transferred to other groups not involved in food production. By the improvement and cultivation of the land an increased division of labour occurs, so that only a part of the rural working society becomes sufficient to provide food for the whole. Conversely, the rest can be employed in non-agricultural undertakings fully focused on providing manufactured goods or on satisfying people's needs other than their basic ones (Brewer, 2011). This leads to an expansion in communal economic undertakings which accelerates the urbanisation process. At the same time market forces attract both people and industries to settle in cities. To some extent the process of development in economic terms involves a par-

---

[1] The term "urban" is used here to refer to the spatial agglomeration of population and business activities settled within a high-density and continuous built-up area that is separated from other urban areas by much greater, mainly agricultural and sparsely populated areas. It ignores the administrative and political boundaries of an urban area in its definitional context.

allel development of agriculture and manufacturing, because on the one hand an agricultural surplus is used to supply the manufacturing and service sectors, and on the other, the desire of the agricultural sector to purchase manufactured goods or to avail of services acts as a reason to produce more than its subsistence requirements. This happens when the surplus can be traded by rural producers for goods and services produced in the cities. And in turn the possibilities of trade are directly determined by the cost of transporting the agricultural surplus from the rural areas to the cities (A. W. Evans, 1985, p. 10). Distance from the centre plays a crucial role here because the economic value of the surplus decreases as the distance from urban centres increases.

Admittedly, even if the marketable share of agricultural output allocated to the non-rural population appears to be indispensable to urbanisation process, it is not sufficient to generate cities and explain why they emerge. As explained above, if the productivity of agricultural activities considerably exceeds the required level of consumption of the rural population, the urban and industrial population begins to grow. The population growth is induced by the surplus due to economies of scale in production which puts pressure on the system to shift to more intensive sectors and technologies (W. Robinson & Schutjer, 1982). The division of labour enhances labour productivity and gives rise to increasing returns to scale due to specialisation in particular tasks. The economies of scale resulting from increasing specialisation may arise within the firm because of the use of specialised technologies which force a more relentless efficiency in production. Increasing returns provide, then, the driving force for agglomeration of the manufacturing activity, which is therefore concentrated in or around a unique place (the city). Firms are attracted because cities offer the economies of agglomeration in the form of a large home market, supplies of skilled labour and the presence of supplementary industries. Moreover, the grouping together of firms in one place allows them to benefit from economies of scale that also arise outside the firms. The so-called external economies enable firms, for instance, to use common services, to build up a market or to share the costs of training labour, so that they gain advantages from their concentration in that place. Taking in turn an individual view, cities offer a wide range of social and cultural services, employment, security and well-being. Once the urbanisation process begins, it triggers a self-reinforcing mechanism in which market forces favour a continued movement of factors and population into the cities (Button, 1976, pp. 14–15; A. W. Evans, 1985, p. 10).

Although economies of scale are seen to be the primary reason for the growth of cities, this however, does not alter the fact that many cities came into being at particular locations for other reasons as well. The spatial pattern of economic activity has often been the result of both economic and non-economic forces that not always correspond to the assumptions of economic theory. Nevertheless, irrespective of the time, urban areas have been highly specialised phenomena particularly suited to the specific needs of the given era, including the economic ones. Amongst the reasons for the emergence of cities is geographical diversity and emanating from that the uneven distribution of resources. The geographical concentration of mineral resources encouraged most obviously especially in the past the growth of mining towns and cities which grew quickly and, as quickly, often disappeared when the resources were depleted. Natural habitat and suitable landform features provide the essential background for all human activity, thus allowing people to settle in places offering the most favourable conditions for life. Therefore, the morphological components of the terrain such as natural harbours, watercourses, availability of cultivated areas etc. were the basic reasons for the development of a settlement. It should be noted, however, that any settlement cannot exist solely for these reasons because there are constantly certain reasons for trade. These encompass either some part of agricultural surplus or goods produced elsewhere due to the occurrence of economies of scale or the minerals extracted in other places in return for the output manufactured in that place (A. W. Evans, 1985, pp. 10–11). In this way, settlements initially, and then in their advanced forms, namely cities, became trading "nodes" creating networks for trade in goods. So, cities could grow and develop initially and may continue to do so because of the trade with other entities and areas.

A further reason for the growth and existence of cities is their role as governmental centres. This was especially relevant at the end of the middle ages when preindustrial cities evolved to become as much political entities as a collection of houses. Various political means were arranged to channel agricultural surplus or later different forms of taxes into the hands of a ruler who being settled in a city exercised authority over its surrounding areas. In many ways, cities were governed by their own laws, which often differed from the rules imposed on the surrounding areas. Their privileged position offered a residence exemption from the customary rural obligations to the ruler. Indeed, preindustrial cities assumed those functions that could be most effectively managed from a central position, which means that they could operate primarily as government centres, and secondarily as economic ones. As noted by Goodall (1972, pp. 14–18), market centres emerged, however, because of the existence of fairs in systems of local trade, which were established to ensure the exchange of goods and services. Urban areas as central communities, at that time, were not only the major recipients of agricultural output supplied for coercive or marketable reasons but also, within primitive forms of specialisation, provided comprehensive services for their tributary areas and an agrarian way of life. Economic and political centres of gravity were overcome only by industrial revolution which through the expansion of new manufacturing processes and services became an economic force of considerable acceleration in the pace of urbanisation.

Bearing in mind these considerations, one comes to the conclusion that the strength and persistence of the phenomenon of urbanisation derive from the supreme features of this process that are responsible for managing the use of resources and thereby lead to a high rate of economic growth. Put simply, urbanisation is a relatively good system for using resources with the overriding aim of meeting society's needs. Urban areas, in turn, are commonly seen as a symbol of humans' ability to form natural, economic and social environments in which they can live and work. Note, however, that an efficiency in the use of resources within an urban area and between urban areas is of the utmost concern. In practice, cities never approach the high order of rationality defined by theoretical models in the scientific discourse. Indeed, general equilibrium can never be attained in real life. Although it is true that the price system plays a leading role in allocating the variety of resources (land, labour, goods, services etc.) in urban areas, the complex nature of the urban economy means that it is not able to work efficiently. Its functioning is weakened by urban problems arising from the interaction between economic and non-economic factors, which makes the market mechanism deficient. The non-economic factors relate primarily to the broadly defined behaviour of urban market actors that are not subject to any disciplinary rules of the price mechanism. As a result, this self-balancing market mechanism is vulnerable to imperfections and distortions, and also unable to bring about all the desired adjustments.

According to mainstream economists, there are very important exceptions which have the effect that the price mechanism does not function in practice as it does in theoretical models. They point to the existence of monopolies (oligopolies), externalities and public goods as the main factors that distort the allocation of resources. Moreover, they also argue that the market economy produces a distribution of income that is quite unequal, thus leading to greater inefficiency in the market mechanism (McDonald, 1997, pp. 19–20). The socially efficient utilisation of resources can be yielded by prices only if they reflect the social costs and benefits involved (given that the social costs and benefits encompass private ones). In most actions, social benefits can be greater than private ones where a certain action gives rise to positive externalities. Likewise, social costs will be greater than private ones if a given action results in negative externalities. Therefore, externalities (social costs and benefits) are not reflected through the price mechanism to a single person engaged in an action but they are represented by an increase in private costs and benefits to other persons. Taking into account a situation where marginal social cost is greater than marginal private cost the producer will equate the price with marginal private cost so as to maximise the profit. On the contrary, the level of price reflecting the social marginal cost would be the desirable option from society's point of view. To illustrate this, suppose that a profit-oriented developer, understandably, intends to construct a housing estate in a given urban location. The developer will show little interest in providing a full range of ancillary facilities, while those amenities would be of great interest to the local community (Goodall, 1972, pp. 7–8). Because of this the differences between social and private costs (and benefits) contribute to a misallocation of resources in urban areas (for more see section 1.4). This situation calls for public action to internalise negative or subsidise positive externalities, with the view to obtain the optimal allocation of resources.

Some goods or services are not subject to prices. By this is meant that some aspects of the urban economy are concerned with such collective goods and services as roads, education, police, etc. These public goods, another imperfection of the market mechanism, are a very important realm of functioning for the urban economy, although the market often fails to provide enough of them to match needs. This is so because there are no profit motives that could organise the provision of public goods. More concretely, the distortion arises not only due to the fact that it is difficult to decide upon the values society places on them, but also because of the extent to which resources can be used in their provision. The delivery of these non-profit goods and services is relevant to the efficiency and success of both individuals and firms. The third mentioned market imperfection is the power of monopoly/oligopoly, which is expressed by the intrinsic ability to affect both the production output or service provision and at the same time the price that prevails on the market. In urban areas so-called natural monopolies are not uncommon, especially in a situation where the level of demand in the whole urban area or its part is sufficient to use the output supplied by only one producer. One reason for that is the non-transferability of some resources in geographical space. A clear example of this is land, which is marked by very distinctive features like the nature of the soil by virtue of the landscape. Thus every place has a unique spatial relationship with all other places. The monopoly power of a particular parcel of land will be conditional on the extent to which other places are close substitutes. Sometimes the excessive fragmentation of ownership in urban areas forms a serious barrier to use land in the most efficient way. Such a situation calls for the power of compulsory purchase, when a public party acquires land for use as public infrastructure (roads, schools etc.) to provide collective goods (Goodall, 1972, pp. 9–10). The availability of urban infrastructure is a contributory factor representing the true potential for a city's success. In general, the allocation of resources under the price mechanism in urban areas may not be as efficient as the manner of resource distribution that can be achieved in the presence of market constraints.

With all this in mind, one can argue that, because of the influence of non-economic factors and market failures, urban areas will never reach a general equilibrium, defined in terms of the efficient allocation of resources. These limits affecting the operation of market forces may result in an increase in the economic costs of performing everyday actions. Urban economies cannot be then considered in isolation from the complex interaction of other factors within the city. There is a wide spectrum of problems and processes in which economic concepts interact with tenets of other disciplines. The challenge of urban economics is to draw on the meaningful framework of research that includes an interdisciplinary approach so as to study the complex nature and dynamics of urban processes and problems (W. L. Henderson & Ledebur, 1972). Notwithstanding this, the role of economic forces in these processes must be appreciated and understood if one wishes to design effective remedial polices aimed at successfully resolving many of the problems of urban areas.

1.2 Agglomeration economies and diseconomies

It is evident that industry and population have tended to agglomerate in specific geographical locations. The rationale behind this centralising process is that both firms and people are attracted by cities as they offer measurable benefits in the form of, for example, a large home market, supplies of skilled labour, jobs, markets and the availability of supplementary facilities. These location-specific economies of scale are commonly known as agglomeration economies. This notion means that cost reductions occur because of the increasing returns to scale and the resultant concentration of economic activities in one place. As Marshall (1890, as cited in Duranton & Puga, 2004) has argued, economies of scale are achieved through three possible originating factors: information spill-overs, non-traded local inputs and a local skilled labour pool.[2] First, the grouping in the same location of firms from the same industry facilitates the sharing of tacit information between the participants. The advantage of such spatial clustering is that proximity maximises the mutual accessibility of all individuals within the cluster, thus improving information availability for all local participants and facilitating decision-making. Second, the concentration in the same area of many

---

[2] Mechanisms providing the microeconomic foundations of urban agglomeration economies at the level of cities were surveyed by Duranton and Puga (2004).

firms in the same industry offers opportunities for certain specialist inputs to be available to all of them in a more efficient manner than if they were widely spaced. This kind of input is defined as a "non-traded input" since it represents components that are not consumed – e. g. adequate infrastructure, business environment etc. Third, locating a firm in an area which has an abundant pool of labour with the specialist skills required by a certain industry reduces labour acquisition costs when expanding its workforce. This is of great importance in particular for those firms in which skills-acquisition costs and the opportunity costs of time are significant due to rapidly changing market conditions (McCann, 2001, pp. 55–57).

More recent literature points to the fourth source of agglomeration economies, that is, urban consumption opportunities (consumption amenities) as defined by Glaeser, Kolko and Saiz (2001). Urban residents gain an advantage from their proximity to other people, which generates various benefits of greater diversity and variety in social experiences and consumer goods and services. The variety, in turn, provides opportunity in the form of more as well as increasingly diverse consumption choices and boosts the consumer's utility functions. Moreover, the primacy of urban centres is intrinsically linked to the provision of all sorts of goods and services, even those targeted at niche markets of all kinds. As higher productivity allows firms to achieve an efficient scale of production, individuals are willing to pay higher rents in exchange for such benefits. The point is that if external benefits accrue for the consumers of larger cities, agglomeration economies will continue whether or not the aforementioned causal forms are sufficient (Giuliano, Kang, & Yuan, 2019, p. 380). A major argument for the "consumer city" is that some goods and services and in particular various aesthetic charms are available in large cities and not elsewhere. Urban centres attract a larger proportion of higher human capital individuals because they provide an array of amenities – e. g. cultural centres, high-quality public services, recreational facilities etc. – and a rich variety of consumption alternatives. In turn, places rich in amenities are also likely to attract highly skilled individuals, so firms searching for such workers will follow them and locate in large agglomerations (Florida, 2002; Glaeser, Kolko, & Saiz, 2001).

The sources of agglomeration economies enable individual firms within the same industry to experience localised external economies of scale, but which are internal to the group. Nevertheless, one may argue that in many areas there are groups of firms in different industries that are spatially clustered. Therefore, due to the different nature of agglomeration economies in different places, they are commonly classified into three types (McCann, 2001, p. 58): internal returns to scale, localisation economies and urbanisation economies. Internal returns to scale refers directly to a firm's production and can be simply achieved by expanding production at a single location. These economies of scale are seen as being internal to a firm and result in falling unit cost over a given scale of operation. If the demand for goods and products is sufficiently large relative to these increasingly efficient scales of production, firms can take advantages because the average cost of production declines as output at a particular location increases. Therefore, when firms want to benefit from internal production economies of scale, they attempt to either locate relative to an urban area that provides access to the desired factor inputs or attract these factors to their location. It is an indisputable fact that these economies of scale are associated with a high spatial concentration of capital, labour force, investments etc., and are location specific.

The second type of agglomeration economies, namely localisation economies, are external to a firm and accrue to a group of them within the same industry located in the same place. In other words, they arise because of the size of the local industry – the larger the industry becomes, the lower the costs. The local supply firms can benefit from the close proximity to their major customer firms, which in turn can achieve the internal returns to scale. Firms in the same industry are in competition and due to frequent information exchange with customers and customer firms they increase the mutual understanding and familiarity. Conversely, they are attracted by large markets and local considerable demand to cluster together because of cost savings that accrue, for instance, on advertising, promotion and transportation, and – with all this put together – on acquiring customers. Similar firms tend to concentrate their activities in order, on the one hand, to compete for a given local demand market and, on the other, to meet the local demand of wholesale purchasers and customers who compare commodities and products. The concentration makes it possible to compare differential prices, qualities, styles etc. Last but not least, the spatial concentration of firms along with proximity to demand for their products provides accessibility to a large labour market and auxiliary industries. The point, however, is that the economies of localisation occur within a particular sector.

The final type of agglomeration economies – urbanisation economies – are those which accrue to firms across different sectors. Firms tend to agglomerate within urban areas and create clusters of differentiated industries by reason of productivity and utility created endogenously by larger cities. The advantages reached by an industry in the form of cost reduction arise from the size of the entire local economy. Urbanisation economies are often described as "external economies" since the benefits cannot be used privately by any single firm or group of firms. They generate savings to all firms and incentives for business to centralise their activities in a particular area. To be more specific, the main source of external economies is a centralisation of sources of supply of production factors and the facilities that are a supportive element in production processes. Firms can benefit not only from the accumulation of pools of the labour input that have gathered due to the clustering of industries but also from the proximity of the other supportive and service industries. Another key motivation behind the centralisation is the social overhead capital commonly seen as state-run public goods and services that are necessarily required in the production of virtually all commodities and to enhance, directly or indirectly, private output. A different type of incentive derives from the complementary stages of production when firms being involved in successive stages in the manufacture of the final product streamline operations to be more cost-effective. Finally, firms tend to concentrate within an urban area to minimise the costs of time in carrying out the production, physical transportation of inputs and outputs, and communication and management (W. L. Henderson & Ledebur, 1972, pp. 51–56). The presence of these factors creates strong incentives that draw other firms to a particular location so as to take advantage of their availability, thus reinforcing the concentration of business activities and people in urban areas.

In the context of this discussion, reference should be made to the vast theoretical discourse developed under the heading *new economic geography* (NEG), which brought valuable input to the better understanding of the role of distance and space in regional and urban economics. A key breakthrough was Krugman's seminal research putting particular attention on the concentration of economic activities and the formation of economic agglomeration. A core–periphery model developed within this research demonstrated how increasing returns at the firm level in relation to transportation costs and mobile productive factors may lead to the emergence of an industrial centre supplying goods to agricultural areas. The spatial economic general equilibrium (the spatial patterns of population and production) is defined as a result of the interplay between two opposite forces – centripetal forces which can bring about spatial concentration and centrifugal forces which lead to dispersed economic activity. Table 1 summarises these forces.

Table 1: Forces affecting geographical concentration

Centripetal forces	Centrifugal forces
Market-size effects (linkages)	Immobile factors
Thick labour markets	Land rents
Pure external economies	Pure external diseconomies

Source: (Krugman, 1998, p. 8)

In line with the remit of this theorem, agglomeration economies are driven by the interaction of three key factors: (1) increasing returns at the firm level which cause individual producers to concentrate their production; (2) transportation costs that encourage locating close to a larger market and shipping to smaller ones; (3) mobility factor – labour is attracted to these central places due to increasing returns, which makes firms more productive, this in turn results in higher wages, which consequently increases the size of the market and the varieties of goods and services. To put it differently, a large market generates bi-directional linkages – on the one hand, the proximity of large markets is preferred as a good location for the production of goods prone to economies of scale (backward linkages), while on the other hand, large markets strengthen the local production of intermediate goods, cutting costs for downstream production (forward linkages). Firm concentration reinforces a thick local pool of labour, notably for highly skilled workers, allowing them to easier find employers and vice versa. Because of information spill-overs a local concentration of firms will create more-or-less pure external economies. At the same time, however, some forces work against agglomeration. These include mostly immobile factors – e.g. the availability of a special fixed infrastructure or land and natural resources. Concentrations of economic activity entail an increase in land rents that are undeniably higher in areas of greater economic density. In fact, higher land rents and traffic congestion represent pure external diseconomies that reduce returns to scale in dense locations (Krugman, 1998). These relate to centrifugal forces causing firms and people to disperse.

The refinement of this general theory of equilibrium was provided in subsequent works by Krugman, Fujita and Mori (Fujita & Krugman, 1995, 2004; Fujita, Krugman, & Mori, 1999). The authors proposed a dynamic continuous–time adjustment model in order to analyse the dynamic pattern of equilibrium allocation of economic activity. Following McCann's view (2001, pp. 86–90), the Krugman-Fujita models show how cities grow (or decline) within the core–periphery framework as national or international market areas expand. Large cities with a wide range of firms and a high variety of goods will be relatively inexpensive to live in (in real terms) as the high variety of products and services will enable the achievement of any level of utility at lower real cost. Simultaneously, due to intense local competition, these centres will offer products at relatively low cost and spread them over large market areas. Since transport costs increase when the quantity of goods being shipped decreases, smaller cities or peripherally located ones, which are characterised by relatively low local competition and high source prices, will be able to cover only small local market areas. Under this model the distance-transport cost is offset by the effect of localised increasing returns to scale that are definitely associated with major cities.³ To sum up, what clearly emerges from the Krugman-Fujita approach is the dominance of cumulative processes which, induced by means of agglomeration economies, can lead to the formation of the spatial core–periphery structures even in the absence of some natural advantages (agglomeration economies unrelated to natural endowments). Processes favouring the concentration can be sparked off by even a small event. The emergence of agglomeration economies is determined by the interplay of transportation costs, the strength of scale economies and the factor mobility (Schmutzler, 1999). However, the centripetal forces that operate for the benefit of agglomerations are undermined by counterbalancing centrifugal forces. Indeed, agglomeration diseconomies can trigger processes that repel economic activities.

The reason for the generation of centrifugal forces is that many of the economies gained from increasing industrial and urban concentration may be exhausted beyond some optimum scale of operation. If urban and industrial growth exceeds the optimum scale of functions and operation, it will engender diseconomies of scale being the source of many of the critical urban problems that characterise urban and metropolitan areas (W. L. Henderson & Ledebur, 1972, p. 48). Provided that market forces (centripetal vs. centrifugal) in the long term can bring about some general equilibrium between broadly understood costs and benefits of life in the city, it is doubtful whether the result being a response to these forces would represent an efficient spatial-economic configuration (Verhoef & Nijkamp, 2003, p. 4). Agglomeration economies undoubtedly cause movements towards cities, until they are stopped up by congestion costs, high land prices and the extent of the market being limited by the presence of spatially dispersed demand for output. These negative externalities discourage agglomeration but their occurrence is tied in with income inequalities within a particular location (J. V. Henderson, Shalizi, & Venables, 2001). Since cities are denser and proximity matters, the existence of agglomeration diseconomies seems to be more important in urban areas than elsewhere. This also means that the negative unpriced effects imposed by some agents upon others make cities locales that generate plenty of undesirable impacts. Therefore, many researchers have highlighted the relevance of negative externalities related to growth in agglomerations, pointing out in particular: the occurrence of crime, environmental decay, traffic congestion, pollution concentration, the devalua-

---

3 As McCann (2001, p. 90) argues, this research framework provided not only a key contribution to a dynamic vision of spatial structures by renewing the Christaller-type urban hierarchies but also showed, through a clarification of the rank-size rule, that it can still be applied to explain the spatial economic development patterns over time.

tion of property, noise and smell, waste, social exclusion, ethnic segregation, urban anonymity, urban sprawl etc. (Borck, 2005; Capello & Faggian, 2002; Glaeser, 2014; Regnier & Legras, 2018; Richardson, 1995; van den Bergh, 2010; Verhoef & Nijkamp, 2003, 2008). Note that agglomeration diseconomies convey the tenet of human interdependencies which are outside the control of the market mechanism. Indeed, someone's performance (utility or production) depends on factors that are imposed upon the recipient without his or her consent, but are determined by other producers or individuals and, especially important, cannot be omitted from someone's activity.

Theoretically, a person who is going to make a decision to produce more output, makes that decision taking into account his own marginal costs and marginal benefits, while ignoring costs or benefits that embrace others. A good example of this relationship is illustrated by air pollution – one of the so-called *producer-upon-consumer negative externalities*. A firm makes its decision on output on the basis of its own marginal costs without taking into account the cost of air pollution. However, from the urban perspective the additional cost of air pollution caused by the firm is required to be included as the marginal cost of the entire city (McDonald, 1997). In order to see the effects of the external diseconomies of urbanisation on the whole urban area we can use a theoretical model depicting those relationships, as shown in Figure 1. The diagram presents a perfectly competitive labour market in an urban area where employment reflects the size of the urban area. Labour is demanded by firms to produce goods and services for both export and local use, and the demand curve for labour is denoted as *D*. Labour supply is represented by the labour curve *S*, drawn with a positive slope which, understandably, is faced by the firm located in the urban areas. The horizontal axis gives the quantity of labour and the vertical axis the nominal wage per unit of labour. Hence, if firms want to expand their output, they need to increase employment, but to do this, higher wages must be paid. As a result, a market equilibrium wage can be achieved at the point w^*, and employment is fixed at the point L^*. The wage level represented by w^* is then the wage rate that firms use to determine how many employees to hire.

Now, we assume that the demand curve for labour (*D*) is the same thing as the value of labour's marginal product (*VMP*), which equals the price of output multiplied by the physical marginal product of labour. Furthermore, it is also assumed that when a firm hires an additional worker, that worker manufactures a marginal product for the firm and at the same time causes output to the detriment of other firms. By way of illustration, let us consider an interrelationship between employment and traffic congestion. The decision taken by a firm to employ another worker (driver) means that there will be more traffic in the urban area. This can happen because drivers working for the various firms will have

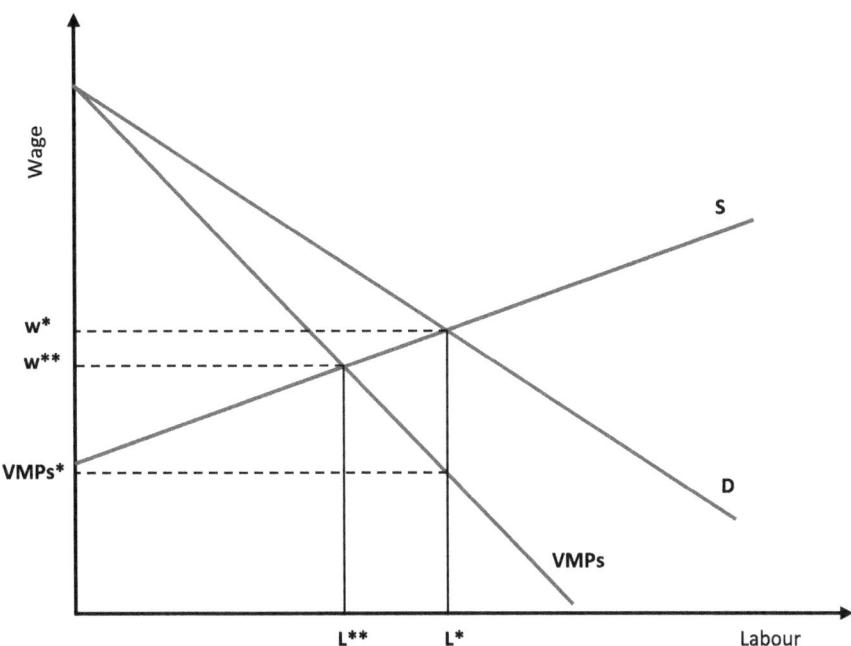

Figure 1: External economies of urbanisation
Source: (McDonald, 1997, p. 43)

to spend much more time to carry goods or provide services, so their day's performance will be less efficient than before. If we imagine that the other firms within the urban area do so, the value of the labour's marginal product to the whole urban area should be drawn as curve *VMPs* in Figure 1. As we see from this figure, the *VMPs* curve is below the demand curve *D* by the amount of the external diseconomy at the margin. At the point L^*, defined by the employment level, the wage rate equals the value of labour's marginal product to the firm hiring the last worker, but the real value of the marginal product of the last employee for the entire urban area is set at the level *VMPs** (McDonald, 1997, pp. 43–44). This means that all the additional workers generate a marginal product to the firms in the entire urban area which is lower than the marginal cost, thus making the employment level inefficient.

If the level of employment L^* is inefficient, and firms paid wages defined at w* to increase the employment, but they could only reap a benefit of *VMPs** as described by Figure 1, it raises the question of which employment level is then efficient. This question is particularly relevant as the appropriate level of employment in the whole urban area would enable some firms to achieve tangible business benefits without worsening the situation of other firms. As we can see, it is not economically viable for firms to employ additional workers because the profits earned from hiring the last worker are relatively small. The efficient level of employment for the entire urban area would be at the point L^{**}, which is the point at which the supply curve of labour crosses the value of the marginal product of labour to all firms. At this point employees could earn a wage rate equal to w^{**}, and all the firms gain output that would be worth the same amount by hiring the last worker (McDonald, 1997, pp. 43–44). However, such a situation is unlikely to happen in the spatial-economic urban reality. As noted by Venables (2005), in the expansion of a city there is a point beyond which some negative externalities may come to dominate and further increases in city size reduce the productivity. What is important is that negative externalities operate at the city level, so they are external to the actions of individual workers or firms. To put it simply, they do not have a decisive influence on the decisions taken by individuals and firms. Nevertheless, externalities are present, giving rise to market failures, unless some intuitions exist that are capable of internalising them.

Agglomeration diseconomies are inherently associated with the city size. They become centrifugal forces that repel economic agents from one another. Conversely, there are some consumer goods and services that are more likely to be available in a larger city and their quality is also likely to be better in a larger city. These are mostly social and cultural amenities desired by many residents, so they can compensate for the overall costs of living in larger cities. As Evans (A. W. Evans, 1985, p. 72) argued, these positive consumption externalities quite often outweigh unpriced agglomeration diseconomies.

1.3 The importance of "place"

The functioning of a city is inextricably linked to a place, often in complex ways. Looking for possible explanations of this fact, one may point to the physical geography as a driver which makes some places more productive than others due to the availability of the more favourable living conditions. However, bearing in mind the economic nature of the urbanisation process, such reasoning does not seem sufficient, given the "agency" of several factors discussed in the previous section that stand out in the formation of cities. Population and economic activity tend to agglomerate in a place due to the attraction of the economic benefits of economic agglomeration (spatial co-location of economic agents). Spatial concentration and specialisation drive urbanisation because they rely on increasing returns to scale and thereby make production cheaper. They deliver intrinsic advantages that facilitate finding jobs, wealth creation via scale, productivity, diffuse learning and expertise, and efficiency gains. Consequently, the spatially concentrated wealth enhancing city liveability attracts people, which in turn increases further wealth creation potential in a virtuous cycle that ultimately accelerates urban growth. Nevertheless, it can be observed that, although the same market-oriented forces are involved in the formation of urban places, there are many differences between the different places. Employment patterns are different; facilities and services are different; life chances vary between places. This is because the nature of a place is shaped by the multitude of interactions within the particular place and with other places. These interactions are moulded by the multilateral flows of people, goods, capital and information, and also by location decisions made by firms. The arguments discussed so far provided understanding on why it is that firms and people are often clustered together. However, it is also clearly seen that not all economic activities are located close to each other. Mostly activities in primary industries are spatially dispersed due to their basic needs of land as an input to the agriculture-based production process. But there are many commercial and industrial activities which also tend to be loosely spaced. This applies usually to those firms and markets where the competitive advantage takes the form of the alternative spatial pricing strategies. In these cases, firms in some markets will offer the delivered prices no matter the location or only partially dependent on spatial distance. Explanations of prices loosely associated with distance can be found in the value–weight ratio which means that the higher the price of each unit of the product, the greater will be the average distance of shipment. To put it simply, the high-value products (largely non-standardised products) will be transported over a large distance as the high value can significantly compensate the greater distance transportation cost, while for the low-value products the transport cost remains relatively high in relation to the value of the goods even over a short distance, thus having a large impact on restricting the distance required to ship these goods. The result of this is that high-value non-standardised products tend to be produced in a smaller number of locations and by a smaller number of producers compared to low-value standard products. Obviously, low-value goods will be produced in many places, thereby limiting the average transportation distance. Different types of production will then take place in different numbers of locations. Conversely, production based on lower technology will occur in many places, and new production or higher-technology production actions will tend to happen in a smaller number of locations (McCann, 2001, pp. 66–70). The main conclusion to draw from these arguments is that the size of the particular product areas and the average distance of transportation from producer to customer are different for different products, and moreover the spatial market areas are different for different firms.

Drawing on Reilly's evidence (1931, as cited in McCann, 2001), it is clear that the attractiveness of the market areas depends on the variety of goods which can be purchased at the particular locations. The greater the variety of goods available at a single centre, the greater will be the attractiveness of purchasing from there, even from a greater distance. Hence, it follows that goods will be purchased over greater market areas, leading to a situation where these goods will also be moved over a greater geographical distance, from centres which offer a wider variety of goods, ceteris paribus. This leads to the conclusion that greater urbanisation economies, related mainly to larger cities, will also imply larger hinterland market areas, and larger transportation distances for the goods produced there. On the other hand, more local market areas with shorter distance shipments will tend to be dominated by purchases of a lower variety of goods. If we now link the discussions made so far with the agglomeration arguments presented in section 1.2, we can claim that the higher value goods will have a tendency to be produced in a smaller number of locations, thus expanding the market areas and the transportation distance of these goods, and vice versa. At this point, it becomes more and more apparent that the high-value goods will be manufactured in major urban centres since such locations provide the necessary technology input, labour force, skills, know-how and information needed in the production of these types of goods. In turn, smaller urban centres without adequate production capacities or retail locations will tend mainly to be the source of lower-value goods being principally marketed within the areas of a short-distance shipment. It is important to note that this observation does not mean that the lower-value goods cannot be produced in large urban centres. These locations are the production places of a relatively high variety of goods, from low- to high-value ones, and their market areas will be larger than those for smaller centres whose production range is also smaller. In fact, the average linkage distance of high-value/weight ratio goods will tend to be higher than for the lower-value/weight ratio goods, which also implies that many of them can be bought locally. However, the production of the high-value/weight ratio goods will be spatially scattered across a small number of locations, often very distant from one another. At the same time the production of the lower-value/weight ratio goods will be inclined to be concentrated in a larger number of locations, thereby covering a smaller market area (McCann, 2001, pp. 70–71).

All of these considerations form a good basis for some models which are applied to describe the evolution of the urban system and predict the growth of urban areas. One of the first general discussions regarding the development of urban systems came from Christaller (Edwards, 2007, pp. 57–58). His *central place theory* (CPT) illustrated the tendency of settlement patterns to be organised in a cascading spatial hierarchy. The concept uses the population threshold and the geographic range to provide a top-down explanation for the emergence of the spatially hierarchical organisation of the urban system. It assumes that there are market areas for individual goods and services on a homogenous plain, where each market area reflects a certain threshold size. In addition to that, every consumer must have access to every good. For each size of central place a different variety of goods and services is offered. The smallest urban places, mostly villages and towns, deliver goods for basic needs (level-one goods) to the population of their small market areas. What is more, there are a very large number of these villages and small towns, which with their market areas form regular hexagons with no gaps and overlaps (hexagon is the one polygon that most easily covers discrete interlocking areas). Above villages and towns in the urban hierarchy are a smaller number of larger urban places which offer less-commonly purchased goods (level-two goods) to the population of larger market areas, but they are not able to produce all of the goods and services to satisfy local demand. These secondary central places, consequently, put demand pressures on the most central places for those goods and services which cannot be produced in second-order central places. All goods and services that are available in first-order locations are also available in second-order locations. The highest order goods are produced in only one city, that is, the core central place which is regarded to be capable of producing all of the goods and services to meet local demand fully. The whole land area is then seen as being divided up into a series of sets of adjoining hexagon-shaped market areas. A graphical illustration of the relationships between cities of different levels is presented in Figure 2. Note that the centres of the higher order hexagons overlap the centres of the lower-order hexagons. This kind of coincidence of hexagons for goods of different levels exists since each central place of a higher order produces and sells all of the goods that are purchased by populations living in the lower-order locations (Edwards, 2007, pp. 57–60). All in all, the entire spectrum of goods and services is considered to extend from high-order items having large thresholds (specialised goods) to low-order items distinguished by small thresholds and ranges (mostly standardised commonplace and convenience goods). The most central places in the whole system have exhaustive economic production capabilities to offer goods and services that satisfy completely the respective population's desires. When moving down through this spatial-functional arrangement, other central locations provide some but not all of the goods that are available at the most central locations. But regardless of their place in the spatial hierarchy, all of these locations induce market forces to differentially attract customers from their surroundings, and thus are regarded as central places. This inter-locking spatial hierarchy continues to cascade outward, reflecting the hierarchical levels of the urban system. All of the central places through their individual hexagonal market areas reflect the number of goods and services tied to each place of production (Mulligan, Partridge, & Carruthers, 2012, pp. 407–408).

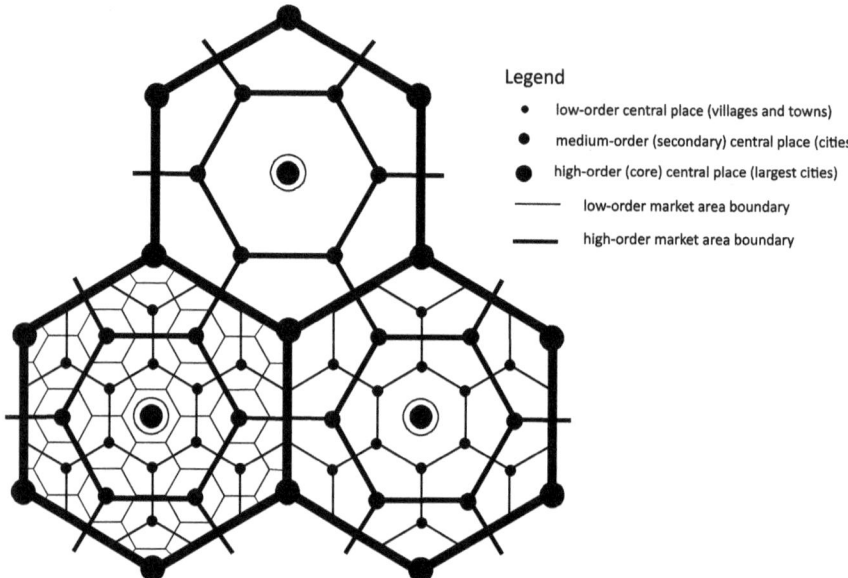

Figure 2: The spatially hierarchical organisation of the urban system
Source: adapted from (A. W. Evans, 1985, p. 67)

A crucial contribution to CPT was provided by Lösch (McCann, 2001, pp. 73–74), who refined and generalised the inductive Christallerian approach to understanding the functional hierarchy of urban systems. His entirely deductive approach relied on seeking to explain the spatial distribution of the size and shape of the market areas based on manufacturing. Lösch argued that each of the goods and services has its own specific market area and that, similarly to Christaller's arguments, businesses or production points naturally emerge at the central place of each different-sized market area. Nevertheless, as Löschian results revealed, due to the different price elasticity of demand for goods manufactured by the various firms, the market areas for different types of goods will be different. High-value products are primarily characterised by a low price elasticity of demand because of their heterogeneity and quality. Conversely, low-value products are rather homogenous, so they will tend to be highly price-elastic. As a result, firms producing goods whose demand curves reflect high price elasticity will tend to cover small market areas. The rationale behind this is that their production will be very sensitive to transportation costs that are a significant component of the selling price of the good, and thereby will reduce demand remarkably when the delivery distance increases. High-value products whose demand curves are highly price-inelastic will be largely insensitive to shipment cost mark-up. Consequently, demand for those products will fall only slightly with increasing delivery distance, which will lead to an increase in the market area. Bearing this in mind it can be stated that different firms producing different goods will produce different hexagonal market areas. Firms producing goods characterised by a high price elasticity of demand, e.g. food products, will determine small hexagonal areas and be situated in a large number of places, whereas firms producing goods with a low price elasticity will determine larger hexagonal market areas and be located in a smaller number of places (McCann, 2001, pp. 73–77). Lösch's most important contribution to CPT was to determine the economic landscape, that is, the general locational equilibrium given the system determining the most efficient spatial allocation of economic activities (Fischer, 2011). Following his line of argument, the most efficient economic landscape is where the maximum number of firms are located at the same point because such a concentration allows agglomeration economies to occur within each of the sets of firms located in the same place. The major feature of the economic landscape will be the domination of a central city over its hinterland with smaller cities and towns, and alternating areas of firm concentration and dispersion. However, business activities and urbanisation can arise independently of local properties or attributes (McCann, 2001).

Although CPT is criticised for not being general enough (it fits predominantly the areas of agricultural, services and basic manufacturing activities), it provides an explanation for two urban phenomena. First, it explains the existence of an urban hierarchy. Second, it explains not only the hierarchical organisation but also the spatial structure of the urban system – the spatial linkages between cities of different size (A. W. Evans, 1985, pp. 66–67). Indeed, one can argue that some kinds of goods and services, such as high-technology production, specialised retail, higher educational facilities, high-tech business services, live performing arts, fine arts and museums can be almost exclusively found in large cities, if not in the largest (central) ones. Most of these services cannot be shipped to buyers at other locations or need a relatively large threshold population to make a service viable at a particular place. They must be utilised on the spot, and therefore have to be located where a financially well-off audience (consumers) is large enough to purchase goods or avail themselves of services. As stated in the literature, the minimum number of these end-users required to sustain these services/activities are found almost solely in metropolitan areas (Edwards, 2007, pp. 59–63). Within this context, it is important to note that CPT, in spite of its limitations and a favoured-by-former-times approach to explaining the spatial patterns of economic activity and urbanisation, is experiencing a re-emergence as part of the core epistemology of regional and urban science by providing a fundamental framework to easily compliment more recent theories (Mulligan, Partridge, & Carruthers, 2012). As put forward by McCann and van Oort (2019) the modern concepts and recent treatment of agglomeration and regional and urban growth, in particular a new economic geography, do indeed build upon previous classical insights including the merits of CPT. This is because the assumptions of CPT integrates, at least conceptually, a number of key concepts in regional and urban science, namely: consumer choice, firm agglomeration and the functional hierarchy. Driven by market forces firms have an incentive to concentrate production in a limited number of places. Firms strive to occupy locations with good access to markets, and at the same time they also attempt to cluster in order to reap mutual advantages – e.g. reduction of transportation costs. Simultaneously, consumers try to minimise costs involved in purchasing goods and services by residing near spaces where they are available. The results of these adjustment processes are on the one hand the concentration of population and, on the other, the clustering of firms, which leads ultimately to the formation of a hierarchy that efficiently supplies all possible goods and services (Mulligan, Partridge, & Carruthers, 2012, pp. 410–413). Hence, it is undeniable that these insights are reminiscent of the result of CPT.

Besides being adequately specified to describe the spatial and functional ordering of urban centres over the regional and national economy, CPT was also extended to cover the distribution of retail and service activities within urban areas (Clark & Rushton, 1970; van Meeteren & Poorthuis, 2018). The two key components of CPT, that is, threshold and range, are still in use here. What seems to be evident is that, all other things being equal, the threshold can be reached more quickly in densely populated areas, whereas the range remains independent of density. However, boundary determination is difficult, if impossible, because in high population parts of urban areas the demand tends to be several times greater than the threshold level. The landscape of ranges and thresholds is defined by a geographical opportunity structure that determines which central functions are viable for provision to which parts of the population. Under these conditions providing some central functions both consumers and firms make decisions to (re)locate appropriately, which consequently reshapes the landscape. In fact, two opposite situations can be considered. On the one hand, firms can attempt to monopolise the market to supply all potential customers in a particular area, and at the same time, to settle as far as possible from potential competitors. The result of this is that the range will become equal to the threshold. Nevertheless, on the other hand, firms may decide to optimise the total number of potential customers. If so, they will try to locate where the highest number of potential customers are concentrated, even if this will be the most rational location for competitors. In the face of competition firms would earn only normal profits. The long-run equilibrium would be in practice representative of monopolistic competition. It is clear, however, that such competition engenders – e.g. through a division of labour between firms and innovative applications – the specialisation of and complementarity between firms. As a consequence of this, central places experience an increase in the variety of central functions (goods and services) simultaneously becoming more attractive, better equipped and, importantly, moving upward in the urban hierarchy. Which of the two business directions is chosen depends on the type of goods. The more specialised and higher value the goods and services, the wider the spread between the range and the threshold of those goods and services. Contrariwise, for firms offering mostly standardised goods and services, proximity to the consumers is a priority, therefore the spread between range and threshold remains low or they even overlap each other. Following on from this, a traditional distinction between standardised and specialised goods and services (convenience vs. comparison goods and services) remains of crucial importance, where central function patterns are presupposed to be more spread out with standardised, in comparison with specialised, goods and services (Goodall, 1972, pp. 134–135; van Meeteren & Poorthuis, 2018).

In seeking further explanations for both industry locations and settlement patterns within the functional urban system, the literature draws attention not only to the advantages deriving from increasing agglomeration but also to the various costs which vary with the city size. Spatial concentration is frequently limited by offsetting agglomeration diseconomies – e.g. high land rents and wages (Richardson, 1995). To begin with, it holds true that the costs of residence are the highest at the centre of a city and fall at a decreasing rate with distance from the centre. Put simply, the larger the city, the longer the distance over which the rent increases and the larger the difference between the rent of agricultural land and the rent of land at the city centre. An explanation for this is the cost of travel – high at the edge of the city and low at the centre. Households, trying to avoid bearing higher commuting costs, are inclined to pay more for housing nearer the centre. Given that the distance which has to be travelled is higher in larger cities, one may expect that land rents in the centres of these cities have considerably higher values. This fact is compounded by costly high-rise apartment and residential buildings in areas of high population density constructed by developers who seek to maximise their profits so as to compensate for the use of expensive land. A second type of agglomeration diseconomies varying by size of city are labour costs. It is supposed that the larger the city, the higher the wages. Since those living at the centre of the city must pay higher housing costs, and those living at the edge of the city decide on bearing higher commuting costs, we should expect that wages, through a labour market adjustment mechanism, will be higher in larger cities. In addition to that, higher land costs may also result in some goods and services being more expensive in larger cities, which reinforces the pressure on higher wages as well (A. W. Evans, 1985, pp. 69–72). These agglomeration diseconomies are borne by both firms and residents. The costs of them increase with the city size, so in order to maintain a long-run equilibrium within an urban hierarchy both firms and residents must obtain some benefits to make up for the external diseconomies.

Overall, CPT allows for a better understanding of how cities and towns of different sizes are organised and how human processes are embedded in space or stimulated by a given location. It emphasises that the spatial patterns and distribution of urban areas and human settlements have an impact on the type and range of economic activity within a location. Moreover, it indicates what kinds of goods and services are delivered at the particular levels of urban hierarchy, thus illustrating that the highest order settlement is distinguished by very peculiar activities. It is clear that some products and goods will not be demanded evenly over all cities and even within cities.

1.4 Market failures in urban growth

An urban area is a place where commercial relationships formed by firms and the allocation of goods and income to people occur to satisfy various needs. These interactions and flows are determined by demand and supply forces operating simultaneously in many different goods and factors markets. However, neither the given urban area nor the entire urban system can be viewed as solely economic mechanisms understood in classical terms. The urban area is created by humans and should be regarded as social unities. In addition to that, urban areas have a political identity and represent a physical setting as well as different land cover types. Thus, the urban system is a result of a complex interplay of physical, economic, behavioural and technical factors, and reflects a dynamic composition of different zonings and functions (Goodall, 1972). This is because there are many distortions in urban environments caused by numerous factors, including especially people's behaviours, that are not subject to any disciplinary forces such as price. In such a situation, when the market mechanism cannot allocate resources and income with a view to achieving an improvement in the quality of life and urban environment for residents, the state must interfere with the diseconomies of urbanisation to remove any divergence between social and private costs and benefits, and to countervail market failures.

The scale and scope of the authorities' responses is a function of the performance of the market mechanism and the limits to which market forces lead to a net social welfare loss. Hence, authorities should act to compensate market failures when the market mechanism is not capable of addressing the problems of negative effects and social costs. According to Henderson and Ledebur (1972, pp. 72–80), the main market failures related to urban market activity can be classified into four general categories. The first category refers to the fact that *individuals are excluded from participating in market activity due to their imperfections related to quality with social, educational, income and other standards set out by the institutions that control market behaviour and participation*. To put it simply, the market mechanism cannot work efficiently (in socially and publicly desirable terms) because of some potential consumers' and workers' inability to participate fully in market processes. Individuals characterised by lower levels of income, education, asset position and training opportunities are mostly pushed out of participating in the institutional arrangements that are accountable for generating supply and demand forces. People living in urban districts affected by deteriorating housing, low-paid jobs, inadequate job access, poor public facilities and lower standards and quality of life, possess comparatively lower economic capacities than those living in other urban areas. These factors make them more socio-economically marginalised and exclude them from engaging in the urban mainstream. Their consumption capacities determine their impact on resources and goods distribution. Since their effective demand is lower, their influence on productive processes, exchange of goods and service availability is also correspondingly weaker. As a consequence of the lower level of education, they are forces to be employed in low-skill and low-productivity jobs which in turn hinders their access to new and different skills and job training. This also discourages them from starting self-employed business activity. Discrimination in education and job access negatively affects productivity and income, thus contributing to widening socio-economic inequalities in urban areas. In connection with this, it is noteworthy that impartial economic processes driven by market forces tend to reinforce or even widen existing patterns of discrimination and inequality.

The second category of market failures encompasses the wide term of *social costs that accrue to individuals in consuming or using products that contribute to or cause personal harm*. These failures are described by increased real and money cost from the use or consumption of goods and services. Originally, individuals can be directly involved in processes induced by supply and demand forces in urban markets and accordingly their decisions/choices operate to allocate goods for their personal use. Even though this system functions well in the allocation of goods and services, giving the distinct role to consumers to determine the flow of resources and goods, and to have a decisive impact on pricing the factors, it seems to be not necessarily effective in other situations. For instance, consumer sovereignty is impotent in solving urban problems. Goods and services consumed within an urban environment may lead to an increase in consumer disutility instead of an increase in consumer satisfaction. This can happen because consumers, when making decisions that, via the market mechanism, affect the allocation of goods and services, lack the necessary knowledge, expertise and economic power to ensure that these goods and services will be of an appropriate quality and improve their well-being. Living in urban areas encompasses many spheres and domains where a high social cost would have been incurred by consumers attempting to satisfy their utility with urban goods or services if they had been delivered without appropriate societal health, welfare and safety standards. If many decisions related to the functioning of the urban system and social life had been left to market rivalry, their consequences would have contributed further to, for example, noise, air pollution, and many other health-related and societal problems in urban areas. Therefore, the market mechanism should function within a control framework guaranteed by legal regulation to prevent or mitigate social harm.

Agglomeration diseconomies are the third category. *Diseconomies accrue to the general public because there is no applicable private mechanism for public goods. Goods provided by governmental agencies bring about production diseconomies as well as uncompensated private cots in consumption.* Residents of urban areas are the recipients of goods and services in public as well as private markets. In general, communal services (road construction/maintenance, water service, waste-water treatment, refuse collection, public transport, education etc.) are provided by urban authorities rather than by private firms. However, even the public market operates under the forces of supply and demand that determine the quality, quantity and distribution of municipal services in urban areas. If the public market acts to deliver a high quality of services that are available to everyone in an urban area, it is generally assumed that the public market functions well. But when the allocation of services is managed in a public market in such a manner that private demand cannot be met sufficiently or residents must incur uncompensated costs, it is unquestionable that the public market contributes to private disutility. A good example of uncompensated costs or, in other words, "public market negative externalities" significantly decreasing private utility are intra-urban motorways that are characterised by traffic congestions. Individuals and firms use these roads for transportation purposes, incurring actual out-of-pocket costs for the use of these facilities. For practical reasons, the marginal cost of using the motorways for the average commuter is zero. The only effective market mechanism aimed at reducing the congestion is the congestion itself. Thus, the real cost and incipient money cost of the time lost dissuade commuters from using the motorways. It is therefore concluded that public markets do not necessarily function to deliver the adequate levels of goods and services to all urban citizens.

Finally, the fourth category of market failures are *social costs or negative externalities that accrue to the population as a whole as by-products of the production process*. This sort of failure, figuratively speaking, takes the form of urban economic ills caused by the production of negative externalities. By way of example, air pollution is an negative externality that occurs when polluters shift some of the costs of operations to society, which results not only in contaminated air in the atmosphere, but also creates a potential health risk to anyone who breathes it. In addition, psychological annoyance and aesthetic factors translate into decreased property values, damage of structures or materials, and damage to crops and other plants, the costs of which are incurred by third parties outside the production process. Given that most of the population lives in urban areas, transportation accounts for a major source of social costs. Residents are thus continuously exposed to air pollution emissions. This has a fairly wide range of consequences from the point of view of the medical costs associated with polluted air. Besides health costs, air pollution also directly affects the productivity of the labour force in terms of total people-hours with time lost at home, health facilities or attending for the care of others. Moreover, as historical structures are usually located in central urban areas with heavy traffic, they are damaged by oxidation/demineralisation, which entails restoration costs that are passed on to society (Rodrigue, 2020). This means that various kinds of spill-overs or by-products such as air pollution have economic costs that are borne by society in particular in urban areas where the most advanced allocation occurs for the productive use of resources.

Urbanisation is typically deemed to lead to greater economic growth of regions and nations. But economic growth generated in urbanised areas is directly connected with the spatial growth of cities. By reason of both the growing populations and their rising incomes, cities expand spatially, which brings about the conversion of agricultural land into residential land. This phenomenon, termed *urban sprawl*, is rather undesirable on environmental and aesthetic grounds. Urban spatial expansion is driven by market forces that, beside growing populations and their incomes, covers also such factors as investment in motorways and growing automobile ownership. Economists argue, however, that urban sprawl can be criticised on efficiency grounds only if the operation of these forces involves market failures. As noted by Brueckner (2000, 2001), there are three fundamental market failures that may lead to the excessive spatial growth of cities: (1) *a failure to account for the amenity value of open space around cities*; (2) *a failure to account for the social costs of freeway congestion*; and (3) *a failure to fully account for the infrastructure costs of new development.*

The first market failure results from the fact that one does not take into account the social value of open space when land is converted to urban use. This means that intangible open-space benefits are not incorporated into the income earned by the land when it is in agricultural use. The disappearance of these benefits is not recognised in the transaction as a monetary loss when the land is converted to urban use. As a result, the invisible hand of the market ignores the open-space benefits and leads to the situation where too much rural land is allocated to urban use, thus causing the excessive spatial growth of cities.

The second type of market failure has its origins in the perception of commuting costs by individual commuters who recognise only partly the social costs of congestion created by their use of the road network. An average citizen perceives only the "private cost" of commuting she or he actually needs to pay. This cost includes the out-of-pocket costs of vehicle operation as well as the "time cost" of commuting expressed as the value of time consumed in transit. Note that while commuting to work, another cost is generated during the trip. This cost is above and beyond the private cost and also covers the cost of the extra congestion caused by other commuters being present on the road. Thus, the true social cost of commuting for an individual includes the "private cost" and the costs imposed on other commuters by the extra congestion. Although the extra congestion cost is slight from the point of view of an individual commuter, its impact is significant as it influences many other commuters. On account of the fact that congestion costs are incurred by others, the individual commuter has no incentive to take them into account. This missing motivation represents a market failure, the result of which is that commuting on congested roadways appears to be unnaturally cheap to individual commuters. Consequently, this leads to excessive commuting and cities that are spatially large, and the fact that congested roads are overused from society's point of view.

The source of the third market failure that significantly affects urban growth is rooted in the fact that real estate developers do not take fully into consideration all of the infrastructure costs generated by new development. When building new housing developments, many other facilities or amenities are needed such as roads, sewers, schools, parks, recreation areas etc., which are provided mainly from the public side. These infrastructural public assets are financed by residents through the property tax system. The market failure arises because, under typical financing arrangements, the infrastructure-related tax burden on new residents is disproportionately less than the actual public costs spent to establish infrastructure that enables living in the city. Hence, new urban development seems to be relatively cheap, from the point of view of the developers, which encourages excessive urban growth.

It should be added here that unpriced traffic congestion is definitely seen as a stimulus to the spatial expansion of cities. However, alongside this there are also other kinds of vehicle-related externalities leading to excessive urban sprawl, namely, air pollution. This happens because low-density suburban development provides incentives for movements towards rural areas which in turn leads to an increase in commuter vehicle journeys and longer commutes, thus causing greater air pollution released by the city's residents. Vehicle emissions are commonly seen as an important source of urban externalities. Nevertheless, the sprawl effect of the emission externality is not based on the effect of the congestion externality. This implies that emission externality is an independent source of market failures contributing to the excessive spatial growth of cities. Although both congestion and emission externalities are linked with excessive urban sprawl, their sources are different. When it comes to traffic congestion, urban sprawl is unwelcome because longer commuting distances arising from spatial expansion give rise to additional external congestion costs. Concurrently, urban sprawl is also not desirable with regard to the emission externality because residents in widely spread cities prefer to use less fuel-efficient vehicles, thus putting more contaminants into the atmosphere (Kim, 2016). In the first case, the additional congestion costs are caused by the commuter's longer presence on the road, while in the second case the higher social costs are generated by vehicle emissions. In both cases the additional social costs are incurred by society as a whole and not by individual commuters, hence constituting market failures in urban growth. Since these costs are not passed on to particular commuters directly, the commuters are, one can say, motivated to draw away from the city centre.

It would appear that the last four discussed market failures are surely associated with urban growth but affect a city's spatial expansion rather than its intra-urban development. This, however, is not true. Both new suburban areas and older inner-city areas compete for mobile residents. Thus, the same market failures that lead to urban sprawl also contribute to urban blight. As reported by Brueckner and Helsley (2011), urban sprawl, understood as excessive investment in new suburban areas, and urban blight, defined as deficient reinvestment in older inner-city properties, arise from the same fundamental economic process. Both phenomena are responses to underlying market failures influencing urban markets. Operation of these market failures gives rise to a situation where the cost of living in suburban areas is inefficiently low. This distorts the allocation of population through encouraging residents to leave the downtown for leafy suburbs and rural quiet areas. As a result of the population shift, housing and real estate building prices are, in turn, reduced in the centre, which diminishes incentives to maintain or reinvest in existing structures. If the filtering process accelerates, the areas that are thus being drained of their residents and purchasing power are naturally grouped together, blighting chances of further growth. Their structures progressively deteriorate, and new capital flees from or is not interested in entering the area and making investments there. Moreover, this process makes the central parts of cities the best locations for poor households, and the residents' low income translates into low housing quality. Low-quality buildings are used by whoever is willing to take them. Because of the owners' earnings incapacity or landlords' insufficient profitability to better maintain or redevelop the properties, all structures become progressively obsolete. This leads to a subsequent reduction in demand for accommodations and urban decline, which extends contagiously across the entire neighbourhood. Additional buildings become run down or may even be abandoned, resulting in a further decrease in demand for living in the neighbourhood. In this way, the blight of inner-city areas is driven by a process of self-fulfilling expectations.[4] It follows that urban blight is likely to stem from the interaction of neighbourhood externalities and exogenous forces causing an initial decline in the maintenance or redevelopment of buildings. However, the main trigger of urban blight is the natural operation of the land market taking place under sprawl-generating market failures (Brueckner & Helsley, 2011).

The reality is that in urban areas residents are both most positively and most adversely affected by the successful functioning of the market mechanism. They enjoy, bear and cause the performance and by-products of the urban system. The extent to which social benefits accrue is a function of income, education, health, wealth, etc., but the extent to which social costs accrue is a function of market allocation. However, as Cinyabuguma and McConnell (2013) noted, limiting urban sprawl may also lead to an increase in the negative externalities associated with (greater than optimal) density. This distinctly shows that sources of urban increasing returns are also sources of urban inefficiencies. Private and so-

---

[4] Surprising evidence on this point was provided by Glaeser, Kahn, and Rappaport (2008), who investigated the relationship between the location of poverty and access to public transport. They reported that the poor are likely to live in cities with more public transportation, whereas cities with a smaller gap in public transit facilities between suburbs and city centres are characterised by less poverty centralisation. This means that public transport plays a major role in initialising the process of urban poverty concentration. Notwithstanding, transportation is vital for the growth of cities. These results suggest that transport technologies and transportation modes determine the structure of cities.

cial marginal returns do not often coincide in a city environment. What follows is that urban production is inefficient in the sense that it does not ensure the best possible allocation of local resources. The existence and growth of cities is driven by various mechanisms that can generate both similar and different outcomes. Hence, the precise identification of the sources of urban agglomeration and their related market failures seems extremely difficult (Duranton, 2009). Nevertheless, knowing about both the type of market failures and their causes is required to initiate an effective policy intervention. This is of particular importance because the market failures associated with urban mechanisms require different corrective policies to internalise externalities, thus bringing a city closer to optimality.

1.5 The intra-urban effects of agglomeration economies on cities

Cities are always changing. As they are still affected by trends of transformation, they undergo a constant process of adaptation to changing conditions in their social and economic environment in order to remain competitive and create growth. While some cities inevitably grow continually and experience a long period of flourishing, others are characterised by extreme difficulties of adjustment and suffer from many problems – e.g. decreasing average wage levels, concentration of inequalities in terms of poor housing, low-quality education, unemployment, increasing social disparities and difficulties in accessing certain services. There is no single overriding reason for urban decline, although the term "market failures" is frequently used as a synonym for describing some undesirable changes that occur in the socio-economic sphere (Brueckner, 2001). Among many causes leading towards a deterioration of urban life (having a social, political or psychological nature) most studies assign the causal role to economic factors (W. L. Henderson & Ledebur, 1972; Lang, 2005; Roberts, 2008). According to Lang (2005), the most relevant economic factors affecting changing cities are:
- (international) industrial restructuring in pursuit of maximising returns including deindustrialisation;
- globalisation and economic concentration as forces for economic structural change;
- the problems of adapting to new demands of economic activities and factor constraints (including the availability of land and buildings).

Urban economy is dominated by some industries and to a large degree depends on the type of production. The more labour-intensive and heavy the industries, the bigger the risk of change that causes a need to adapt. And vice versa, the more advanced and innovative the activities requiring a skilled or highly skilled labour force, the lower the risk for the local economy. More advanced production or services are closely linked to more urbanised areas. The rationale for this is that more innovative production and services need highly qualified employees and capital, which are available in agglomerations. In turn, smaller cities are characterised by poor economic structure or even depend on only one industry, causing serious problems with adaptation. In recent decades, especially since globalisation processes have become even more apparent, there has been a strong demand for rationalisation in the production and service sectors. There was a significant transition from an industry-based economy to a service-based economy, with a growth of employment in services and a need for different and more specific requirements in the labour market. This process affects adversely in particular those areas with traditional production sectors that face increasing difficulty in adapting to newly emerging needs. In such changing contexts and the growing importance of business networking large companies (international or national) and smaller enterprises motivated by means of agglomeration economies locate their production facilities, service and financial centres in or near large urban centres. As a consequence, current processes of internationalisation and inter- and intra-firm relations reveal a tendency towards concentration of the most important business activities in a relatively limited number of sub-national regions or agglomerations. Such tendencies manifestly promote the concentration of population and economic activity in capital cities and other large core cities (Lang, 2005).

Indeed, large urban centres have legacy advantages that give them a strong competitive edge over other areas to attract both people and business. Urban concentration is commonly deemed to lead to greater national economic growth and produce a wide range of benefits (Brülhart & Sbergami, 2009; V. Henderson, 2003). However, the advantages aside, cities, even the core ones, encounter difficulties in adjusting to the changing economy and can experience an imbalance of demographic and economic development. Many cities face a significant loss of inclusive power and cohesion, experiencing an economic slowdown and an increase in social problems and social disparities. Adjustments to changing supply and demand conditions are not without difficulties and may lead to really serious problems in intra-urban development patterns. Urban growth is largely dependent on an increase in the adequate infrastructure (transport and communications systems, housing, business spaces, public structures) and/or direct or indirect contacts between people and business. Put simply, if the channels of transmissions are overloaded, the result is disorganisation. The provision of transport or other components of urban infrastructure is removed from the impact of price mechanism, and changes in supply (e.g. new infrastructural investments) are not essentially tailored to changes in demand but to the public financing capacities. This works particularly where no direct price is charged for the use of urban facilities (e.g. roads). The disorganisation resulting from the overloading of urban structures can drive intra-urban relocation, so that more and more business activities, but also people, seek non-central locations (Goodall, 1972). Firms opt to invest in those areas where they can avoid diseconomies of agglomeration or at least they can attain locational equilibrium. People, in turn, are interested in more comfortable conditions for living, work and leisure. Such a tendency explicitly represents the phenomenon of urban sprawl seen as a natural process of expansion of large urban areas, under market conditions, mainly into the surrounding undeveloped areas. The old housing stock, due to technical obsolescence or physical exhaustion, does not meet basic standards and are not a subject of interest, or are even abandoned. The increasing worker mobility results in the geographical dispersal of work places which, in turn, leads to the creation of new linkages between home, work, trade and leisure facilities. Consequently, the old urban structures and buildings no longer comply with the new functional plans, and it may even be argued that some urban areas "fall out of a play" for a city. These disadvantaged areas lose their competitiveness because the old urban tissue, due to its morphology (e.g. difficult roadway access, lack of green areas etc.), is not able to adapt to new functions (new services or forms of production). Furthermore, it should also be noted that old urban areas and their residential properties rarely evolve in line with the rhythm of city's development. In fact, they are eroded by the profound structural economic shifts, which leads to the creation of "set-aside urban zones" – in these areas, historically rooted industrial sectors disappear and new ones do not emerge because no one is interested (Skalski, 2016).

These inner-city areas become not only physically marginalised and suffer degradation but also lose well-educated people because of job shortages or unattractive living and working conditions. As Goodall (1972, p. 219) pointed out, buildings and areas constantly react upon one another. The greater the proportion of obsolescent buildings in an area the less desirable it is as a location for new business activities and the more difficult it is to maintain the proper value of buildings or redevelop particular sites. Obsolescence spreads throughout an area accelerating the displacement of people and business activities, thus making it deprived. These areas face acute problems of urban decay and social exclusion, and become synonymous with urban blight. Given that a blight is regarded subjectively by the non-acceptance of obsolescent buildings and areas with their factual features, there are two types of real property depreciation, namely: functional and social. The former arises from a decline in a building's capacity to render service or from a decline in the demand for the service rendered. In addition to that, both causes depend on changes in supply/demand conditions and are reflected in a loss of earnings. The latter, that is, social property depreciation, is associated with a loss of prestige. The negative characteristics of blighted areas seldom represent a simple aggregate of defects in individual properties, for often important service facilities are lacking in these areas. What is crucial in this context is that causal factors of urban blight generally stem from economic progress and urban growth. The conflict between fixed infrastructural resources and highly mobile social and economic demands emphasises many of the basic maladjustments in the spatial structure of urban areas (Goodall, 1972).

As can be seen, the deterioration of inner-city areas is based on mutual causality and interactions. To some extent, it can be explained by Myrdal's *cumulative circular causation* (1957), where social systems tend to amplify difference, thereby engendering inequalities through ongoing processes of interactions (Dannefer, 2020). Therefore, drawing on Henderson and Ledebur's (1972, pp. 162–167) genesis of deprived inner-city areas, the process can be determined by the following factors.

1. Economic discrimination. The market mechanism tends to discriminate, through its rationing function, against those inhabitants who have purchasing power significantly inferior to that of other consumers in the market. Low-income earners with a low disposable amount of money are simply priced out of the market. They cannot afford to purchase commodities that would make for a decent standard of living. Conversely, they do not have adequate qualifications that are needed in a labour market characterised by structural change. These people possess a weak entrepreneurial mindset and often suffer from being dependent on difficult circumstances (e.g. public income support) rather than being able to make their own living.

2. Decreasing employment opportunities. A decreasing income makes people marginalised, which exerts the effect of social polarisation that in turn leads to spatial segregation. The phenomenon of socio-spatial segregation creates an environment that is not conducive to the retention of business. The locational influences that initially attracted and maintained business in the central parts of cities are successively eroded. Positive locational factors such as rapidity of contact and proximity of the market are being offset relatively quickly by technological improvements in both communication and transportation. The remaining positive locational factor of the disadvantaged area – a cheap unskilled labour force – is crowded out by technological advancement. Business operations are becoming increasingly capital-intensive, involving less labour, and employees with higher skill levels. These factors have resulted in a trend of businesses moving out of the central parts

of cities and into the suburban rings. The employment opportunities and respective services are increasingly shifted to the suburbs. Note that they are becoming difficult to access in both geographical and qualifications-related terms.
3. Inferior training and support. Residents face in particular significant difficulties in access to employment. Decreasing employment opportunities are partly responsible for their low income. In turn, low income makes it difficult to take action aimed at upgrading the professional skills or helping professional reorientation. Because of the insufficient income, they are not able to obtain adequate education or training in order to strengthen their potential and adapt their qualifications to changing labour market needs. The problem is exacerbated when social assistance institutions and public employment services do not work effectively or, due to limited public financial capacities they are powerless against the extreme magnitude of the problem. As a consequence, inferior skills cause low productivity in the labour factor in the area. Low productivity results in low income and the chain of causation starts again. Residents suffer from work-related discrimination and experience increasing disutility effects.
4. Deteriorating physical facilities. Factors 2 and 3 produce the economic profile of the deprived area. By reason of the combination of decreasing employment opportunities, inferior training and support, and low productivity, extensive unemployment develops within the area. All this makes it increasingly difficult for people with low income to find decent housing at an affordable price. Hence, the residents often live in poverty in the midst of a rapidly deteriorating physical environment. The quality of buildings decreases essentially with the present residents because they are not able to maintain these facilities on the grounds of their age, rate of deterioration and the residents' low income. The successive use of these buildings by group after group of low-income people accelerates the rate of obsolescence. In the deprived areas landlords are less interested in keeping up property than making profit while maintaining it for a stable economic productivity as long as it does not becomes completely obsolescent.
5. Separate neighbourhoods. The cumulative interaction of the aforementioned factors leads to the classical picture of deprived areas – i.e. separate and segregated neighbourhoods characterised by an urban fabric with the variety of public facilities inferior to the ones that exist in the other areas of the city. The rapid deterioration of the physical environment results in declining property values. These areas are regarded as exclusion enclaves that have emerged especially in central areas or in old industrial districts. To complement this picture, the processes of spatial segregation are usually

accompanied by a gentrification[5] which, changing some attractive historical districts, further exposes the socio-economic inequalities in a spatial dimension. The combination of the residents' low incomes, decreasing real estate property value and relatively low levels of entrepreneurial activity with the out-migration of businesses results in the lack of an appropriate tax base to ensure the desirable level of public services.

6. Insufficient public services. Deprived inner-city areas experiencing the hardships of unemployment, economic disinvestment, social disorganisation and in general urban blight do not provide an adequate tax base to support the necessary public services. In addition, if urban authorities struggle with limited financing possibilities for needed services and investments, these areas are confronted with inferior public facilities such as roads, education, sanitation, green and leisure areas, cultural sites, public amenities, etc. This deepens the negative impacts because such facilities are necessary to create a level of environmental quality in which individuals do not suffer from the deteriorating appearance of their neighbourhood. What is more, the inability to provide basic public facilities leads to inefficiency in the services in general called *social overhead capital*. This term refers to the whole spectrum of publicly provided services, and in its wider sense includes all public services from law and spatial planning (order) through education and public health to transportation, communications, energy, water supply etc. The important thing is that this capital ensures the fundamental base necessary for economic development to occur. Following Hirschman's line of argument (1958), it enables economies of scale to be achieved in particular locations, thus accelerating business activity growth.

A graphical representation of these factors, which interact in the process of cumulative circular causation and result in the formation and persistence of deprived urban areas is provided in Figure 3. As can be seen, economic factors are driving forces for an urban deterioration in spatial terms. By reason of the

---

[5] Gentrification is a process of neighbourhood change in which an initially poor urban area experiences an influx of higher-income and higher-educated residents who redevelop buildings and businesses and which often brings about an increase in property values. This takes place largely in historically marginalised areas located in the urban core where certain historical and cultural features as well as the availability of specific jobs or services are factors that make them more attractive to newcomers. Moreover, these factors are a powerful driver of physical and socio-economic transformation of the areas. Nevertheless, the redevelopment pressure entails the loss of affordable housing and causes the displacement of the usually poorer residents, thus changing completely the character of the place. For more see: Goetz et al. (2019).

inability of residents to meet changeable market needs, in a narrow sense, or the inefficiency of the whole urban system to spark adequate adjustment processes, in a wider sense, some inner urban areas experience population decreases and a degradation of the urban fabric. Depending on a particular location, different factors accounting for urban decay can affect both people and businesses in various ways and to varying degrees.

What is interesting about the influence of particular factors and the interactions between them, as shown in Figure 3, is the fact that only the cumulative interactions of all of them may lead to a serious and chronic deterioration in the state of a given area.[6] However, urban authorities have a role to play in advance, by establishing anticipated strategies and effective local policies aimed at addressing the economic tendencies and concerns. Urban deterioration is undeniably a diseconomy of urban growth, and the misallocation of resources is such that it should become a major policy issue for urban authorities at the proper time.

Although there are many disadvantages caused by urbanisation which push some residents and districts out of the urban mainstream and bring about a concentration of inequalities, urban areas continue to grow, showing relatively high rates of growth. This indicates that the disadvantages of urban growth do not outweigh the advantages. Cities do play a crucial role as engines of the economy, being centres of knowledge and sources of innovation. They provide a wide range of public services and facilities and possess unique cultural and architectural qualities. As long as the advantages of cities' social and economic development can be "internalised" by people and firms, the urban disadvantages are more likely to be "externalities" (Goodall, 1972).

---

[6] However, the arrows running from the particular factor-triangles to the deprived urban area hexagon mean that the various factors may affect the formation of the deprived urban areas with varied intensity. Furthermore, depending on specific local circumstances, not all of them may occur to form such an area.

48 — 1 Background – urban economics

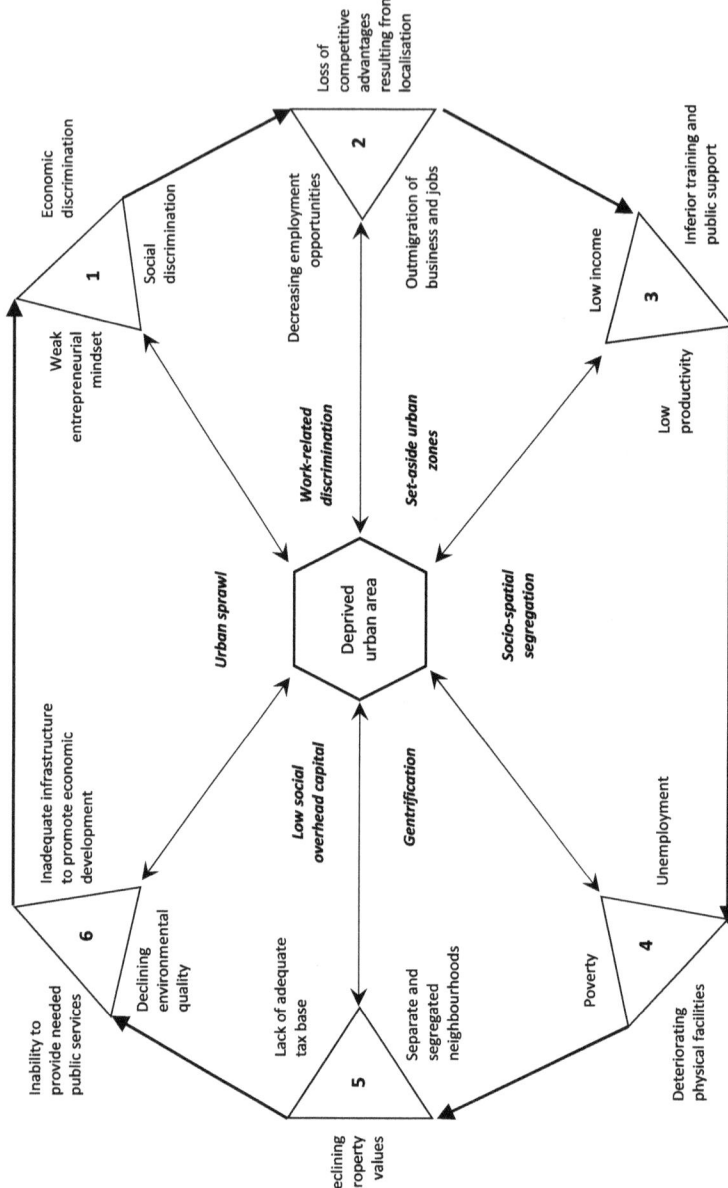

Figure 3: The formation process for deprived urban areas
Source: Adapted and modified from (W. L. Henderson & Ledebur, 1972, p. 164)

2 The theoretical underpinning of a place-based perspective on sustainable urban development

2.1 Urban policy as a response to urban needs

2.1.1 Urban land use planning and policy-making

The use and structure of urban land plays a decisive role in shaping the potential of residents to access jobs, services, and consequently create productive and sustainable growth. Land use planning (LUP) is perceived, in its regulatory function, as one of the most important instruments of public interventions applicable to the imperfections – by nature – of market mechanisms for the location of building infrastructures in the space (Markowski, 2018). Since land markets are characterised by endemic market failures there is a need for LUP in order to create benefits in the form of public goods such as roads, parks, street lighting and other amenities provided by the authorities. The aim of urban LUP is to design and implement regulations that lay down the pattern of how land can be used in cities. Such a policy should be focused on coordinating private investments and complementing private land use. By doing so, as Collier and colleagues argued (2020), it is possible to support cities to allocate land adequately for public infrastructure with the view to improving productive density. Moreover, active and well-designed land use policy can also enhance social cohesion and reduce socio-spatial inequalities in cities by planning integrated neighbourhoods, thus addressing the existing market failures pertaining to land. Among the main challenges regarding policy decisions on urban land use planning, they point to three aspects:
- urban spatial master plans, that design plans for the future spatial structure of a city;
- density regulations, that set limits on the density of development in a city;
- the acquisition of land for urban transformation.

Regarding the first aspect, a common phenomenon associated with urban development is urban sprawl. It does not always have to represent land market failure but it is often caused by restrictive density regulations or discontinuous leapfrog development (it occurs in areas that are not adjacent to the existing development). Therefore, land use plans should determine adequate connections be-

Piotr Idczak

https://doi.org/10.1515/9783110762198-006

tween firms and workers, via roads, public transport systems and non-motorised transport. In addition, the designation of land for socially desired public spaces will produce significant benefits for residents in recreational and psychological terms. By ensuring conditions for better connectedness and greater desirability of surrounding property, LUP provides a credible signal of planned future investments in surrounding areas. As regards run-down urban areas that lost their liveability consequent to the operation of market-driven forces, land use plans establish believable frameworks and directions of future development, thereby improving coordination and providing guidance for private decisions to initiate new investments or meet expectations within a given urban area. In order to do this effectively, proactive planning is desired which takes into account future changing needs and tackles the future challenges of a city in advance (Collier et al., 2020).

In the sphere of urban LUP, there is a special control tool, termed "zoning", for regulating the type and range of actions to be taken in a particular area. Zoning means a regulatory mechanism whose purpose is to provide for orderly community growth and development by delineating some areas where different land uses are deemed incompatible (Brown, Sanders, & Reed, 2018). It is of particular importance in the context of deprived urban areas, against which zoning can also provide the opportunity to stimulate a specific kind of processes. Zoning regulations can be applied to launch spatial plans and define more detailed requirements of buildings in an area. Moreover, they can set out special regulations for individual permitting decisions to facilitate some actions in an area which should result in higher efficiency regarding the formal arrangements on an area of land.

Density regulations, the second aspect, lay down limitations on density and are useful to coordinate land use with the needs of firms and households because they can reduce adverse effects of higher density on living standards, pollution and productivity through overcrowding and congestion. Nevertheless, these regulations can also lead to an increase in land prices (as a result of the reduced local housing supply), excluding lower-income households from the land market (Collier et al., 2020). High density and rising land prices due to a lower housing supply can also stimulate urban sprawl, which in turn may give rise to the deterioration of previously densely inhabited inner-city areas. Hence, these regulations should be established carefully, keeping in mind the city's needs and the broader context of land uses.

Finally, acquiring land for urban transformation purposes can stimulate the city's growth. It is generally accepted as legitimate when its aim is to release land for the public's general interest. The compulsory acquisition of urban land by authorities, also called *eminent domain*, is expected for the realisation of vital infrastructure investments or public spaces and amenities with the intention of improving a city's liveability. However, *eminent domain* can become a field for abuse, especially in urban regeneration. Many examples from the past show that regeneration projects implemented simply for the modernisation of a city did not do much to contribute to improving the lives of previous residents who were resettled in disconnected locations (Collier et al., 2020).

In general, LUP is a special domain of public intervention which is specified through territorial and horizontal dimensions, and influences long-term processes. It should not be equated simply with the placement of public goods investments. It is strongly associated with market failures in real estate markets and all the challenges linked to them, such as: speculation in land, speculative bubbles, economic and structural crises, urban deterioration, etc. LUP determines solutions and methods of intervention that are important in the long run. In this area, policy-makers can establish key conditions for sustainable development to introduce regulations that diminish the negative effects of activities introduced by other policies. LUP, depending on the needs, can be decomposed into other specific policies of which, undeniably, the major policy is urban policy (Markowski, 2018). Notwithstanding this, both urban policy and LUP, at the planning stage, need to take into account market-led modes of thinking as cities are organic systems driven by market forces. As Adams and Tiesdell (2010) noted, a new balance between public planning and business expectations towards land use is possible and capable of offering new solutions, provided that planners demonstrate a clearer appreciation of markets as social constructs.

2.1.2 Strategic approach and urban policy fundamental for effective interventions

Cities have never operated in a vacuum. They grow rapidly and irreversibly and always struggle with resource and capacity constraints to manage the process of urbanisation. Although urban markets bring resources to their optimum and possibly best use, because of the existence of externalities, market allocation does not ensure the optimality of the solutions. Many of the problems faced by cities cannot be solved within cities alone. Urbanisation becomes a crucial issue not only for local but also for national economies. Urban growth, if it is uncontrolled, can generate serious social and environmental problems, including social inequalities and poverty. To a very large extent these problems stem from a lack of or scarce land use plans which often push cities to the limit of their capacity to provide services such as transportation, health care and security, energy etc. Therefore, there is a need to take into account the interrelation between urban areas and their surroundings, especially with respect to planning issues. Strategic planning is then a management tool that determines the direction of development of a city. Nevertheless, urban strategic planning and plans cannot substitute for the spatial planning process and spatial plans designed at other administrative levels of the territorial division of the states. The strategic planning process must guide development in the common direction of those strategic priorities identified by all stakeholders through vertical and horizontal collaboration.

Although cities, thanks to decentralisation, can make decisions closer to the people and are endowed with competences for managing new responsibilities, in many cases inequality of available resources and administrative capacities exists between different levels, limiting in practice administrative autonomy and possibilities to implement polices imposed by central government. In fact, local authorities have often weak instruments for regulating urbanism. Since cities are perceived as engines of large potential for economic and social development, creating jobs and offering new opportunities, their urban development plans must be inherent in key documents shaping the socio-economic and spatial development of the country (Górniak & Mazur, 2012). In other words, urban issues should be an integral part of overall development policy that encompasses series of interrelated activities carried out to ensure the sustainable development of the country, and social, economic and territorial cohesion. This represents a functional approach, presenting development policy from a managerial point of view, thereby providing an overall strategic vison and a wide range of general objectives, related both to different public policies and to different territories. All public polices and strategies should make up the strategic management of the country's development that is used to initiate directions for actions and implement specific measures (Hausner, 2008). Urban policy should then take a prominent place within the framework of this system, which means that, with other relevant public polices, it should constitute a complementary and consistent programming whole entailing the need for the implementation of the appropriate decisions and actions.

As for the urban policy, it is a form of public intervention in urban development conducted at a level higher than that of the municipal authority. Intervention levels are then the national and regional levels. However, the primary level of intervention is still the local level – i.e. the municipal authority and various structures that create local governance. External interventions towards the urban level are justified by a relatively high efficiency of local authorities in pursuing operations, which also results in better adjustment to the needs. Note, however, that "top-down" intervention is also justified by the complexity and supra-local nature of contemporary urbanisation processes. The essence of urban policy is to solve those issues that cannot be solved by individual cities on their own (Kuźnik, 2015). Therefore, cities taking part in the management of the country's development contribute not only to the improvement of the social and economic conditions within their boundaries, but also influence the growth of surrounding territorial entities and accordingly the whole country.

Bearing in mind the above, cities, in order to benefit fully from being part of this system, must design their own urban strategies or plans, including land use plans, that will be fully integrated and consistent with the priorities and objectives set out in the national development policy. Urban planning should encourage residents' participation in local policy decisions as a condition to develop sustainable and suitable projects in line with local needs. Urban planning should be based on a good urban governance basis where social participation and wide partnership are the key requirements (Badach & Dymnicka, 2017; UN-HABITAT, 2007). Participation and civic engagement should be ensured at various levels and through different solutions such as cross-sectoral teams, specific working groups and public consultations. Civil society as well as the public and private sectors should create networks rather than hierarchical relations, strengthened by knowledge and experience. Moreover, city authority should also ensure transparency and accountability by virtue of participatory action planning, resource mobilisation and resource allocation. Through mobilising and involving stakeholders in the implementation of urban projects as well as in the operation and maintenance of services, it is possible to improve the efficiency of all local efforts made to improve a city's liveability.

2.1.3 Territorial integrated approach

In his groundbreaking report of 2009, Barca argued that policy interventions are superior to spatially blind interventions, which too often assume a top-down approach (Barca, 2009). This began a shift in thinking from sectoral and top-down interventions to place-based policy thinking. The debate on this new approach was especially influential on the measures of EU cohesion policy. The fundamental assumption of the integrated place-based approaches is that exogenous interventions (one-size-fits-all) appeared not to be efficient enough. The exogenous state is not regarded as knowing better the particular needs of various areas. But this state should set a policy framework that invites local and regional actors to express their views, to cooperate, to develop new ideas, and to build trust. According to Zaucha, Świątek, and Stańczuk-Olejnik (2013), integrated place-based approaches rely on:

- *a long-term development strategy with the objective of reducing persistent inefficiency and inequality in specific places;*
- *the production of bundles of integrated, place-tailored, public goods and services, designed and implemented by eliciting and aggregating local preferences and knowledge through participatory political institutions, and by establishing linkages with other places;*
- *being promoted from outside the place by a system of multi-level governance where grants, subject to conditionalities on both objectives and institutions are transferred from higher to lower levels of government.*

Integrated place-based approaches emphasise the local context, and directly indicate that local knowledge is necessary to determine the most appropriate solutions for a particular place. They encompasses a number of interlinked dimensions (van der Zwet et al., 2017). First, a *geographical dimension* which involves the integration of "specific places" and provides "linkages with other places". This means that development interventions should be integrated territorially and tailored to the specific needs of certain places regardless of their administrative boundaries. The second dimension refers to an increase in the *integration of interventions*. Through combining intervention measures under different sectoral polices (integration), it is possible to improve their effectiveness and to establish a more integrated approach to, for example, urban development. It is also foreseen to implement development strategies through joint approaches between local administrations that at the same time are part of a functional territory. Third, *knowledge integration* stresses domestic institutional structures in particular at the local level. The aim is to provide opportunities for capacity-building at the local level, and empower local communities in implementing development initiatives, thereby promoting strategic thinking and dictating the concentration of actions and resources at local levels. Finally, the *governance dimension* relates to "participatory political institutions". The assumption here is that the integrated approach should be based on a strong vertical and horizontal collaboration between partners and common responsibilities that are shared appropriately. The integration of territory should be achieved by mechanisms which enable the harmonisation of interventions across administrative territories. In order to do this, vertical and horizontal relationships between partners should be strengthened with a view to facilitating multi-level partnerships. Taking all these dimensions into account is a necessary condition for achieving territorial cohesion.

Regarding the urban question, Medeiros (2019, p. 3) argues that there are several urban problems to be dealt with when implementing territorial cohesive policies, namely: "avoiding diseconomies of very large agglomerations and urban sprawl processes, combating urban decay and social exclusion, avoiding excessive concentrations of growth, promoting access to integrated transport systems and creating metropolitan bodies". The importance of the urban dimension seems, therefore, essential for facing the opportunities and challenges of cities themselves but also for achieving the endogenous growth potential of territories. Hence, drawing upon Faludi's territorial cohesion thinking (2009), it is argued that intervention measures designed for urban areas should acquire an added value by forming coherent policy packages which take into account the specific opportunities and constraints of a given place. More substantively, such an approach strives for providing a more cohesive and balanced territory through reducing socio-economic territorial imbalances, promoting environmental sustainability, improving territorial governance processes and, fundamentally, reinforcing a more polycentric urban system (Medeiros, 2016, 2019). In that respect, urban measures have to provide a trade-off between people- (sectoral-) and area-based interventions in order to, on the one hand, preserve the original social characteristics of a particular area and, on the other, to carry out in-depth physical upgrading and restructuring with the main goal of combating a variety of problems in deprived areas. This, however, requires horizontal, vertical and territorial integration,[7] otherwise implementation of urban measures will remain effectively irrelevant. The integration of various policy measures in a local area that has to be embedded into higher-level (regional and higher) polices and made under the conditions of multi-level governance enables the creation of a joint territorial development policy (Tosics, 2015). The important role played in this complex process by the integrated approach is key to ensuring a greater complementarity and synergy between various urban measures designed to counteract multiple deprivation. Sound urban programmes and projects must therefore shape the form of urbanisation which provokes a desirable territorial cohesion path counter to common patterns of territorial development and trends.

---

[7] In the literature, *horizontal integration* is generally understood to mean establishing and coordinating the policy fields in a specific area. It combines investment measures focused on improving the physical environment with social measures for helping local people into jobs to ensure that they benefit from economic renewal of the area. *Vertical integration* refers to bringing policies from different levels of government together. It means that the various levels of authorities communicate and work together for commonly agreed aims and methods. In turn, *territorial integration* tends to be used to refer to reshaping functional areas to make them evolve into a consistent geographical entity in which policy interventions are not limited only to deprived neighbourhoods, but constitute an inherent part of development policies for the entire entity. (For more see Böhme et al., 2011, pp. 23–28; Ramsden, 2011, pp. 53–56).

Returning to the problems of urban deterioration, it is important to acknowledge that diseconomy forces become sufficient enough to create a pattern of spatially unbalanced urban growth. Consequently, some inner urban areas emerge that are vulnerable to cumulative risks. From Myrdal's theory of cumulative causation, which sought to explain the spatial imbalances in the economy and the spatially uneven development (Myrdal, 1957), through the "new" economic geography of Krugman, where a mix of economies of scale, specialisation and transport costs are used to clarify the growth of urban areas (Krugman, 1991), to the place-based approach proposed by Barca, who traces underdevelopment in some places to the lack of a tailored policy response to the location-specific needs (Barca, 2009), it has been certain that these agglomeration diseconomies can be tackled through the place-adjusted public interventions addressing the tendencies towards urban inequalities.

2.2 Urban regeneration

2.2.1 Purpose and concept of urban regeneration

Urban regeneration is widely regarded as a significant component of wider *urban policy*, which is not solely related to regeneration (Tallon, 2013, p. 4). It can be seen as a response to social and economic decline that occurs in urban areas and societies as a result of urban transformation and insufficient capacities for adaptation to structural change. Urban areas are complex and dynamic systems being affected by many processes which continuously induce economic, social, physical and environmental transition. Urban regeneration is then regarded as the outcome of the interplay between these many processes that is stimulated by public and private policy response (Roberts, 2008). This means that urban regeneration entails any significant interventions that involve coordinated actions carried out under the auspices of urban authorities in run-down urban areas in need of lasting improvement (de Magalhães, 2015). It includes a wide range of various local policies and strategies established to deal with urban decline, decay or transformation (Lang, 2005). They aim to implement a joint set of remedial actions that will produce desired outputs that, in turn, will affect core outcomes like employment, quality of the environment and people's lives and social inclusion (Tyler et al., 2013). Hence, urban regeneration is a process geared toward improving deprived areas' qualities and creating the favourable conditions for a sustainable and social inclusive growth. It intertwines architectural and urban dynamics with economic development, social inclusion, spatial order and environmental protection (De Medici, Riganti, & Viola, 2018). All this comes down to the general conclusion that the key purpose of urban regeneration is to make run-down urban areas attractive and vibrant again, and promote economic growth and improve quality of life for their residents.

However, as structural changes provoke a greater or lesser degradation of some parts of urban areas due to their variegated impact on all aspects of urban development, urban regeneration has to be a multidimensional and multifaceted response which covers not only the economic and the physical aspects of urban transformation in the long run, but also pays particular attention to the social dimension. Urban regeneration is done for people so as to develop places where they want to be, and, equally importantly, by people so as to make them involved in the decision-making process on the development of those places. To better express the comprehensive nature of urban regeneration Turok (after Tallon, 2013) identified three distinctive features of this concept:
- it is intended to change the nature of a place and in the process to involve the community and other actors with a stake in its future;
- it embraces multiple objectives and activities that cut across the main functional responsibilities of central government, depending on the area's particular problems and potential;
- it usually involves some form of partnership working amongst different stakeholders, although the form of partnership can vary.

These features clearly show that urban regeneration tends to focus on both people and places. It addresses the urban problems through an adequate response to new conditions and thereby cannot be a static phenomenon. Given the fact that urban areas, including deprived ones, are dynamic socially and economically constructed places, regeneration aims to re-connect marginalised urban areas with the functional dynamics of the whole city to which they belong. Problems of deprived urban areas count often amongst the most intractable in society, therefore a successful regeneration response calls for a deep understanding of the processes of decline (Tallon, 2013). This implies the need to recognise the particular situation as regards the nature of social, economic, physical and environmental problems in the context of specific inner-city areas. While there is no *one-size-fits-all* solution, regeneration decision-makers are expected to provide appropriate support and tailor actions to meet these areas' needs under the strategic framework for city-wide development. As Stouten (2011) argues, two major concerns that are prevalent in recent times on the agenda of strategies for urban regeneration are the search for lasting solutions and an integrated approach to physical, environmental, social and economic programmes.

The complexity of urban regeneration is highlighted by the multitude of definitions and approaches on what urban regeneration does mean and, more operationally, how it should be carried out. The fact is that its definitional connotation depends on the level of development of particular urban areas and the magnitude of the challenges that need to be tackled. Roberts (2008, p. 17) defines the essence of urban regeneration as *comprehensive and integrated vision and actions which lead to the resolution of urban problems and which seek to bring about a lasting improvement in the economic, physical, social and environmental condition of an area that has been subject to change*. A priority for urban regeneration, according to Couch, Sykes, & Börstinghaus (2011, p. 3), is *to enhance the quality of life of local people in areas of need by reducing the gap between deprived and other areas, and between different groups' economies*. In turn, Lang (2005) places special emphasis on the casual context of urban regeneration and explains it as a *holistic process of reversing economic, social and physical decay in areas where it has reached a stage when market forces alone will not suffice*. A more contemporary definition is provided by Marra and colleagues (2016, p. 379) who, following the European mainstream in urban issues, interpret urban regeneration as *an integrated policy promoted by a partnership of public and private stakeholders, aimed at comprehensive, long-lasting and holistic renewal of degraded urban areas from a wide range of points of view (physical, environmental, social and economic)*. Although these definitions do not exhaust the entire range of definitional considerations on urban regeneration in literature, and provide different backgrounds and views, they show a high degree of consistency to be regarded as a necessary far-reaching intervention towards urban decline. (For a detailed review on the topic of urban regeneration definitions in contemporary literature see e.g. Jadach-Sepioło, 2021; Xie, Liu, & Zhuang, 2021).

Bearing in mind the above-mentioned review, in what follows, it can be stated that regeneration plays an important role in the process of reversing economic, social and physical degradation in urban areas, where such a stage has been reached that market forces are no longer sufficient to maintain a path of sustainable development. In the face of such a situation, there is a need for intervention by the public authorities, which are directly or indirectly required to implement a wider range of measures in the areas affected by the accumulation of states of emergency (Musiałkowska & Idczak, 2016). In this context regeneration needs to respond to new conditions and aims to modify the urban fabric with the view to adapting to new conditions, social requirements and demands (Stouten, 2016). More precisely, it should be a coordinated process, run jointly by local authorities, local communities and other stakeholders, which is an integral part of a development policy focused on achieving such objectives as preventing degradation of urban spaces and crisis phenomena, stimulation of the development and qualitative changes through increasing social and economic activity, improvement of living conditions and protection of national heritage, etc. (Wojnarowska & Kozłowski, 2011). This approach primarily emphasises the need for coordinated action, both public and private, which should be implemented in accordance with the principles of sustainable development. As noted by Evans and Jones (2008), the concept of sustainability lies at the core of the urban regeneration agenda. The implication of the term "sustainable" was a holistic approach widely applied to regeneration which involves governance and multidimensional partnerships in getting regenerative actions done. Multi-agency governance and a collaborative style of planning and implementing together with goals of sustainable development are perceived to structure the realm of urban regeneration. Following this line of reasoning, it can be argued that urban regeneration is a narrower category in relation to sustainable urban development. While urban regeneration actions must be done in line with the sustainable urban development paradigm, a variety of actions pursued according to the sustainable urban development paradigm cannot always be termed urban regeneration. A distinct basic characteristic distinguishing both categories is the context of the place. Urban regeneration refers directly to urban areas (some parts of a city) affected by long-term deprivation (also referred to as run-down urban areas or deprived urban areas). To put it differently, urban regeneration is sustainable urban development targeting deprived urban areas. Hence, hereafter, wherever mention is made of sustainable urban development, it relates mostly to deprived urban areas and it should be thereby considered as urban regeneration.

The regeneration process covers a wide range of measures to be taken in degraded inner-city areas in order to ensure their renewal: starting with diagnosis of the main problems and ending with identifying solutions and their implementation in the form of specific actions (Jarczewski & Ziobrowski, 2010). This approach makes this concept frequently applicable, especially in the context of the creation of infrastructural solutions. Consequently, the concept of regeneration is used interchangeably with terms such as renewal, reconstruction, restructuring, renovation, restoration, reclamation and rehabilitation (S. Kaczmarek, 2001). It should be emphasised, however, that regeneration moves beyond all the previously mentioned terms. It includes all of them and presents the comprehensive nature of the general processes focused on sustainable urban development. Regeneration goes beyond the process of urban renewal, which is often regarded as carrying out the physical changes, as well as beyond the process of urban development, which is in turn identified with the mission and objectives of a properly defined development policy (Roberts, 2008, p. 18).

When analysing the regeneration process of degraded urban areas, one must keep in mind that its key elements are social aspects. Social sustainability is a basic component of any plan to improve the living conditions of residents. Therefore, regeneration cannot be restricted to re-stimulating economic activity in an area where it has slowed down or even disappeared. This process forces decision-makers to plan and undertake comprehensive action in the dysfunctional areas in order to guarantee the restoration of social functions and enable social integration (Couch, Fraser, & Percy, 2003). It should be stressed that the regeneration takes place primarily in a social context. Its primary purpose is social development and this is what the regeneration actions should ensure, including those aimed at modernisation of the buildings. However, regeneration measures cannot be undertaken outside the society. The success of public policies and welfare of the local community depends on the involvement of citizens in the regeneration process at every stage. It is a necessary factor to ensure the success of regeneration actions (Musiałkowska & Idczak, 2016).

The theory indicates that due to the nature of urban regeneration, a strategic and long-term view in combination with tactical principles should be taken into account when programming regenerative measures. In order to address the complex dynamics of urban areas and their challenges by reversing the deprivation of inner-city areas, urban regeneration policies and programmes are needed. The implementation of sustainable urban regeneration makes it necessary to take into account the spatial, social, economic, environmental and governance dimensions of particular urban areas. Detailed aspects of these dimensions are shown in Table 2. Failure to do so may lead to ineffectiveness of actions taken, or to achieving unintended results. Focus only on the purely infrastructural renewal of run-down areas without providing actions directed strictly at the local community can deepen social stratification and as a result further the persistence of or even increase social polarisation. Therefore, the implementation of regeneration projects should follow an integrated approach – i.e. covering the implementation of consistent and coordinated action in the following areas:

- Spatial – this stresses the importance and the specificity of a given area as an unique place in terms of the existing problems as well as opportunities. The regeneration initiatives must take into account special characteristics of the urban space and respond in a precise manner to the particular needs reported in a specified time. This includes the requirement to cover long-term strategic land use planning as a determinant of the sustainable development of urban areas. This dimension should serve as a coordinator and a verifier (Markowski, 2011) of the regeneration actions.
- Social – the measures are targeted at preventing social exclusion and the dominance of social pathologies. These are also required to reverse adverse demographic trends, the impoverishment of society or struggles with low levels of education. It is also important to ensure equal opportunities to persons with disabilities, elderly people or those professionally inactive by en-

abling them to participate equally in social and economic life (Wojnarowska & Kozłowski, 2011). Empowering the society through the inclusion of citizens in the decision-making process plays an important role in this dimension, particularly in terms of formulating the goals and directions of the regeneration process (Lorens & Martyniuk-Pęczek, 2009).
- Economic – this refers to the economic recovery of a run-down area. Regeneration actions implemented under this dimension should lead to the restoration of economic activity, especially the creation of new jobs. To this end, it is necessary to support local entrepreneurs, create incentives for external investors, and attract new residents and users (Wojnarowska & Kozłowski, 2011). The economic dimension also includes the economic effectiveness of undertaken measures.[8]
- Environmental – this aims to reduce environmental impact and improve the environmental quality of urban systems and lifestyles. The effort of decision-makers should be focused on physical interventions in urban areas and consider innovative low-carbon and energy-efficient actions while taking into consideration the wider relationships to other dimensions. Environmental actions promote the "recycling" of land and buildings and the reduction of the demolition waste and new construction materials. Through all these actions, it contributes to reducing demand for peripheral urban growth and favours intensification and compactness of existing urban areas (Turcu, 2012a).
- Governance – this involves multiple stakeholders including local authorities (and authorities at a higher policy level), residents, representatives of business, culture and education, and other civil communities of interest. As a special mode of the decision-making, it structures the collaboration and the institutional arrangement for dealing with urban regeneration issues. Since it formalises policies, standards and procedures for directing the decision-making, it should constitute a key component in urban regeneration management (Xie, Liu, & Zhuang, 2021).

---

[8] The authors understand the concept of economic efficiency as both financial efficiency (narrower category) and economic efficiency (which is a broader category). Financial efficiency is related to the viability of the actions to be taken, and therefore indicates whether the investment will be profitable and will bring a certain return. Due to the public nature of many regeneration measures, it is not a necessary prerequisite for success of an investment. Economic efficiency in turn broadens the category of financial efficiency by specific benefits, which the investment will bring to society. In regeneration, it is indispensable.

Table 2: Dimensions and initiatives of urban regeneration

Dimension	Initiatives to be addressed
Spatial	connecting land use planning to strategic planning preparation of urban spatial master plans that draw the future spatial structure of a city greater consistency and certainty in an area – adequate space for transport links and other public spaces zoning regulations restricting certain types of land use in certain areas of a city acquisition of urban land for urban "transformation" by authorities, if needed
Social/cultural	the restoration of social functions enhancement of integration among persons increasing people's access to culture, education and training, information, sport and recreation etc. improvement of people's health and the overall level of safety facilities for people with disabilities, health effectively combating criminal activity and preventing violence housing quality of life, quality of social public services
Economic	special market incentives for business providing a new or renewed functional quality and creating opportunities for growth job creation employment and professional skills employability and income financial viability of urban projects spill-over effects and multiplier effects of actions taken concentration on knowledge generation and innovation
Environmental/ physical	measures to protect against, and adapt to, climate change (e.g. extreme rains and floods, heat waves and droughts) innovative low-carbon and energy-efficient actions recycling of land and buildings reduction of the demolition waste and new construction materials greater scope for high-quality landscapes and habitats local energy generation general open-space leisure activities infrastructure, built and natural environment public transport and communications
Governance	multi-level cooperation cross-sectoral collaboration engagement of local community involvement of other interest groups

Table 2: Dimensions and initiatives of urban regeneration *(Continued)*

Dimension	Initiatives to be addressed
	style of local leadership
	more deliberative decision-making
	integrated approach

Source: the authors' own elaboration

Urban regeneration is inherently a public intervention, the aim of which is to restore the functioning of market mechanisms in the deprived areas. Although the main forms of interventionist activities are state-led, it is desirable in the case of urban regeneration to correct market failures under the broad public–private consensus (Roberts, 2008). The reason for this is that regeneration requires the combination of the various activities that need to be carried out by relevant agencies in a "joined-up" holistic approach to solving the interrelated problems of unemployment, crime, low educational attainment, poor health, and housing and the local physical environment. Therefore, wide strategic partnerships focused on local regeneration matters and bringing together all the major agencies – including local authorities, housing providers, business partners, development and community organisations etc. – are needed to formulate common strategies and supervise their implementation (Couch, Sykes, & Börstinghaus, 2011). One should not forget that a crucial role in the regeneration process is played by a spatial dimension, responsible for the proper matching of actions and measures to the problems accumulated in specific locations. Successful regeneration is the result of the integration of actions and concentration of resources in the areas requiring support.

2.2.2 Urban regeneration policy framework

Hence, urban regeneration constitutes a major field of public policy that deals with the regrowth of economic activity, the restoration of social function or social inclusion and the re-establishment of environmental quality in cities that have experienced those elements. Such a policy should be applied at a very localised level and by local authorities, however, within the agreed wider national policy framework. All in all, the main thrust of urban regeneration is to tackle market failures arising in cities through, on the one hand, safeguarding the interests of inhabitants, while, on the other hand, providing strong incentives affecting the possible gains from urbanisation. This means that degraded or deteriorating urban areas cannot be left to market forces. Therefore urban regeneration needs relevant regulations and redistributive policies to mitigate the undesirable effects and to reconcile market forces with social and economic goals.

Urban regeneration measures should be neither limited only to the areas affected by long-term deprivation or degradation nor counteract solely the consequences of urban sprawl. Regeneration processes should not only cover substituting parts of the city but also contribute to densifying and improving the compactness of the city fabric (Marra et al., 2016). This implies a comprehensive approach to urban regeneration which, although it emphasises the area-based and target-oriented tendency (favouring the most deprived inner-city areas and/or socially excluded residents), engenders the need to take into account morphological, social and economic issues occurring across the whole city. Hence, the current framework of urban regenerating policies must be based on a *holistic approach*, that is, dealing with spatial, physical, social and economic issues together as a combination of several horizontal policies – physical, social, economic, ecological, cultural, psychological, financial and others – adjusted depending on the specific needs and local context (Marra et al., 2016). This significant turn in the approach to urban matters in the last decade means that, after the focus on the physical dimension of urban transformation processes and a subsequent incorporation of social and economic issues, the urban agenda was extended by two more key areas, namely, integration and safety. Following this, a more tailor-made approach highlighting the importance of the local context became a widespread tendency, as it was reported by the decentralisation of budgets for urban transformation from national governments to urban authority, but also to private stakeholders (Mak & Stouten, 2014).

Due to the complexity and scope of the operation, urban regeneration involves many different players in many policy areas and occurs at different spatial levels. It initiates both publicly funded and market-driven actions which relate to flagship projects as well as small community-based initiatives. This signifies the conviction that the regeneration actions can be performed by the public, private or community sectors or by some combination of them acting in multi-level or multi-sectoral partnership. Following on from this, it is deemed that urban regeneration takes place at different spatial levels – national, regional, local (urban) or particular inner-city area levels (Parkinson, 2014). Therefore, taking the holistic approach's line of argument, actions and resources under regeneration should be concentrated in an integrated way to target urban areas with specific challenges and, at the same time, they should be integrated into the wider objectives of sectoral policies governed by different administrative levels. To be successful, urban regeneration actions must be mainstreamed into the integrated approach within a wider policy framework encompassing different administrative levels (local, regional, national), and in partnership with entities representing different policy areas and relevant representatives of inhabitants.

Policies implemented in urban areas being of concern cannot be fragmented and limited purely to on-the-spot measures – i.e. mostly taking the form of physical regeneration. Policy decision-making must address the urban areas as a whole perceived through the lens of the complexity of the urban system and multi-dimensionality of processes of urbanisation. In order to have a better understanding of the impact of urban policies implemented depending on the scope of the adopted intervention, it is important to use case-based analysis conducted by Jacquier, Bienvenue, and Schlappa (2007) who illustrated the possible options and policy outcomes. The results of their analysis are shown in Figure 4. To begin with, there is an urban area market by A that at time t_0 can be regarded as a good place to live. Due to the changes taking place in the socio-economic and physical sphere of this area over time, it is being degraded and consequently experiences urban decay, which happens at time t_n. This is the time regeneration actions should be implemented, which, conditional on the effectiveness and content of public and private interventions run at time t_n, may occur in four different options. Each of them results in further changes within the area itself and also its relative position in relation to the whole urban area. These four options are:

- *A1 (decline)* – there is no public intervention or minimal one. As a result, the area continues its dynamics to date and subsequently its situation deteriorates further, leading to an increase in social and economic disparities associated with urban decline. The area suffers from a series of serious difficulties such as physical degradation, departure of people capable of representing the community, downgrade of commercial and service functions, weakening of public services, negligible or absence of voluntary associations and civic organisations, etc. This process is often perceived as a process of "disintegration" of the area as it leads to further exclusion in physical and socio-economic terms, thus making the area and people living marginalised and disadvantaged.
- *A2 (maintenance)* – as a consequence of public intervention, the process of deepening deprivation will be stopped. However, the given area remains in the same position in an intra-urban hierarchy as it has occupied so far. Urban authorities tend to invest in socially essential infrastructure through the renewal of housing units and public spaces, development of public transport, provision of urban amenities. These measures are pursued to maintain some state of conservation and can be seen as nothing more than a purely cosmetic or superficial improvement. The implemented projects without a doubt provide significant assistance to the area in question but they do not spark changes that would radically reverse current trends

and launch a process of urban regeneration. Such actions are of a temporary nature and frequently, in the absence of further interventions, the deprivation can continue.

- *A3 (gentrification)* – this option is often described as uncontrolled revaluation because it relies on a spontaneous market-led improvement. Although the redevelopment can be initiated and promoted (explicitly or implicitly) by urban authorities (through some strategies or programmes), in fact, it is mostly based on the reclamation of an area by private external investors who expect a certain financial return due to increases in rents for land and property. This process requires the combination of three factors: a territory which ensures high qualities (good architecture and good location within the city); high rental incomes, and weak resistance by current residents (people facing eviction); acceptance by urban authorities for such a development process. As a result, new housing developments and recreational areas are built which attract new residents of higher status, thus pushing out the original residents who are forced to leave the area. In general, this process results in "gentrification". Admittedly, it shows to some extent the integration between an area, people and intuitions, and it is extremely likely to be even a part of a coherent wider development plan. But these arrangements are achieved independently of the people who lived there, not for them, and not with them, and often at their expense. Although this scenario results in an increase in the urban value and is a relatively frequent one in European cities, it does not resolve the problem set out at the start.
- *A4 (coherence and good practice)* – this scenario refers to urban regeneration understood in the very best sense of that word. Here urban regeneration is done "by", "for" and "with" the local communities. Any regeneration initiatives are implemented within the framework of good collaboration among all the interest groups. Such collaboration needs to be built on a shared understanding of common targets and must pinpoint joint objectives that lead to the sustained improvements of the particular urban area. To do so, highly skilled and competent practitioners are needed, on the one hand, and also individuals, on the other, who have the spirit and talents for encouraging people to take action and forming a community capable of creative co-operation in various spheres of their daily life. Urban regeneration tends to link both people and institutions of a city and to integrate them around the inner-city areas in need of transformation. Therefore, it is important to reach an agreement on the diagnosis with the various stakeholders present at the local level (inhabitants, urban authorities, business representatives and others). This solution has the advantage of being in a spirit of partnership and proactive cooperation, allowing the avoidance of confusion be-

tween reality and symptoms (the balance between inhabitants' needs and public–private responses is based on a shared diagnosis) and thereby enabling to work efficiently to achieve shared tasks and objectives.

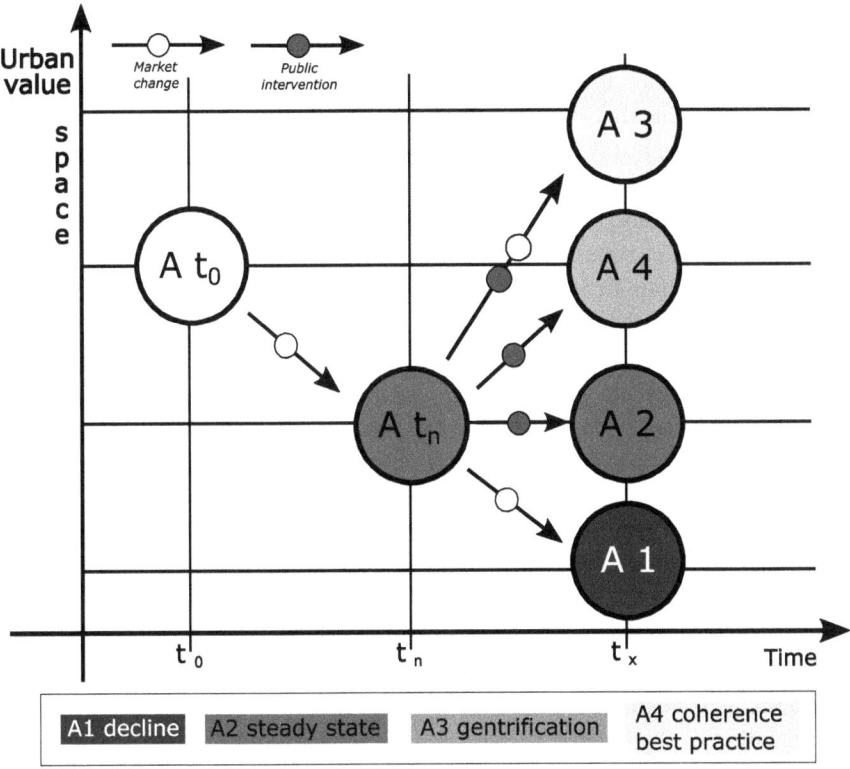

Figure 4: Different options for area-based regeneration at the local level
Source: (Jacquier, Bienvenue, & Schlappa, 2007, p. 27)

The above-described analysis clearly shows that regeneration actions depending on the type and scope of the adopted intervention can lead to different outcomes. Option A4, which envisages a full complexity – i.e. integration of different sectoral policies and broad cooperation between actors from the public and private sector, including individuals – is considered to be the best solution. Concurrently, this optimal and the most desirable option is the most challenging one for the sake of the results that are the most difficult to achieve. Hence, as Jacquier, Bienvenue, and Schlappa argued (2007), an integrated programme for sustainable urban regeneration is required to manage and make the interactions between all three components – place (environmental/physical dimension), people (social dimension) and institutions (economic and governance dimensions) – more effective. This is a necessary prerequisite to provide opportunities for the disadvantaged areas to become a "normal" part of the city. The integrated area-based programme for sustainable urban regeneration must assume complex interventions which cover all issues related to the particular dimensions of urban regeneration (see Table 2) depending on the specific needs and circumstance of particular run-down urban areas. Notwithstanding this, such a programme should neither discriminate against other urban areas nor create a dependency culture in the deprived areas. It is undeniable that, in practice, such interventions are needed because they can address market failures (investment capital shuns risk disadvantaged locations), empower the residents and increase their capacities in accessing the labour market, thereby linking the deprived area to the bigger urban area. Nevertheless, there is always a risk that place-based programmes may simply shift or spread problems between different inner urban areas and not contribute to the overall economic and social well-being of the city as a whole (Tosics, 2011). Focusing only on the separate areas to solve their problems may break down because many of the root causes of the problems and the potential solutions to those problems do not lie only in the particular narrow areas. Regardless of whether they are of a social, economic or environmental nature – as regards the causes, or involve the variety of regenerative measures – support instruments or institutional resources (programmes) – as regards the solutions – are found often outside the run-down areas (Vranken, de Decker, & van Nieuwenhuyze, 2003). According to this line of argument, the problems of the most disadvantaged areas cannot be solved simply within these areas. Instead, an integrated approach is recommended which implies a combination of the horizontal interventions (poverty reduction, increase in the level of education, increase in employability, housing etc.) and physical (environmental) interventions (development and improvement of urban infrastructure), which should also address larger territorial areas (Tosics, 2011). What is more, initiatives and projects taken under the urban regeneration programme should be consistent with the mainstream policy framework set out at higher administrative levels which delineate the policy orientations and objectives for urban development at a larger scale.

Although urban regeneration is pursued at the local level, it should be governed and managed jointly by all the administrate levels of a particular country. Being an integral component of a wider development policy, urban regeneration can significantly contribute to economic development and social cohesion on a broader territorial basis thereby boosting prosperity in the country as a whole. Therefore, the process of urban regeneration must be framed within a coherent overall development policy (or strategy) in order to be efficient. It should be considered in terms of systemic management, which enables looking at activities and processes from the point of view of a systemic understanding of the functioning and role of various public authorities, jointly responsible for urban regeneration. This implies the use of strategic management involving, in particular, a strong link between urban regeneration and overall national development policy. Consequently, it is deemed necessary to integrate social and economic development planning and land use planning at different levels of policy implementation (Noworól, 2010). The interlinked nature of urban development necessitates the greater involvement of a government in planning and regulating urban land use. Effective planning coordinates all activities undertaken in urban space in such a way that it is matched to complementary private investments to existing conditions and ensures adequate provision of public infrastructure that provides important benefits to society at large. Moreover, it also diminishes the negative effects of some types of activities that can put whole cities at risk of unintended development directions. Active land policy secures a future urban expansion before it actually takes place. This is extremely important with regard to land markets that are characterised by endemic market failures. Hence, the role for policy in urban land use planning is then to deal with these failures through coordinating and anchoring both private and public investments accordingly (Collier et al., 2020). Moreover, urban regeneration processes should also secure the interests of all the regeneration participants against adverse socio-economic effects. Actions and projects executed without respect for the complex nature of regeneration may lead to unintended results in the form of deeper social segregation and pathology. Therefore, the right of the inhabitants of the regenerated areas to remain in the place of residence as well as their interests should be guaranteed in advance by the state (Billert, 2008). All possible actions in terms of regeneration should lead to transformations in urban areas in a way that will best take into account the requirements of the constantly changing and evolving society. This comprehensive and simultaneously integrated approach is consistent with the nature of the regeneration process and should be included at every stage of regeneration initiatives.

With this in mind, there is a consensus on the involvement of different layers of government in urban regeneration. First of all, a national government is expected to set out the national institutional policy framework in which urban policy, including urban regeneration, is of particular importance. Through powerful coherent national strategies and a policy framework for cities, national governments acknowledge the need for a comprehensive approach to urban regeneration, and at the same time empower and support cities by resourcing them with funds and tools. However, no single government level is fully responsible for a city development. Policy-making for cities needs to engage different territorial levels of government together with the appropriate division of responsibilities between them. The polices and resources of the mainstream policy framework that affect cities directly need to be committed to urban areas. This concerns such spheres as: housing, education, transport, social security, health etc. Note that urban policy supports both places and people. Therefore, it should take into account an integrated approach and recognise the linkages between housing, education, transport, health, social security policies so as to create a tailor-made and complex response to urban problems. Since the urban problems are not separated into functional spheres and extend beyond the administrative city limits, the policies working under the umbrella of urban policy have to be governed by different administrative levels. This poses a great challenge for the urban regeneration process as a very complex issue. On this account, it is recommended to enhance vertical policy integration between national, regional and local governments in order to strengthen the synergies of different actions run by different authorities, but focused on common goals (Parkinson, 2014). Urban regeneration is about dealing with places where people live and work on a daily basis, and hence they themselves and their concerns are the focal point of policy responses. What follows is a need for broad partnership which engages on an equal footing people, the private sector and public parties. This means that the policy framework must envisage the provision of horizontal policy integration between public, private and community sectors. The engagement of local communities and other groups of interest in urban regeneration policy can give both legitimacy and effectiveness to regenerative actions executed at the local level and deliver outcomes also desired at the regional and national perspective. Such a policy framework based on a more sophisticated multi-level and cross-sectoral governance arrangement should adopt a wide territorial focus which links the various challenges diagnosed at a particular inner-city area to the larger urban, sub-regional, regional and national economic scale. As many problems of deprived areas are often created outside them, solutions to those problems can be found through networks and functional collaboration between different territorial entities. At the heart of the policy in question is the achievement of the right spatial balance, so that every territorial entity can benefit when the interests of larger and smaller entities are reconciled without the domination of larger ones in the decision-making. This can be done within the national policy framework that is based on broad collaborative governance (Parkinson, 2014).

A key component of this integrated urban regeneration policy is a place-based and integrated urban regeneration programme. It should be a spatially focused programme that targets a complex set of regenerative actions and projects at particular deprived urban areas. It must focus on the needs of local communities and involve them in order to jointly participate in the process of shaping the framework conditions for urban regeneration, and regeneration as such. Urban regeneration programmes should be from the very beginning embedded in, and contribute to, a hugely complex environment. The reason for such complexity is partly due to the huge number of actors and the enormous number of interactions across and between organisations (Larsen & Engberg, 2011). A place-based approach and participatory governance arrangements result in diversity and interplay and then are expected to enable actors to coordinate problem solving and decision-making. This certainly causes a tremendous challenge to the planning and implementation of urban regeneration as well as urban planning and policy generally. However, this must be on the agenda and cannot be ignored. Non-public organisations and various actors (residents, families, individual businesses, non-governmental organisations, ad hoc community-based associations, other market-based actors etc.) were in the deprived areas a long time before urban regeneration started and will be there after its termination. Therefore, urban authorities' ability to engage them in reciprocal and trust-based relationships is decisive for the socio-economic viability of the regeneration measures. As a matter of course, an urban regeneration programme should consists of several activities each of which embraces dozens or even hundreds of micro-actions or projects, meetings, conferences etc. (Larsen & Engberg, 2011). In this way, the bottom-up approach is used to reinforce and complement the public efforts aimed at leading the disadvantaged inner-city areas out of deprivation.

In essence, it should be noted that at the heart of the urban regeneration is the public intervention aimed at improving the quality of life in deprived urban neighbourhoods. Urban regeneration represents a challenge for public authorities because in the context of the governance of the development it focuses territorially the public intervention on specific urban areas where the most relevant negative phenomena build up (Noworól & Noworól, 2017, p. 134). Integrated urban regeneration links cross-sectoral interventions and multi-agency governance, while emphasising practices of consultation and participation, especially through wide partnerships and the involvement of the communities, and seeking to transform the state into an enabling partner. The key to success is planning policies and a governance model which integrate robust national-, regional- and city-level planning polices into a common policy framework (Colantonio & Dixon, 2011). To put it more precisely, urban regeneration should be an inherent element of the development policy of the state (Ciesiółka, 2018). The central instrument of an effective regeneration is an integrated urban regeneration programme that should be linked to city-, region-, country-wide development policies and strategies. Its success largely depends on local community participation and empowerment.

2.2.3 Urban regeneration themes

As mentioned in Chapter 1, urbanisation and its features show that it does not always lead to a desired effect. Undoubtedly, the concentration of business activities and individuals is important, and short distances between actors enable smoother and less complicated interactions. Nonetheless, there are many factors that may affect urbanisation and consequently the efficiency of cities. As Moretti (2014) argued, market failures in urban areas are rife, both in terms of the positive externalities (increasing returns on agglomeration economies) and the negative externalities (e.g. congestion arising from living close to one another). Therefore, the nature of urban processes allows the claim to be made that urbanisation is "policy intensive" and as such requires public interventions and regulations to be successful in reinforcing cities. A sound urban policy can not only heavily influence the structure of city growth and thereby direct the trends in urbanisation but also shape the form of urbanisation enabling a sustained socio-economic transformation (Miller, 2014; Roberts, 2008). Hereby, such a policy is also regarded as a response to structural and functional deficiencies that hamper cities' capacities to address the needs of their residents. At this point, a significant body of literature on the subject calls for urban regeneration as a catalyst for inclusive and sustainable cities. The rationale behind launching the renewal process is that even if market forces commenced the regeneration of deprived urban areas, provided that could actually happen, the market-led, self-renewal operation would be exceedingly long. More importantly, an unacceptable wide variety of social, economic and environmental costs would follow in its aftermath. The life-restoring role of urban regeneration comes from a particular understanding of the causes of socio-economic decline in cities and of the appropriate policy responses to the diagnosed problems (de Magalhães, 2015). Regeneration interventions realise the need to counter localised market failures and to achieve an equity objective (regarded as social cohesion). These actions lead to attaining additional social, economic and environmental outputs and outcomes which would otherwise not have occurred or which would have been yielded at an unsatisfactory level.

Of particular importance in this context is a holistic approach. This stipulates that any regeneration initiatives should be implemented by bringing a wide range of social, economic and environmental considerations into the decision-making process on an integrated programme of urban development. The idea considers the regeneration programme as relating to a complete city system, and rejects a piecemeal approach. To address the issues resulting from this comprehensiveness, the needs and aspirations of local residents to redevelop their locality are supposed to be met in the wake of the coordination of a number of private and public sector actions (Couch, Sykes, & Börstinghaus, 2011). Moreover, the formulation of solutions to the problems of deprived urban area residents and people living in the neighbourhood should take place by way of a common vision, agreed objectives and priorities, pooled expertise and common decisions for the allocation of resources. In this respect it should also be underlined that, following de Magalhães's view (2015), the core understanding of what socio-economic decline in cities means must be seen as social, economic and environmental problems *of a city (locality)* rather than as social, economic and environmental problems that happened to take place in that locality. Therefore urban regeneration through holistic approach policies seeks to address the problems of cities in all their multiple dimensions. It is then characterised by agendas of inclusiveness, multi-agency partnerships, and a shift from government to governance (J. Evans & Jones, 2008). These considerations suggest that the approach to urban regeneration requires work to be done within all three dimensions: cross-disciplinary (sectoral) involvement – horizontal integration; close collaboration between all stakeholders from different levels – vertical integration; and local regenerative measures being an inherent part of a wider development plan for the entire territory – territorial integration.

Although there is no single excellent European model for successful urban regeneration, it is possible to point out, on the basis of many good practice examples implemented across Europe, some pathways of actions that to a large extent refer to the approach as discussed above. These pathways can be used not only for formulating the guidelines of how to implement regeneration projects at the local level, but also for drawing up a policy framework of urban regeneration applicable in the more general context. This reasoning follows from the fact that there is no single commonly accepted theory capable of explaining in a comprehensive and exhaustive manner the cause–effect relationships associated with urban change. In addition, cities vary considerably in their location-specific problems, the size of underused land or distressed and decaying inner-city areas, the range of social exclusion and their functional importance in regional or national economies. Different regeneration challenges entail widely differing views of how to tackle the issues of decline and urban decay, and also the use of the distinct operating methods aimed at achieving the given place-related outcomes and expected impacts. Yet, there is no *one-size-fits-all* approach to urban regeneration. Regardless of the local context, however, some lessons and knowledge should be gathered, kept and transferred to other places after prior formation into a generic model. Such a simplified framework can be applied to describe the workings of the urban regeneration realm at the European level. The model will essentially constitute a theoretical construct providing a structural foundation that the decision-makers can use to debate and decide on the best regeneration scenario. But it can also perform the function of an analytical framework which allows the study of particular components and processes shaping urban regeneration policy-making.

In developing the structural model of urban regeneration applicable at the European level, the theoretical contributions draw also upon practice-oriented works providing both positive and negative insights on the subject mentioned above. This aligns with Roberts's (2008, pp. 21–22) viewpoint on the understanding of urban regeneration as a distinct activity *rooted in practice rather than theory*. In spite of the fact that urban regeneration theory delivers a number of important features which facilitate the defining of the content and mode of operation of this process, a high level of similarity between the characteristics of theory and practice should be expected. The theory of urban regeneration focuses predominantly on the institutional and organisational dynamics of the management of urban change, therefore the theoretical features are supposed to be supplemented by ongoing practice. Drawing upon the examples of good practice and expertise which have been proven to be successful in combination with a theoretical background makes it possible, appropriately, to take forward policy debate on how to improve the performance of cities in deprived areas. In essence, any ineffectual efforts and unsuccessful solutions should be avoided as they are usually punitive. Yet, despite this, in policy-making some reliable lessons can be also learnt from bad examples. For instance, assume the situation where similar policy solutions have brought about varied performance. It is then possible to isolate factors that contributed to the success or failure of the programmes' implementation. Thus, to produce a theoretical construct of urban regeneration providing a good framework for this study we used a vast amount of literature that discusses features and effects of regeneration policy and operations Europe-wide, while taking all the foregoing issues into account. We used *inter alia* theoretical considerations focusing on the explanation of why urban regeneration is necessary and how it works as a major component of urban policy (Aalbers & van Beckhoven, 2010; André et al., 2012; Ciesiółka, 2018; Ciesiółka & Rogatka, 2015; Cornelius & Wallace, 2010; Jadach-Sepioło, 2017; Janas, Jarczewski, & Wańkowicz, 2010; Lang, 2005; Neto & Serrano, 2011; Roberts, 2008; F. Robinson, Shaw, & Davidson, 2005; Rode, 2018; Xie, Liu, & Zhuang, 2021). Some of the learning and good experiences were derived from a number of case studies which disseminate the knowledge about urban decline and its causes as well as successful regeneration schemes (Almeida et al., 2013; Bartocci & Picciaia, 2020; Billert, 2019; Cervelló-Royo, Garrido-Yserte, & Segura-García del Río, 2012; Couch, Sykes, & Börstinghaus, 2011; Ferilli et al., 2017; S. Henderson, Bowlby, & Raco, 2007; Lepore, Sgobbo, & Vingelli, 2017; Medda, Caschili, & Modelewska, 2012; Pastak & Kährik, 2016; van der Pennen & van Bortel, 2016; van

Kempen, Wassenberg, & van Meer, 2007; van Meerkerk, Boonstra, & Edelenbos, 2013). We also employed information from the research reports published by various organisations which provide vital insights on the effects of regeneration initiatives/projects and strategies implemented in run-down parts of European cities (Cadell, Falk, & King, 2008; Carley et al., 2000; Jacquier, Bienvenue, & Schlappa, 2007; Urbact, 2013; Wassenberg & van Dijken, 2011; Wassenberg, van Meer, & van Kempen, 2007; Weeber, Nothdorf, & Fischer, 2011). This literature lays down a solid basis for the framework for conceptualising the integrated approach to urban regeneration that is proposed in the present study.

Evidence from much of the reviewed cross-disciplinary literature on urban regeneration indicates at least a few significant conceptual issues that need to be addressed prior to constructing the model. The identified issues are as follows.

Strategic perspective
Cities are strongly affected by market forces and thus they face accelerated and continuous structural change. In response to new challenges cities must constantly adjust their local policies and develop a confident new approach. Counteractions to the unfavourable consequences of urban transformation should take the form of tailor-made operations that are constructed within a longer-term and, in particular, strategic approach with a clearly defined purpose in mind (Roberts, 2008, p. 18). Successful regeneration actions take a very long time and for that reason maintaining the success of a city, in a constantly changing world, should be seen as a never-ending process. Therefore, the successful outcome of the regeneration of a particular deprived area depends on the success of a wider economic development strategy established by a city which at the same time should constitute a coherent component of the strategic frameworks adopted at higher territorial levels (regional or national). As cities are greatly exposed to competition they need especially to attract job-creating firms or individuals capable of working and generating new values. In this context, setting and managing a strategy is seen as an adequate way to transform the local economy and to adapt it to the current market needs, thus counteracting any adverse effects that impact primarily on structurally less developed districts of urban areas (Cadell, Falk, & King, 2008). Literature reviewing European experiences show evidently that the ability to effectively react to change and use its possible benefits directly follows the strategic approach, rather than the merely aesthetic-design approach, when the transformation is done in conditions of governance and multi-sectoral coordination (Lepore, Sgobbo, & Vingelli, 2017, p. 186). In short, urban regeneration can only be successful if it embarks on

the appropriate measures and actions undertaken within the wider strategic framework of development policy. Regeneration can succeed if it is part of the wider economic success of the entire city.

The decisive role of local authorities
Since cities always change and are in constant transition, local authorities are at the forefront in struggling with the challenges on the ground and providing viable solutions for their communities. As the custodians of a place, a city's authorities understand the wider context thereof as well as challenges and opportunities faced by local communities. They are closest to citizens and due to this fact they have key responsibilities for carrying out inclusive policy-making and inducing sustainable development. In this respect, they are also obliged to demonstrate a long term and full commitment to improve deteriorated situations in the deprived districts of cities. Put differently, a city's authorities should take the leading role in driving forward a regeneration scheme which is not limited exclusively to a run-down area but also implies a change in the image of the whole city. This is because the core competencies of local authorities are the decision-making and implementation of many local policies, including e. g. spatial planning policy, which constitute legal frameworks and determine the directions of economic development (Ciesiółka & Rogatka, 2015). In a study exploring the role of local government in urban regeneration, the authors revealed that the implementation of regeneration in the form of a top-down approach cannot be taken as given because of local contingencies, including patterns of resistance (S. Henderson, Bowlby, & Raco, 2007, p. 1444). Local authorities are expected to define a new economic role for a city that would found solid development bases for its future prosperity. Therefore the real power in this field should be devolved to city authorities. They must take responsibility for both the regeneration of the deprived area in question and the future development of the entire urban area. In addition to the devolution of power a real transfer of resources is required to match the city authorities' responsibilities (Cadell, Falk, & King, 2008). In a nutshell, responsibility for urban regeneration should be vested in city authorities which, taking a strategic socio-economic view, in conjunction with other key players, are required to cope with multiple issues and complicated problems arising as a result of the transition processes.

Cross-sectoral collaboration
Urban regeneration is not a one-actor process and regeneration actions cannot be performed without the involvement of the different kinds of stakeholders root-

ed in the urban environment. A strong and well-functioning partnership involving governments, local business, non-profits and philanthropic groups, housing associations, communities, educational establishments, and the public as a whole is vital for the success of regeneration projects implemented in areas of urban deprivation (Carley et al., 2000; Cornelius & Wallace, 2010). Quite often some actors belonging to the authority or administration sector are accused of being ineffective if they work on their own. Therefore, every form of wide collaboration becomes an expression of the actors' awareness of their incapacity to deal with serious problems on their own. Public administration should create a platform for the wide-ranging cooperation and collaboration of private companies, non-profit organisations, various groups of interest and even lay citizens so as to work together for a common long-term goal. Establishment of a general strategic agenda and its implementation under conditions of cross-sector integration helps to build up trust and legitimacy for the performance of challenging regeneration actions (Bartocci & Picciaia, 2020). Since urban regeneration is a long-term endeavour, long-term persistence and collaborative working across sectors and across actors is required to make sure that it succeeds. It is then crucial to ensure interactions and communication between all stakeholders involved at all stages of city regeneration actions/projects – from the planning phase through negotiations concerning deliverables and governance to continuous monitoring of progress (Cornelius & Wallace, 2010). Literature reports evidence that a relatively well-performing solution is a city authority-owned and -driven institutional entity with jurisdiction over a particular area which is responsible for developing some kinds of partnership among different stakeholders. This entity's essential task is not only to manage the urban regeneration scheme but also to share the management functions, entitlements and responsibilities for a given urban area between certain groups of interest. This body is expected to act as a networking initiator, bringing a wide range of public and private partners to work together, organising a required range of knowledge and skills, allocating tasks and resources among actors involved in the partnership, and having regard to the legitimate interest of residents (Bartocci & Picciaia, 2020; Cadell, Falk, & King, 2008). All of this is at the root of various forms of, what is described by Jacquier, Bienvenue, and Schlappa (2007) as, horizontal (or transversal) cooperation. Such an approach makes it possible to initiate long-term interactions between actors from different sectors, and foster greater integration aimed at achieving mutually beneficial outcomes. However, it is important to realise that horizontal cooperation is the hardest thing to get under way due to relatively hermetic boundaries between the professions of the representatives of housing, culture, business, security, education, social affairs etc.

Multi-level governance

Most studies report that greatly successful regeneration plans have been coordinated at the city level and carried out by powerful local authorities or by their duly authorised body under a highly decentralised system of governance. This clearly indicates that governing urban regeneration must include all the institutions and actors involved, all the legal and managerial capacities and resources needed, and all the ideas and concepts proposed. Therefore, governance of urban regeneration strategies has to go beyond the formal structures of the state and its legal system and judiciary, and encompass wider networks of relationships between government acting at different levels, business and civil society actors through which power flows and is exercised in society (Couch, Sykes, & Börstinghaus, 2011; Lang, 2005). In this context, the governance approach seems to make the decision-making process more cooperative, democratic, inclusive and transparent, and, as a result of this, contributes to empowering civic and social groups. It entails devolution of responsibilities and financial resources for joined-up urban regeneration actions to the city level (Aalbers & van Beckhoven, 2010; Xie, Liu, & Zhuang, 2021). Urban regeneration governance should be seen as a conventional way of organising a decision-making process that involves a variety of politically independent but mutually interconnected by a common goal actors at different levels of territorial organisation. From a city's perspective, all actors focus efforts on planning and afterwards implementing location-based initiatives (to address disadvantages in that location) which are designed coherently at different levels of governance. Multi-level governance needs durable engagement and genuine collaboration between various tiers of government, between adjacent governments and authorities, and between all other interested parties involved in urban regeneration. It ensures mechanisms of vertical cooperation to create multi-level policy coherence at the local, regional, national and even European scales. Furthermore, in view of the fact that the core of the urban regeneration is area-based intervention, governance as a powerful ally wishing to bring regeneration forward must also take horizontal integration into account instead of functionally organised sectors which in fact are the pre-eminent domain of higher levels of governance (Rode, 2018). Additionally, following Neto and Serrano (2011) and Ciesiółka (2018), urban regeneration initiatives should not be seen as one more public policy directed at cities. They must constitute an inherent element of the development policy of the state, so that any regeneration actions have to be designed and implemented with all other public policies within the framework of a consistent programming system. This kind of collaboration ensures a locally driven regeneration strategy can be successfully implemented.

Residents' interests first

Regeneration actions stand out by a strong social context because they focus on tackling urban inequalities, with a view to improving life and conditions within marginalised communities. Therefore, any kinds of policies *are not to be imposed on people but developed together* (Wassenberg & van Dijken, 2011, p. 49). In light of this reasoning, local communities must be allowed to participate in decision-making concerning the planning and implementation of integrated urban regeneration programmes that affect directly them. It should nonetheless be acknowledged that although the involvement of communities, i.e. local residents, in the governance of regeneration programmes is far from easy, such an approach can work and influence the improvement of programmes and the position of the participants themselves. The empowerment of communities tends to lead to long-term, better and more desired outcomes than "traditional" programmes that prevail at higher levels of governance (F. Robinson, Shaw, & Davidson, 2005; Wassenberg, van Meer, & van Kempen, 2007). According to Robinson, Shaw, and Davidson (2005) residents' involvement in urban regeneration programming and projects is not just desirable, it is *essential and morally right*. The involvement of the inhabitants of deprived neighbourhoods is key to the success of urban regeneration, as only people, not institutions (multiplicity of formal structures), have the ability to overcome the divide between the system and the daily life of residents (van der Pennen & van Bortel, 2016). A firm belief that these people have a role and a place in the urban regeneration process should be regarded as a mode of enhancing the quality of actions/projects (matching the scope of the urban projects to the inhabitants' particular needs). What is more, local involvement must be carefully nurtured and managed so as to make it possible for people to re-establish control over their daily lives and their immediate environment (Jacquier, Bienvenue, & Schlappa, 2007, pp. 41–42). However, the concept being discussed here it not confined to the people's involvement in the urban regeneration process. It also encompasses the decision-maker's responsibility to secure the interests of all regeneration participants, in particular the inhabitants of deprived neighbourhoods, against possible negative consequences of the implemented measures. Regeneration actions/projects taken without respecting the specifics of the place and the needs of the inhabitants who live there can lead to unintended results in the form of deeper social segregation and even greater urban inequalities (Billert, 2019). Since the stakes are highest for the people who live and work in a redeveloped neighbourhood, every regeneration scheme should be fully understood and accepted by them. The inhabitants (will) shape its future and decide whether it thrives.

Market incentives

Regeneration is commonly seen as the answer to urban decline (physical, social or economic) caused by processes of structural change. Since these processes are induced by forces of a different nature many cities struggle to deal with more or less deep crises due to their various impacts on all aspects of urban development. Extreme difficulties or inabilities to reverse adverse trends spontaneously amplify structural inequalities and gradual deterioration of living standards. Therefore, purposive regenerative actions are required to be induced on the public side through an adequate policy because market forces are not sufficient to trigger and ensure adaptation or transformation (de Magalhães, 2015). As this clearly shows, the foundation for regeneration actions should be to recover the market role in the urban context. Old or new functions can be restored to or launched in the deprived urban areas, but giving due consideration to the market forces shaping urban processes and the central role of the lives of citizens (Urbact, 2013). To this end it is exceedingly important to translate appropriately investment need into demand by combining both a strategic policy response and a key delivery response. While some areas notably related to the social and public domain fail to be merchandised, other investment needs appear to be attractive for the private sector or can remain unfulfilled due to a lack of capacities in the city authorities. In this case, the key role of the public sector is to encourage private investors through demonstrating economic viability, providing evidence of market and offering a reduction in the investment risk. The last of these issues is of particular importance to such an extent that private sector investment depends on the facilitating role of the public authorities. Hence, the public sector can create legislation and regulation to assist the market function and thereby indeed serves to simulate markets so that the positive economic effects are evident at the macro, urban and micro levels (Adams & Tiesdell, 2010, pp. 196– 198). In particular, local authorities are the competent institutions to foster urban regeneration actions by instigating private investment. Local government initiatives usually offer one or more different types of market incentives aimed at reducing risks and leveraging a combination of public funds and private money. They include, *inter alia*, regulatory relief, liability relief, waivers of development fees, property tax abatements, remediation tax credits, subsidised insurance and grants and loans (Almeida et al., 2013; Medda, Caschili, & Modelewska, 2012, pp. 224–226). Economic growth in marginalised parts of urban areas can also be stimulated by public investments in infrastructure and amenities, which can alter investors' perceptions of a locality, enhance its competitiveness and lead to more investment in the city's economy. Moreover, there is considerable evidence indicating that some market-led flagship projects may contribute in certain urban areas (rather not in highly deprived ones) to generating socially and publicly desired outcomes (Pastak & Kährik, 2016). Nevertheless, as Acierno (2013) points out, of particular concern is to keep the balance between public and private investments which allow for the coexistence of the fitting partnership (depending on the programme scheme and context). This will prevent a situation in which a private business takes a leading role in urban regeneration and becomes the main beneficiary of public funding.

Social and business environments
Dealing with urban regeneration requires a concerted effort to change the conditions and the social and economic dynamics of disadvantaged places. Therefore a good strategy obliges all stakeholders, whether direct or indirect, to collaborate with each other and provide each other with the local knowledge that derives from their experiences and practices, to make it work. In doing so, regeneration emerges as a process embedded in dynamic network environments, in which different more or less interested actors – i.e. governmental, commercial, non-profits and residents – rearrange urban areas and are dependent on each other. Local initiatives proposed by inhabitants or businesses seem to be valuable for producing the expected outcomes because those initiatives stipulate a way of carrying out regeneration that starts actually from within the deprived area itself and focuses primarily all efforts and resources in a coherent manner on that area. Such an approach strongly increases the chance that the regeneration fits local needs and conditions, and enhances the involvement of local stakeholders and, consequently, leads to the effective implementation of the whole regeneration scheme and individual projects (van Meerkerk, Boonstra, & Edelenbos, 2013). Concerns about the stakeholder-catching environment lie in the necessity to ensure advantageous circumstances for collaboration, and, just as importantly, to encourage newcomers to settle (irrespective of whether for residential or investment purposes) and discourage locals from leaving a place under regeneration (e.g. as a result of initiated urban transformation). Therefore, the principal task of local authorities is to stress quality in all aspects of the development, in particular through creating attractive and balanced residential neighbourhoods. This is important especially with regard to the fact that transforming the prospects of a deprived area depends mainly on creating environments which are attractive to enterprising businesses and people with choice. The creation of an environment favourable to business will attract private capital flows, thus contributing to the desired increase in investments (Cadell, Falk, & King, 2008). The environment refers to both more formal structures – such as business environment institutions (Jadach-Sepioło, 2017) – but also numerous less formal organisations and bottom-up forces that act as catalysts to empower residents and stimulate a

unique set of opportunities to keep mainstream service providers accountable for the activities that are needed (Wassenberg & van Dijken, 2011). It should not be forgotten, however, that local authorities must take care of securing the most appropriate consent route, balancing actual local residential deficiencies with specific well-tailored solutions, instead of being an afterthought to private investors' commercial considerations. Nonetheless, most of the examined cases showed that many run-down areas were turned into attractive residential ones through a physical upgrading (combination of refurbishment and modern infrastructure), thereby shaping an attractiveness which also provides an inspiring environment for people and businesses. Yet, as van Kempen, Wassenberg, and van Meer argued (2007), physical urban restructuring projects are necessary but insufficient and thus do not guarantee success.[9] A right mix of physical and non-physical measures is conducive to the social- and business-friendly environment that is sought to spark proactive behaviour and entrepreneurial capacities among all stakeholders committed to the redevelopment of a given deprived area.

Education and training

Local communities are directly affected by ongoing structural changes in urban economies. A lack of sufficient capacities or social resilience to effective adaptation to the new socio-economic conditions decreases significantly the chances of individuals or even larger groups of society achieving a happy and prosperous life. Negative effects of structural changes in societies manifest themselves distinctly in some parts of urban areas which by reason of the industrial collapse were left blighted by unemployment and socially excluded from more vibrant districts. These changes escalate many social problems, including not only unemployment but also, for example, social inequalities, decreasing wage levels, crime, physical decay, worsening living standards etc. In order to counteract these unwelcome tendencies, it needs to provide educational and training activities and events targeted at disadvantaged groups. It is widely agreed that education is a key factor of long-term development and an effective instrument to combat poverty and exclusion, and in consequence enables people to improve their living standards. Education tackles social exclusion by providing individuals with added marketable skills that are required by the dominant institutions

---

9 It is worth noting that according to Ploegmakers and Beckers (2015) the physical improvements of the industrial sites implemented within the framework of the regeneration strategy in deprived urban areas have a negligible effect on economic outcomes. These effects relate primarily to the overall policy goals such as: increases in employment and number of firms, increases in the value of property and in the intensity of land use.

in society, mainly the labour market. Moreover, as regards urban regeneration in particular, education and learning are also decisive in affecting social groups and their spatial forms in dynamic collective ways (André et al., 2012). Education remains one of the main pathways to supporting social and urban cohesion, especially through the development of skills and competences that are vital for economic success and work as a crucial vehicle for social mobility. Drawing on the work of André and colleagues (2012) educational processes in marginalised urban areas should comprise two strategies. The first one deals with local learning communities applying the concept of *communities of practice*. This approach implies that learning is a fundamentally social, experiential and situated process by which people learn through their engagement in social practice. Groups of people sharing common problems deepen their knowledge and expertise, which make a difference to their ability to act individually and collectively (Dawley, Conway, & Charles, 2005). The process focuses on the area where people live and encourages cross-fertilisation – both between formal methods and grassroots practices, and between institutionalised education and tacit knowledge. The commitment to education, mainly technical, and job-related training bring the disadvantaged residents closer to the labour market and increase their employability, thus contributing to social inclusion (Cadell, Falk, & King, 2008). In this way, people who fell outside the labour market and missed out on their professional qualifications can gain new ones and through their reintegration into employment ensure themselves a decent life. The second strategy in turn accentuates the role of educational institutions as proactive agents of urban regeneration processes with the intention of making deprived areas socially more creative. This is reflected above all in their embeddedness in the urban community and their active involvement in the governance model of decision-making on area-based regenerative actions. Importantly, as highlighted by Atkinson (1999), knowledge and expertise acquired in this way are necessary to be an active participant involved in governance decisions and capable of articulating convincingly the needs and proposals of local communities. Involving the education-affected community can be not only a means to ensure that regeneration schemes are more effective in achieving their goals but also a stimulus that engages those people in the mainstream of urban social and economic life.

Leveraging culture and creativity
Arts and culture as distinctive features of humankind are conceived in their broadest sense as a catalyst and engine of urban regeneration (G. Evans & Shaw, 2004). In an anthropological sense culture refers to a shared system of meaning created by knowledge which is learnt by people and then put into prac-

tice by virtue of interpreting experience and generating a particular form of behaviour. The central tenet of cultural discourse (*a complex system of meaning created and maintained by people*) has several decades ago been incorporated into contemporary discourse of economic policy and its subdisciplines, as e. g. urban policy and regeneration, for a dual effect of more successful urban policy-making. First, culture in its widest sense actively supports urban development strategies through cultural industries and events. This approach should give a boost to residents, attract external investors and in the long run ensure urban competitiveness. Second, culture-led urban regeneration strategy can be applied to address issues of social inequality. This *modus operandi*, in turn, stems from the strong belief that creating a culturally competitive city contributes significantly to social cohesion through accommodating social diversity and governance (Degen & García, 2012). Although cities have always had cultural functions, the rapid expansion of the service-oriented economy has put culture at the heart of urban development. Moreover, culture became a commodity with a market value, an economic asset, and importantly, a valuable producer of creativity and marketable city spaces (García, 2004). Cities began to build and promote urban cultural life as a way to develop local economies and trigger the implementation of the sustainable urban regeneration of deprived areas. The rationale behind culture-led urban regeneration is a wealth of benefits that can be generated for residents and businesses, particularly at the neighbourhood level. According to McCarthy (2000), there are three closely linked strands of argument relating to the culture-led approach and its impact on reducing social and spatial marginality in disadvantaged districts.[10] To begin with, the expansion of local activity in the cultural/creative industries leads undoubtedly to economic diversification and employment creation. The upkeep and restoration of facilities used for cultural heritage, the restoration of historic built heritage or its adaptation to the changing realities and needs of society, the additional urban structures and arts infrastructure including theatres, concert halls, galleries and co-

---

10 Several authors (e.g. G. Evans, 2005; McCarthy, 2000) have called into question the unambiguously positive role of the culture-led approach to urban regeneration. They underline that an excessive focus of attention on some high-profile flagship projects in the most deprived areas to achieve physical improvements can lead to an increase in social polarisation, gentrification and a regressive distribution of benefits. More recent evidence (Ferilli et al., 2017) reveals that urban regeneration based on a cultural/creative approach can be effective if there is a good balance between the aspiration of achieving short-term outcomes (mainly addressing neighbourhood branding and real estate marketing purposes) and a vision of functional integration taking into account all dimensions in the long-run (eliciting the involvement of local people through inclusive cultural participation).

working spaces etc. often lead to the creation of completely new business and non-business activities with new employment better equipped for the future (Cervelló-Royo, Garrido-Yserte, & Segura-García del Río, 2012; G. Evans, 2005; Palazzo, 2017). The second strand refers to the positive externalities generated by the image enhancement or physical redesign of place. High-profile cultural projects (including iconic architecture) can help to transform the image of an area and have an impact on attracting more investments and urban economic recovery. These externalities can create a unique urban brand and promote a new sense of place. As a result, building and branding urban cultural life involve all the factors considered as improving the overall quality of place and, consequently, influencing people's and businesses' choice of location. In this way, an amenities-based place provides inputs for the entrepreneurial spirit of residents and newcomers to induce both standard business activities and creative industries, thus creating new types of localised advantages with income-enhancing effects (Cadell, Falk, & King, 2008; Degen & García, 2012; G. Evans, 2005; Wassenberg & van Dijken, 2011). The final strand concerns the benefits of personal development that result from the increasing local participation. Stated more precisely, no less important are "soft" measures and local projects which engage local residents in such activities as the visual and performing arts, preservation and promotion of local heritage, sport, city-wide festivals, gastronomic activities, holiday celebrations, entertainment, street performances and a wide range of activities related to creative sectors. These activities can give inhabitants – e. g. talented young people, midlife career changers, active retirees, and particularly those people who are marginalised – access to a vast range of opportunities for, on the one hand, developing their individual potential, and on the other, cementing the fabric of society and promoting social cohesion by furthering integration and mutual understanding between diverse groups of local community (Cadell, Falk, & King, 2008; McCarthy, 2000; Pratt, 2009). Collective cultural activities and participation affect social change and build connectedness, thereby reducing isolation. In what follows, these encourage local residents to be more responsive to the local needs and through their transformative role have an impact on the overall well-being of the area.

Spreading the benefits of regeneration
Many studies and reports emphasise the need to strike the appropriate balance between the physical change (infrastructural recovery of vastly run-down areas) and a cross-sectoral, multi-layer and multidimensional approach to urban regeneration. Hence, the focal point is that a regeneration scheme should cover measures aimed at upgrading the visible face of a city, but also involving those is-

sues of important economic and social significance. This means that investments in public infrastructure facilities, structures, and a high-quality public realm must be accompanied by actions giving local inhabitants motivation to acquire and develop personally or collectively new skills, capacities and behaviours that will be of great help in a new reality. The combination of physical morphology change with more ineffable aspects of social life in relation to a particular deprived urban area is essential to reverse the negative urban trends in that place and social deprivation of its inhabitants. This should be so because urban regeneration is expected to put local residents at the core of decision-making on the place where they live, work and want to be. It is therefore fundamental for place-making to build a genuine place that ensures safety, aesthetics, amenities, environmental quality and an environment supportive of lifestyle choices. By bringing it back into the city, it will meet, within the urban organisation of the whole city, the needs and aspirations of the local inhabitants. However, urban regeneration is not only about people and places, it is also about both creating benefits and spreading them throughout the community. As Cadell, Falk, and King (2008) rightly noted, *spreading the benefits of regeneration is just as important as generating them*. Inhabitants of all parts of a city need to feel that they can take advantage of the development of the city and in this way create their attachment to the city and commitment to city matters. A sense of community is a basis for the effective transformation of marginalised areas and disadvantaged people. Accordingly, city authorities are responsible for creating the better connections of the deprived neighbourhood to the whole city, on the one hand, and enhancing the city's solidarity with the neighbourhood, on the other (Weeber, Nothdorf, & Fischer, 2011). The most practical expression of this is informing the inhabitants of the other parts of the city about improvements in the social and physical spheres that occurred in the disadvantaged area, and motivating them, through a variety of events and festivities, to visit this neighbourhood. By doing so, it is possible to get rid of negative images and to achieve a characteristic and positive neighbourhood identity which contributes to strengthening the deprived area's (re)integration into the city. The more coherent image of the city is then fabricated by a bottom-up approach through the agency of *communicative culture* challenging local people and the whole city's community to be jointly involved in the socially integrative and city-wide development (Nussbaumer & Moulaert, 2004). Spreading the benefits of regeneration makes it possible to ensure a greater understanding of the implementation of the major structural changes and, more importantly, to obtain a greater social acceptance of actions and projects aimed at improving the quality of life in disadvantaged areas and social groups.

2.3 Model of integrated approach to urban regeneration

All the points emerging from the review of literature and policy practices discussed in the previous section provide solid arguments for developing a more holistic conceptual framework for the integrated approach to urban regeneration valid across Europe. This new conceptual framework seeks to capture the different dimensions to as well as the factors, processes and actors in the nature of urban regeneration through the concept of sustainable urban development. However, it would be too easy to think that urban regeneration is a simple complete system consisting of a number of components (stakeholders, decisions, goals etc.). The literature review shows that an attempt to provide an explanation of complex components in terms of every particular issue (places, processes, areas) is not sufficient. Urban regeneration requires systems thinking. Drawing upon Janas, Jarczewski, and Wańkowicz (2010), urban regeneration denotes, then, a system in which not only its components are important but also the interactions between the components. Put differently, relations that describe the entirety of urban regeneration cannot be deduced only on the basis of the principles of rights governing components but on the basis of the components and interactions that exist between them. At the core of this systemic approach is finding an understanding of what role each component (stakeholder, place, decision) pays in the accomplishment of the desired result. Since heterogeneity is an intrinsic and pivotal feature of urban regeneration, it is essential to take an epistemological perspective with a view to achieving a better understanding of the target system. An explicit epistemological framework serves to reflect upon the researchers' actual modelling practices because it obliges them to be very precise in making the design choices, and thus facilitating the research concept and a clear understanding of a phenomenon of interest covered by the model. Epistemological reasoning is also useful for linking results obtained by means of different research methods (Graebner, 2018).

The system of urban regeneration consists of the urban regeneration policies and regeneration schemes which lay down an intent to act on diagnosed particular urban situations, and more specifically, on the negative phenomena concentrated in some parts of the cities. These two kinds of public "statements" are framed by factors contributing to an urban regeneration environment which the literature (Janas, Jarczewski, & Wańkowicz, 2010) divides into two subsystems, namely regulations (political, legal and financial) and fields (socio-economic and spatial). In fact, the system is strongly institutionalised with policy instruments, budgets, rules, interest groups and various organisations focused on the urban development issues. In addition to that, the system of urban regeneration has to reflect fundamental social agreements about how cities will keep being built and transformed, and not least, how their residents will relate to each other across the city. The complexity of the regeneration issues and its direct impact on socio-economic development and quality of life in cities requires an equally wide range of different components and circumstances to be taken into account. As the systemic approach connects the components of a system, it can be applied to examine the system of urban regeneration as a whole. In order to highlight the role of the chosen approach, as already mentioned, systems are seen as a methodological support that links the theoretical background, knowledge, expertise and data from various disciplines relating to the same system (Garbolino, Chéry, & Guarnieri, 2019). Consequently, the systemic approach is used here to define the model of the integrated approach in urban regeneration at the European level in response to urban decay in European cities.

The essence of any modelling is to develop a representation of the study area of interest at an appropriate level of detail to reinforce the reasoning of the researcher. The model functions as an aid, giving an insight into the complex relationships between particular components of the research subject under study. In this work, modelling concerns constructing a representation of the system – the model showing the integrated approach in urban regeneration developed on the best knowledge and good practices from all over Europe. The central role of the model is to simplify, at least in part, the structural and functional properties of the system of urban regeneration. In many ways, it seeks to maintain, to the greatest possible extent, intelligibility, reliability and usefulness (Garbolino, Chéry, & Guarnieri, 2019). Therefore, in order to adequately represent the normative attributes and applicability of the conceptual model, its construction should be done with reference to epistemological characteristics such as ontology, structure, function and integration. The ontological approach refers to what the system *is*. It allows for a detailed description of the structure of the specific system area. Ontologies establish semantic relationships with real-world conditions and processes, thus making it possible to link information that is required to be included in the conceptual model with information that is depicted in a readily understandable way for one's perception. In other words, ontologies are a means to diminish semantic heterogeneity and clarify knowledge access and knowledge transfer so that the semantic model can be applicable, reliable, efficient and conclusive (Guarino & Giaretta, 1995). In this case, the ontological foundation is used to define the overall structure of the urban regeneration system (on the basis of general terminology) that underpins the understanding of the reality the model of the integrated approach in urban regeneration at the European level attempts to describe.

The second characteristic, namely structure, refers to how the system *is* (*built*). The structural approach builds on the concept of the system that is formed by interconnected elements, including the legal rules establishing the framework for its functioning. All interlinked elements compose a structure that has such features as: it is a whole, relevant unit; it can be transfigured over time, it is not static; and it possesses self-regulating mechanisms that ensure its preservation as a system. The structure can be formalised with a view to anticipating how it will work. Note that this specific characteristic is of particular scientific interest related to the structural approach. It should also be added that the structure constitutes the theoretical model that is applicable to reality, and not reality itself. The structure is not natural but it occurs as a result of a researcher's formulation that involves the identification of the relationships of the phenomenon's elements and their formalisation in the theoretical model (Wachelke, 2013). The arrangements of the particular elements of the conceptual model, and their reciprocal relationships demonstrated through modelling language constructs and domain terms, express the claim of the model. By this reason, the structure (model) can be used to present a certain dynamic or static pattern of the application domain, and its terminological content to reflect the framing conditions of a theory (Pfeiffer & Niehaves, 2005). In this context, taking into account the main theory, and the structural processes and properties of urban regeneration, the structural approach covers in this work the static description of the organisation process of the urban regeneration system, its particular elements together with their mutual interconnections from the perspective of the managing institutions, participating interest groups and governed organisations (particular deprived urban areas).

The third characteristic, that is, the functional one, refers to what the object *does*. From the theoretical point of view, the functional approach considers any social, economic or political institutions by identifying the functions they perform within a wider systemic context. Those functions can take several forms from basic conditions or needs to fundamental processes or activities indispensable for the functioning of the system. Interestingly enough, the functions are a series of actions that may only occur over time and within a system including the aforenamed institutions (Jackson, 2002). According to the systems theory, the main functional aspect of the system is characterised by goals which in turn can be operationalised by identifying specific functions. Following on from this, it is a researcher's task to define a function as the intended outcome that the system will produce. Each element of the system can have an assigned function, and hence it may be expected to attain all element-functions so as to achieve the main goal. The function is performed by a structure (model), even though function and structure are conceptually separate from each other (Worren, 2016). Complementing the role of the functional approach, it should be stated that this approach not only explains what the system does, but also addresses what the system *is for* (Garbolino, Chéry, & Guarnieri, 2019). This means that the system must conform to functional demands such as strategic goals, people's expectations, social inclusion etc. These demands determine the functions that the system must fulfil or, building on an axiomatic design, the functional requirements that need to be satisfied. Thus, a researcher is expected to diagnose these demands and identify a set of functions which dealt with the demands. The follow-up action is to specify how the functions should be performed, that is, to design appropriately the structure (Worren, 2016). On that basis, it can be concluded that the urban regeneration model must incorporate an illustrative description of the processes taking place within the system, i.e. actions and measures to be taken, their sequence and interdependencies, and the goals to be achieved.

Finally, the integrative characteristic refers to how the system *works* as a whole. An urban regeneration system, due to its complexity, requires holistic solutions that involve working across different authorities, sectors, rules, principles and tools. Hence, all components of the system should build an integrated whole, so that the system can be able to address adequately and efficiently the existing needs (demands) and the system itself can finally be a functional part of a bigger system (or groups of systems) and contribute to it (or them). The systems theory provides for a system that is characterised by its structure and its behaviour. Whereas the structure mirrors the system components that are interconnected to form the entire system, the behaviour describes the operations and processes of the system and focuses on the interactions between its particular components (Hieronymi, 2013). In order to create human consciousness and cognition, the integration of the system structure and behaviour is made by exploring and visualising the system components and functions, and the interconnections between them. Such an integrative conceptual framework has a great explanatory power vis-à-vis the system. It clearly shows how it functions in general or how it can be applied in reality to control given goals and establish future ones, concurrently organising and integrating all the system components and functions. It can be done so because the integrative approach is commonly seen as a multidimensional system perspective for creating change that uses systems thinking to engage people (whatever role they play in the system) and resources in a process of continuous improvement. Moreover, the outcomes that result from applying the integrative approach are always focalised on optimising both the socio-economic and physical dimensions of the system as they are symbiotic co-factors. It can also work either as a regulatory force or as a catalysing force aimed at implementing pattern-breaking change (Cavaleri, 1992). Therefore, taking account of the deep roots of the integrative approach in systems theory, the model of integrated urban regeneration needs to provide an appropriate integrative conceptual framework for understanding the multidimensional relationships at the level of policy issues, interest groups, development factors, other impact areas (other systems) and adopted goals.

Bearing in mind the above-examined characteristics of the systems thinking, it is possible to develop a conceptual model of the integrated approach to urban regeneration which can be applied generally to the implementation of urban policy by countries. However, taking into account the specific context of multi-level governance presented here, it is in particular applicable at the European level. The model provides a simplified graphical representation of the system of urban regeneration which shows how policies, decisions, structures and stakeholders are interrelated to influence the regrowth of inner-city areas. In this sense, it is a cognitive model as, focusing on the system's operational rules and specific future goals, it constitutes a reliable representation of the system itself and expresses the best state of knowledge thereof. It defines the system's elements (authorities and stakeholders) and the functions (activities and processes) of their causal interactions. In other words, the model describes what and how decisions made in concert with all interest groups within the framework of urban regeneration policy influence the way the run-down areas may emerge effectively from the urban decay. There are two major reasons by which this reasoning can be justified. One the one hand, the model represents a formalised theory of the regeneration processes that objectively states which decisions and activities, and how, affect the overall performance of regenerative initiatives run in urban areas most in need of change. On the other hand, it is also built on experiences, practical examples and best practices on regeneration measures and projects implemented in nearly a hundred cities across Europe. Specifically, the model translates explicit theoretical knowledge and practical experience on urban regeneration into graphical formulations of the arrangement of the system's components in such a way that accurately reflects its functions and processes.

Figure 5 illustrates the model of the integrated approach to urban regeneration applicable at the European level. It summarises the findings discussed above and all the considerations made so far. The model constitutes a graph-theoretically oriented and practice-based conceptual framework of implementing the regeneration activities. Given the importance of integrated urban regeneration and its strategic potential for sustainable urban development in Europe, as stated in the *Toledo Declaration* (2010), it needs to be framed in the wider concept of integrated urban development which, in turn, should come within a common and strengthened policy framework at the EU level. The most tangible expression of this was the incorporation of the urban dimension into the EU cohesion policy and the earmarking of a special financing envelope within European funds for sustainable integrated urban development (De Gregorio Hurtado, 2017). It has since become apparent that the concept of sustainable integrated urban development and integrated urban regeneration, as its basic component, forming the so-called *Urban Acquis*, require a multi-level policy to tackle effectively complex challenges faced by European cities. Since cities do indeed have a crucial role to play side by side with the regional authorities in implementing EU and national policies, multi-level and multi-stakeholder cooperation is critical to solve many of the most currently pressing and future concerns. Therefore, putting the integrated approach into practice in this context means addressing the whole complexity of urban development, all policy areas and resources as well as the importance of each part of the city in the whole policy structure. It requires cities, regions, Member States, the EU and other key stakeholders to come together to deal jointly with urban issues and deliver policy actions for the benefit of people. Such an extensive cooperation should be built on the principles of vertical coordination between all administrative levels, i.e. EU/national/regional/local, by means of special arrangements for multi-level governance. The EU is requested to establish a more integrated and coordinated approach to policy framework with an impact on urban areas. This does not imply the need to initiate new regulation or instruments, but rather the need to concentrate on a more effective and coherent implementation of existing EU policies. By doing so, it is possible to overcome some obstacles in EU policy which do not enable local authorities to be more powerful partners in the decision-making process on integrated urban development. As a result, urban authorities can act in a more systematic and coherent way so that they can achieve specific local objectives, and thereby contribute to achieving overarching goals. The EU regulatory framework considering the relevance of the urban dimension in EU policy development (e.g. cohesion policy) should constitute grounds for the implementation of integrated and sustainable urban development strategies and place-based approaches through urban projects.

Authorities at the national level are expected to ensure the good coordination of the sectoral policies and provide a legal framework for the organisation of multi-level governance at all the administrative tiers. In accordance with the provisions of the *Leipzig Charter* (2007), national authorities should also take responsibility for establishing urban development policy that as a separate policy framework serves the needs of a coherent and coordinated city development. This level, along with the other government levels, should lay down special incentives to develop innovative solutions conducive to protecting, strengthening and developing cities further. Special attention needs to be paid to deprived urban areas that face numerous structural and socio-economic problems. Activities aimed at achieving the objectives of social cohesion and integration within cities should also be embedded in an integrated urban development policy. Moreover, this policy should take into account the existence of a polycentric urban system in which many cities and their functional areas vary by potentials and challenges. It follows that urban policy must endeavour to seek the establishment of balanced territorial organisation and promote competitiveness by developing existing and planned socio-economic and functional ties. In turn, the regional governmental level is seen in the whole system as an intermediary tier responsible for coordinating sectoral and local policies embedded within the context of a broader regional perspective and, in this regard, paying particular attention to metropolitan or rural–urban relationships. Having regard to the polycentricity of the urban structure, regional authorities should foster the development of regional clusters of cooperation and innovation, thus, while applying a well-balanced and integrated approach to development based on a diverse potential of territories, contributing to the territorial economic growth. Moreover, stemming from the recommendations made by the Committee of the Regions in its opinion on *The role of urban regeneration in the future of urban development in Europe* (2010), the regional governmental level should play a primary role in designing, implementing and evaluating integrated urban regeneration strategies and, consequently, contribute to improving the urban environment in general and promoting cohesion within their territories. In addition, sub-national governments and administrative levels play an important role in the formulation and implementation of EU cohesion policy. Regional authorities are directly involved in the negotiation processes and participate in decision-making regarding the usage of EU funds (Dotti, 2013). They allocate EU funds available to them across regions through their operational programmes (OPs) so that they can decide which funding objectives (under a Common Strategic Framework) will be pursued. European funding earmarked for integrated sustainable urban development available under the European Structural and Investment Funds (ESIF) priorities is addressed through most of the regional OPs. Hence, regional authorities have a particular responsibility to adopt measures which provide effective EU cohesion policy support for urban areas.

Urban authorities are those local governments who remain obligated to implement urban regeneration measures. They also bear the main and lasting burden arising from the necessity of constantly tackling structural challenges posed by globalisation, demographic and industrial change, and the development of new technologies. In response to this, they are obliged to develop an integrated vision based on the coordination of actions with the intention of ensuring not only a balanced development of the city as a whole and its particular parts, but also considering its role within the wider territory. This also includes the need to counteract the problems of urban decay and social exclusion through reversing the physical and socio-economic degradation process in some inner-city areas and coping with deteriorating living conditions. Urban authorities, being most familiar with local needs, are the major players to implement sustainable urban regeneration initiatives in order to reorganise and upgrade deprived urban areas. They have a responsibility for this through the exercise of their statutory obligations and public administration tasks, using recognised procedures and applying the variety of local policy instruments. Yet, as many authors have argued, municipal authorities should be given considerable power in matters pertaining to the formal organisation of the regeneration process. As all activities, initiatives and policies carried out in terms of urban regeneration compose a complex, lengthy and funds-demanding strategy, the overwhelming majority of cities experience insufficient administrative capacities or regulatory empowerment to fulfil this mission solely on their own. Therefore, on the one hand, a specific comprehensive legal framework should be established at the national (legislative) level which ensures a universal nature of the regeneration process and gives powerful tools to help address problems of decline and structural change and, as a matter of course, lead the deprived urban areas out of degradation. This legislation should naturally vest in urban authorities full responsibility for the exercise of urban regeneration. While on the other hand, law- and policy-making, together with the delegation of power, should be accompanied by the ring-fencing of special money for regeneration actions and its direct transfer to local authorities or making its allocation available to local players on specified terms.

Urban authorities represent the public sphere closest to the people and play a crucial role in their daily lives. This is the government level where cross-sectoral collaborations should be initiated with the aim to engage local communities in decision-making about their area. Putting an integrated approach into practice means involving multiple local stakeholders including residents, housing associations or communities, business representatives, non-profits and philanthropic groups, representatives of education and culture etc. in order to build a local partnership capable of developing and implementing an integrated urban regeneration programme (IURP). Such a local partnership appears to be an adequate response to the issues that neither the market, nor the authorities, nor civil society alone, are able to address, these issues being the complex problems of both economic growth and social exclusion which cut across the boundaries and responsibilities of different institutional structures. A partnership-driven urban regeneration, furthermore, should have a bottom-up approach in which inhabitants and decision-makers feel social responsibilities and develop programmes aimed at urban transformation while taking into account varying social needs in differentiated local contexts (Corcoran, 2006; Trillo, 2014). The commitment

2.3 Model of integrated approach to urban regeneration — 95

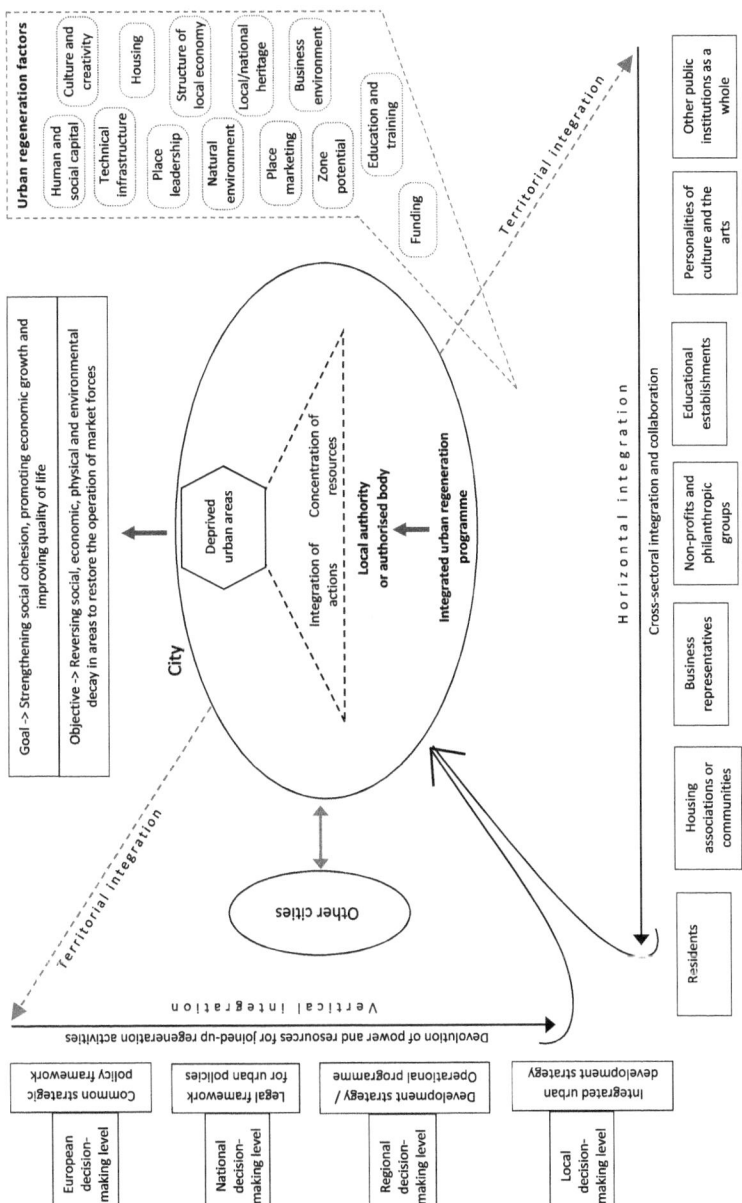

Figure 5: The model of the integrated approach to urban regeneration applicable at the European level
Source authors's elaboration

and collaboration of all local interested groups makes it possible to better diagnose local bottlenecks as well as specific potentials of particular inner-city areas. In this way, cooperative and effective local governance structures are created which place greater emphasis on individual (people) and private (market) involvement. What is more, wide collaboration, greater networking and more arrangements with local groups of actors create grounds for the approval and endorsement of IURP. For local governments this means a mandate for implementing the programme to regenerate deprived urban areas. In fact, the horizontal integration between local actors involved in urban regeneration/city building goes hand in hand with the vertical integration of all administrative levels (EU/national/regional/local) by means of formulas for multi-level governance. Although this two-dimensional integration of various decision-makers ensures a good collaboration, which combines top-down and bottom-up approaches to transform some run-down areas, it may not be sufficient to achieve balanced development in a wider perspective. Thus a more functional view crossing geographical and administrative boundaries is also needed in this case. Even though many urban bottlenecks are of a local nature, they call for wider territorial measures and collaboration within functional urban areas. There is, thus, a need for a territorial dimension of integration which relies on reshaping functional areas to make them evolve into a consistent geographical entity. This implies the implementation of the territorially coordinated policies and, within their frameworks, specific actions that are not pursued as some disjointed undertakings but constitute an inherent part of general development policy (governed at a higher administrative level) for the entire entity (Böhme et al., 2011; Bradley & Zaucha, 2017). Territorial integration refers to different territorial levels depending on the relevance of policy intervention. Hence, cities willing to deal with problems of urban blight must establish integrated and sustainable urban development strategies and ensure their execution for the city as a whole, from its functional areas to its neighbourhoods (New Leipzig Charter, 2020). It follows that integrated urban regeneration programmes should take into consideration a complex network of functional interdependences and partnerships occurring within cities as well as in inter- and intra-regional perspectives.

The consequence of applying an integrated and place-based approach aiming at the balanced and sustainable development of cities is the necessity to develop IURP. The complexity of the urban issues and the need to incorporate the priorities of territorial integration require city authorities to frame such an IURP whose objectives and goals, actions and tools will be to a large extent integrated within the context of the wider geographical realities. Moreover, it must also be consistent with the targets, and underpin the implementation, of supra-local strategies and the general development policy of the state (Ciesiółka, 2018). IURP has here the meaning of a document drawn up and approved by urban authorities. This preparation should follow the basic rules on cooperation and partnership which involve all the interest groups representing local communities and provide an appropriate framework for the empowerment of them, thus incorporating them into the decision-making on their locality. The main task of the programme is to deliver evident improvements in the quality of life in its target urban areas. It must, by means of the integrated approach, address the high concentration of social, economic and environmental problems becoming increasingly visible. Therefore, the overall objective set out in an IURP should lead to reducing disadvantages in the deprived inner-city areas by focusing on such issues as: unemployment, low levels of entrepreneurial activity, poor health, crime, education, culture, and also a radical improvement of local infrastructure. Nonetheless, the physical transformation of buildings and amenities is a necessary but not sufficient condition for successful urban regeneration. Improvements to the physical sphere are if not of secondary importance to social issues, then they should enjoy treatment at most as favourably as the social ones. To put it differently, only a comprehensive programme comprising both social and physical initiatives can transform whole target areas into attractive and liveable spaces as well as reverse the unfavourable processes experienced in these areas (Schuurmans, Dyrbøl, & Guay, 2019). An IURP should include a deep and detailed understanding of local deficits and needs as well as careful consideration for the people affected by it. Assuming the liveability of the target areas in the long run, the actions under an IURP should be tailored to the local needs with a view to restore affirmative urban functions by the reconciliation of old and new development perspectives. Hence, the preparation of regeneration programmes must be preceded by a comprehensive diagnosis of the causes of degradation and the scale of negligence in relation to the whole urban area, and then joint development of actions focused on deprived areas and aimed at bringing them out of the crisis (Jadach-Sepioło, 2021). This is why an IURP should clearly demonstrate a high level of compliance with the functional characteristics of the area, on the one side, and the specificity of problems to be tackled, on the other. All the regeneration factors listed in the model determine conditions for defining the directions of the development of particular deprived areas, and, in a wider perspective, coherent development of the whole city. Such examination of the regeneration issue seems reasonable when considering the need to restore market forces and social activity in these areas, which consequently leads to the improvement of the people's quality of life.

At the core of the model of the integrated approach to urban regeneration is a triad of determinants: (1) urban authorities (or a special body mandated by those authorities) must play a central and decisive role in urban regeneration on the basis of multi-level and multi-sectoral governance; (2) an IURP that covers the entire spectrum of actions and projects to tackle the problems of disadvantaged inner-city areas should take into account the integrated approach as a principle for any regenerative actions and favour the concentration of resources and greater use of incentives on the development priorities; (3) all efforts, actions and resources need to be focused on a specific (deprived) area (or areas) designated within a coherent urban area (city) that is (are) characterised by multiple relative deprivations. The first determinant stipulates that urban authorities (or an authorised body) should be assigned a leading role in the design and implementation of their IURP. The rationale behind this is to have a single competent actor that assumes final responsibility for supervising compliance with the IURP provisions. The second determinant aims to maximise complementarity and synergy effects through setting out objectives and regulatory provisions, programming actions and technical management, and identifying integrated financial tools. By focusing on priorities and concentrating resources, it is possible to reduce waste and boost the multiplier effect that will generate an increase in income and employment. Finally, the last determinant refers strictly to area-based approaches where particular areas of very serious concerns located within cities should be especially recognised and supported under the IURP. Sustained concentration of resources and attention upon carefully specified marginalised areas can effectively contribute to the improvement of the quality of life (Parkinson, 2014). The integration of actions and concentration of resources make it possible to avoid the fragmentation of effects and spreading them thinly. It can really work and contribute to lasting improvement in the social, economic, physical and environmental conditions of the area.

Overall, the model of the integrated approach to urban regeneration applicable at the European level depicts an integrated framework of practices that decision-makers on urban development should have regard to when implementing urban policy, and in particular urban regeneration in cities. In many aspects of its conceptual form, it refers to the key elements of the Pact of Amsterdam which launched the Urban Agenda for the EU (2016) and the *New Leipzig Charter* (2020) which advocates multi-level, multi-stakeholder cooperation and an integrated approach in addressing urban problems. The intention of the model is not to present an exhaustive framework of urban regeneration but rather a view for conceptualising the urban regeneration policy-making that is evident across many theoretical and practical indications.

3 Urban policy as a part of cohesion policy – towards repayable assistance

3.1 Cohesion policy objectives and framework

The overarching objective of the European Union (EU) cohesion policy (CP) is to promote the harmonious development of its regions and cities in order to achieve continuous, coherent and sustainable development throughout the entire Community. More specifically, the EU makes every endeavour to support balanced economic, social and territorial development across all European regions, in particular those "lagging behind". It must, however, be acknowledged that a change in CP has been observed in the last decade towards turning into an approach that builds on a territorial context and enhances the endogenous competitive potential of regions (Barca, McCann, & Rodríguez-Pose, 2012). This signifies a shift from a traditional policy focused on reducing the disparities in socio-economic development between the EU's regions through sectoral interventions (subsidies targeted at relevant entities) to a place-based approach in which policy measures and financial resources are tailored to specific places (Szlachta & Zaucha, 2010). From its very beginning CP has been perceived as a development policy aiming at improving the conditions for growth, jobs creation, well-being and protection of the natural environment at the level of the EU regions, thus reinforcing the integration of regional economies. Initially, it played a role as the driving force for balancing the socio-economic disturbances that arose with respect to the creation of the European internal market. Over time, there has been a shift of emphasis from a focus on the reduction of disparities between regions to identifying and making use of regional (endogenous) potential as a stimulus for national growth. CP has changed markedly throughout its history, driven by both internal and external factors. The former encompass mainly the progressive process of learning, successive enlargements of the EU, the process of deepening European integration and market unification. In turn, the latter include increasing globalisation processes, changing economic contexts, institutional decentralisation and the evolution of regional policy and regional development theories (Ferry, 2013). Indeed, the current CP logic is shaped by modern thinking which results from an advanced understanding of the relationships between economic geography, technology, innovation, creativity and gov-

---

Piotr Idczak

ernance.[11] Following this line of argument, CP should respond to the needs of European citizens in such a way that, according to Barca (2009), *everyone, irrespective of where she/he lives, is able to benefit from the economic gains from unification, to have equal access to the opportunities so created as well as an equal possibility of coping with the risks and threats.*

However, the CP architecture in 2007–2013 could not be said to have provided an optimal balance between basic infrastructure development and more sophisticated interventions that concentrate on promoting competitiveness and job creation through support for such areas as research and innovation, human capital, business services etc. The more traditional approach to regional development support, which is based on improvements in infrastructure, remained in place due to infrastructure underdevelopment mainly in the Member States that joined the EU in 2004 and 2007. This approach represented a sort of flexibility towards these states to achieve an adequate balance between CP objectives and regional and local needs. Thus, less economically advanced regions could allocate more funds to infrastructure-related investments.

Against this background, the objectives of the 2007–2013 CP were formulated so that regions and states could programme appropriate actions for growth according to the extent and nature of their structural deficits, the structure of their economies and specific areas representing their potential or comparative advantages. The actions taken within the framework of the European funds should foster sustainable development by promoting growth, competitiveness and employment, and strengthening social inclusion and improving the quality of the environment. By doing so, the funds should contribute to achieving the following three objectives, as provided for in Regulation EC 1083/2006 (Council, 2006b):

- *convergence* – to promote actions aimed at improving conditions for growth and employment through investments in physical and human capital, support for innovation and knowledge society, improvement of the environment and administrative efficiency – all this should lead to real convergence of the least-developed Member States and regions;
- *regional competitiveness and employment* – to strengthen competitiveness and attractiveness through the increasing and improvement of adaptability of workers and businesses, economic and social changes – regions outside the least-developed regions were eligible for support under this objective;

---

11 It should be noted that considerations on the framework of CP do not extend beyond the 2007–2013 programming period as this covers the financial perspective when JESSICA was launched and implemented.

– *European territorial cooperation* – to encourage cross-border cooperation through joint local and regional initiatives, trans-national and interregional cooperation, and exchange of experience.

The actions taken under the *convergence* objective can be largely perceived as traditional forms of regional development support because, in terms of the structure of financial allocation, they focused mainly on hard infrastructure investments. The arguments in favour of the infrastructure-related actions were, as mentioned earlier, mostly infrastructural bottlenecks, and their elimination was predominantly needed for successful development. The second objective appears to be more appropriate to ensure an optimal combination of "smart" interventions aimed at supporting employment and the business environment. Nevertheless, as Mendez (2011) noted, many of the countries that joined the EU in 2004 and later (including Poland) earmarked a sizeable volume of funds for competitiveness-related investments, although they were formally bound by the rule. However, irrespective of how financial concentration was arranged by regions and states in the programming period, they were obliged to organise their investment programmes, while making a concerted effort, in such a way as to tackle the supply-side bottlenecks and enhance productivity. The intention thereby was to offset the demand-side pressures on their economy which usually characterises the real economy of many transforming countries.

From this study's point of view, it should be stressed that, the regulations and guidelines for the 2007–2013 programming period vis-à-vis the European funds provided for a "stronger" urban component than ever before (Atkinson, 2015). It follows that at the level of regulations CP provided finance for a wide range of urban development projects. This was expressed generally in Regulation EC 1083/2006 as the funds should *in an appropriate manner, support sustainable urban development particularly as part of regional development* (Article 3). This meant not only a significant change but also the adoption of "urban mainstreaming" into CP. As a consequence, the *URBAN Community Initiative*[12] had to be mainstreamed in the operational programmes prepared by the Member

---

[12] The URBAN Community Initiative was launched by the European Commission in 1994 as a special structural action to support urban regeneration. This programme aimed to address the challenges faced by run-down urban areas and with the use of the European structural funds to improve the living conditions of residents, while promoting sustainable urban development. URBAN adopted a strategy based on an integrated approach in which local authorities and other local stakeholders had to participate in regeneration processes. It assumed that the problems of deprived urban areas should be solved through the implementation of the urban regeneration programmes based on a collaborative approach. (For more see De Gregorio Hurtado, 2015).

States and the regions. The rationale behind this was that all European cities could build on the experience derived from URBAN and use them so as to apply an integrated approach to urban areas (De Gregorio Hurtado, 2018). A more explicit reference to the specific requirements relating to the urban dimension was included in the regulation on the European Regional Development Fund (ERDF) (Regulation EC 1080/2006). Article 8 of this regulation entitled "Sustainable Urban Development" foresees that *in the case of action involving sustainable urban development*, ERDF may *support the development of participative, integrated and sustainable strategies to tackle the high concentration of economic, environmental and social problems affecting urban areas* (European Parliament and Council, 2006). In fact, CP introduced the urban dimension into its framework, which required cities to establish the integrated urban development strategies or programmes. Hence, all measures undertaken within the framework of that policy should have promoted competitiveness and social inclusion. Such an approach entails a variety of factors that must be taken into consideration when drawing up programmes of integrated urban development, such as *inter alia* economic growth and jobs, rehabilitation of the physical environment, social exclusion, demographic change, urban sprawl, brownfield redevelopment, the preservation and development of natural and cultural heritage, the promotion of entrepreneurship, good governance etc. (European Commission, 2009, pp. 31–32; European Parliament and Council, 2006). It should be added that in line with the provision of this Regulation the Member States and the regions were allowed to apply Article 8 on a voluntary basis.

Furthermore, the Decision on Community strategic guidelines on cohesion (Council, 2006a) – hereafter referred to as "Decision" – poses an obligation on Member States and regions to take into account, when preparing the national strategic reference frameworks and operational programmes for 2007–2013, specific problems facing urban areas. As a response to the problems, adequate actions and measures should be planned to strengthen internal cohesion inside the urban areas that strive to improve the situation of districts in crisis. What is particularly important, a new instrument was proposed, namely JESSICA, that, operating on a financial engineering basis, would support the implementation of urban projects included in integrated urban development plans.

3.2 Cohesion policy support for sustainable urban development

With the adoption of the regulations and decisions on the 2007–2013 programming period, it became clear that cities play an important role in bringing about social cohesion and the development of European regions. The urban dimension moved up the political agenda, despite not being a legal basis for urban policy in the treaties. Urban actions were incorporated into regional and national strategies, and became vital elements in many of the mainstream operational programmes. When developing the operational programmes Member States and regions should direct their efforts towards specific geographical circumstances in order to adapt appropriate actions to the specific challenges of various places. Providing appropriate assistance for all territories based on their individual deficits and capacities, under the conditions of good governance, according to the Decision, constituted a main mechanism on the road towards the achievement of territorial cohesion.[13] Cities are key players in this process. Therefore, Member States and regions obtained the possibility within the legislative framework to delegate to cities funds addressing urban problems. In addition, to enable the full benefits of partnership, cities were intended to be involved throughout the process and to shoulder their share of the responsibility for the delegated part of the programmes at both the preparation and the implementation stages (Council, 2006a).

Cities are places where desired resources concentrate and thereby can contribute significantly to the creation of jobs and growth, thus offering good living conditions and well-being (Dziembała, 2019). One should, however, remember that, according to the literature, an accumulation of resources in an area with a high density of different activities may also lead to negative externalities such as traffic congestion, pollution, price increases and a lack of affordable housing, urban sprawl, rising costs of urban infrastructure, social tensions and higher crime rates, a degraded environment, health problems and as a result a reduced quality of life, that is, phenomena that frequently are related to overcrowding (Castells-Quintana & Royuela, 2014; Duranton & Kerr, 2018). In order to counteract the concentration of numerous negative phenomena in some city districts, the integration of all relevant sectoral policies under an integrated plan for sustainable urban development is needed. Since urban development is a complex and long-term process, cities had to prepare a long-term and consistent development plan as a precondition for the successful use of the funds. In a nutshell, cities were obliged to apply an integrated approach to sustainable urban development in which every action in one field must be compatible with those in another (European Commission, 2006b). Guidelines and good practices

---

[13] Note that the "territorial cohesion" objective, as such, was introduced to the EU Treaty in 2009 and was the latest goal to be defined when analysing CP as a whole.

worked out by URBAN and the URBACT network[14] in the last 2007–2013 cycle were key elements in building the EU approach to addressing problems of run-down urban areas. In this approach sustainable urban development cannot be confined to physical resources and the environment. It aggregates four basic pillars – i.e. economic, environmental, social and institutional – with a view to manage urban development. Notwithstanding, the starting point under this policy framework remains explicitly the environmental pillar (see Figure 6). For the sake of the relative intensity of economic and social activity taking place in urban areas, they are and most likely will be always net consumers of resources of the environment around them that in turn sustain their existence and development. Therefore, regeneration policy aimed at dealing with urban decay should be applied through environmentally focused actions, while being embedded within specific and complex economic, social, institutional and geographical contexts (Czischke, Moloney, & Turcu, 2015; Turcu, 2012b). This approach was commonly recognised in the EU as the integrated approach to urban regeneration including a wide variety of physical, economic, social and environmental initiatives, capable of integrating local residents into inclusive governance (Acierno, 2017). Integrated urban regeneration seeks to reconcile the objectives deriving from the necessity of climate protection with those of economic growth and social progress. It should be added, however, that throughout this time a policy towards urban issues, including urban regeneration, had an informal character and some of the available instruments were not mandatory.

Despite the lack of formal rules laying down urban policy issues at the European level, the European Commission, and in particular the Directorate General for Regional and Urban Policy (DG Regio) encouraged Member States and regions to introduce some innovative solutions related to urban policy into their local governance systems. This action was recognised by many of them, which was manifested by the establishment of the legal or strategic urban policy framework, especially in those states where a specific national-level policy did not previously exist. This led to a greater involvement of national institutions, regions and cities in the implementation of urban policy. Municipal authorities gained knowledge and technical capacity to design and implement integrated urban regeneration strategies (De Gregorio Hurtado, 2017). These strategies were some kind of precondition in applying for support available under the umbrella of the ERDF. In fact, cities not only got involved in the preparation and execution

---

[14] The URBACT programme was the follow-up initiative of URBAN in the last 2007–2013 cycle. It focused on networking cities involved in sustainable urban development with the aim of sharing experience, exchanging knowledge and learning with peers across Europe.

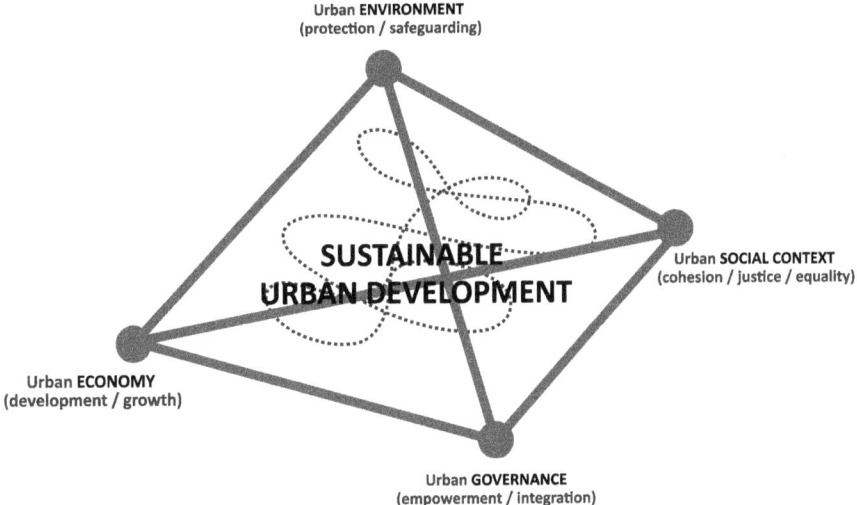

Figure 6: The prism of urban sustainability
Source: (Czischke, Moloney, & Turcu, 2015, p. 7)

of these strategies but also showed a growing interest in implementing urban regeneration initiatives co-funded by the ERDF. A greater involvement of authorities at different administrative levels in urban issues contributed to the use of, on a far greater scale, the instruments of urban regeneration based on the "URBAN method" (a strategic, participative, collaborative and area-based approach). The increasing challenges of urban development – mainly growing socio-spatial inequalities, on the one hand, and the knowledge and experience gained so far through addressing them, on the other – resulted in the so-called *EU Urban Acquis*. This covered a collection of documents on urban development agreed by the EU ministers, thus creating a common ground for the urban policy of the EU. Under the *Urban Acquis*, strengthened from 2007, "sustainable integrated urban development" and "integrated urban regeneration" concepts were adopted which caused them to be an indispensable part of the EU policy discourse. This also gave rise to wide-ranging initiatives on urban development and regeneration taken in Member States at different administrative levels (De Gregorio Hurtado, 2017).

From this study's point of view, two documents adopted under the *Urban Acquis* are especially important. First, the *Leipzig Charter on Sustainable European Cities* agreed at the informal meeting of EU ministers on urban development in May 2007 (Leipzig Charter, 2007). It includes recommendations addressed to European cities to draw up integrated urban development programmes covering an

entire city as a implementation-oriented planning tool. It should enable a greater use of integrated approaches which involve the coordination of spatial, sectoral and temporal aspects of major areas of urban policy. Such approaches integrate the state, regions, cities, citizens and economic actors around the common goal of strengthening the competitiveness of cities. Special attention is paid to deprived urban areas. In this aspect, an integrated urban development policy should enhance social integration which *contributes to reducing inequalities and preventing social exclusion.* To this end, the signatories to this *Charter* recommend *inter alia* the following strategies for action:
- pursuing strategies for upgrading the physical environment,
- strengthening the local economy and local labour market policy,
- proactive education and training policies for children and young people,
- promotion of efficient and affordable urban transport.

Pursuant to the provisions of the *Charter*, Member States and regions are allowed to use the European structural funds for substantial integrated urban development programmes. Moreover, the role of urban development funds was also emphasised. This refers in particular to the JESSICA initiative, which should be applied as a financial engineering instrument to leverage private capital for the realisation of integrated urban development strategies.

The second document is the so-called *Toledo Declaration*, entitled "Toledo Reference Document on integrated urban regeneration and its strategic potential for a smarter, more sustainable and socially inclusive urban development in Europe" (Toledo Declaration, 2010). This was adopted at an informal ministerial meeting on urban development in June 2010, that is at the mid-point of the reference period of this study, but it also significantly affected actions taken in urban areas. First of all, the ministers highlighted the strategic role of urban regeneration in the future of urban development in Europe. Urban regeneration should represent an opportunity to address the key challenges of European cities from the standpoint of the multiple dimensions of sustainability (environmental, social, economic, urban planning, architectural and cultural, and governance). The *Declaration* stresses the importance of integrated urban regeneration that treats the city as a *functioning whole and its parts as components of the whole urban organism*. Regeneration actions should be taken with a view to fully developing and balancing the complexity and diversity of social, economic and urban structures, while simultaneously promoting greater environmental eco-efficiency. In the face of limited public resources at that time, JESSICA was supposed to favour integrated urban regeneration.

Overall, many Member States and regions implemented the "urban instruments" of CP targeted at cities in a sectoral manner reflecting the operational programmes and associated priorities. As a result, cities had to apply for funds in the same way as all beneficiaries. Indeed, cities were deprived of the benefits accruing from the guidelines established due to their special needs. They did not have any assurance to receive funds for the implementation of their integrated urban development programmes (Atkinson, 2015). This certainly made it difficult for cities to achieve their objectives and also hindered the implementation of the integrated approach to urban development.

Furthermore, attention should be drawn to the fact that cities are not isolated places. Changes occurring in one place have an impact on others. This is because markets, trade relations, commuting, communication and governments that cover more than one place form interconnections between places. This means that some decisions made in a single place at a certain time can affect the prosperity of other places at different scales, also having importance for the future. Therefore, intervention actions carried out in one city need to be, depending on particular circumstances, coherent and complementary to actions implemented by neighbouring cities (or regions). In order to deal with this, the European Commission proposed the concept of territorial cohesion as it was stated in the *Green Paper on Territorial Cohesion* published in 2008 (European Commission, 2008a). Although the Commission made it clear that this *Green Paper* does not cover any of the financial aspects of CP within the 2007–2013 financial period, the *Green Paper* itself and the intense debate about it (see e.g. Böhme et al., 2011; Faludi, 2009; Ramsden, 2011) affected to some extent the implementation of the integrated urban development programmes. From this perspective, what this does imply is that the territorial dimension of urban development cannot be ignored. Furthermore, it should be seen as an indispensable element of urban development requiring that particular attention must be paid to the impact of programmes and projects in terms of promoting spatially balanced, harmonious and sustainable development.

3.3 Rationale for the revolving mechanism in urban policy

The process of addressing the major urban challenges, caused by changes especially in economic and social structures and globalisation, was confronted at the end of the first decade of the twenty-first century with a serious scenario of limited public resources. This meant that the public response to the increasing inequalities and economic stagnation might not, due to extraordinary budget pressure, be sufficient. In this situation, CP, with its technical construction, turned out to be useful. The CP funds are never the sole source of financing but, in accordance with the principle of additionality, they need to be supplemented by the financial contribution paid from the Member State side. Co-financing means that CP, in practice, raises additional funds from various sources (public and private) for a particular investment. In other words, CP increases by its nature the leveraging of public spending. Therefore, the European Commission decided to complement the conventional approach, based almost exclusively on grants, with new instruments using financial engineering (Hübner, 2008). The intention was to combine different types of public funding (European funds, national, regional and local funds, etc.) under a new formula with private financial capital. This new approach to funding urban investments aimed to stipulate conditions for the creation of new financial incentives for private firms and other urban actors, seeking to increase the involvement of private property. Since the financial engineering mechanism can gain more by virtue of its revolving nature, the new approach was seen to enhance the effectiveness of traditionally involved European and national funding sources. The revolving character of such instruments means that the same funds, through the cycle mechanism, can rotate several times, thus multiplying their impact and ensuring the long-term sustainability of these instruments. As a consequence, the final impact of these funds can be many times greater than it would have been if they had been used only once. In addition, the general effect is also reinforced by interest and dividends paid on the account of the funds from the capital employed.

Taking into consideration the policy design perspective, CP financial instruments can be seen as an alternative way of delivering funds to finance investments of a greater importance from the point of view of society in general. The main difference between traditional grants and financial instruments lies not in the objective to be achieved but rather in the way the financial engineering mechanism is able to bring about the achievement of that objective and wider policy outcomes. Hence, the main point here is that the financial instruments may be only involved when a given investment is capable of generating revenues or saving costs at the operating level in order to provide the means for the initial financial support to be refunded (Wishlade & Michie, 2018). It follows that public interventions aimed at responding to particular needs justified by the provision of public goods will not always be appropriately tailored to the nature of the financial instruments. As a matter of principle, public investments are not focused on generating a return but on performing important social functions. In many cases they do not demonstrate capacities to produce enough revenues to be deployed for the repayment of the financial support. Therefore, it is possible to consider those investments for repayable support which not only will provide activities on a profit-making basis, but also will be well-suited to the market imperfections being addressed.

With regard to CP, transforming grants into recyclable forms of finance can enhance incentives for better performance in terms of the quality of the projects and accordingly contribute to promoting long-term sustainable growth in regions. Financial engineering instruments (FEIs) are generally supposed to offer a number of advantages, the most important of which are the following (Schneidewind et al., 2013; Wishlade & Michie, 2018).

- Leverage effect. This is seen as the key advantage since FEIs create the possibility to leverage additional capital from various potential sources, including the private or the public sector. The FEI mechanism makes it possible to attract additional resources, thus expanding the common effect of CP resources and the national/regional contributions. In fact, the ultimate impacts on society and the economy should be greater than those induced by grants.
- Sustainability. FEIs builds a foundation for the long-term recycling of public funds. This feature seems especially important in times of public budgetary restraints. Since the funds are repaid, it creates a legacy that, thanks to its revolving nature, can be invested again. Managing authorities are allowed to use the reinvestment of the funds at the regional level beyond the end of the programming period. In essence, public funds employed through the FEI mechanism contribute to achieving better value for taxpayers' money.
- Capacity-building. A fundamental assumption of FEIs is the collaboration through establishing partnerships between the public and private sectors. Such alliance supports the building of institutional capacities by means of joint involvement and the exchange of knowledge and experience. It also requires the involvement of a broader range of stakeholders, namely, financial intermediaries/institutions that are inserted into the process of the CP implementation, pooling of expertise and know-how. There is a strong commonality of interests and shared objectives in which public policy objectives that characterise public institutions are pursued with the use of the commercial market mechanisms typical for private investors. As a result, it is possible to achieve synergies resulting in a better quality of projects.
- Risk coverage. Note that public instruments should be focused on addressing market failures, that is, the situations where, due to inefficient outcomes, private investors see no interest in the deployment of business activities. Investments in such markets are regarded too risky from the point of view of the financial institutions. These types of investments are not attractive without public intervention. Therefore, the role of the FEI mechanism is not only to offer private investors better terms than exist in financial markets, but also to place emphasis on requirements that are important for the public interest but not necessary on the grounds of financial institution interest. The use of

FEIs should reduce the risk of investing, thus encouraging investors to invest more in areas in need of support.
- Speeding up programme implementation. This feature seems to be more crucial from the managing authority perspective. When the funds earmarked for FEIs under a particular operational programme are set up, they are perceived as being implemented. This significantly reduces the risks of automatic de-commitment. Moreover, the main burden of managing EU funding shifts to an authorised body that becomes responsible for this. From the investor perspective, it means that the procedures are less bureaucratised compared to grants and the process to obtain funding should be faster.
- Urban development. As the aforementioned features refer to FEIs in general, this one highlights a particular role they take with regard to support under the JESSICA initiative earmarked for the development of urban areas. FEIs can act as a catalyst for the establishment of wide partnerships established between regions, banks, investors and the European Investment Bank (EIB), to help tackle the problems of urban areas. This special financial vehicle is focused on encouraging new actors (other than public ones) in the urban development arena, helping leverage additional funding, e.g. in the form of public–private partnerships (PPPs), and mobilising additional support beyond grants. Compared to grants, FEIs are also more effective because, from a particular project perspective, they make it possible to achieve multi-use purposes and hence meet more than only one need.

Overall, FEIs in comparison to traditional grants provide the availability of financial resources in advance, i.e. the pre-financing of investments. Grants in turn cover expenses on an ex-post reimbursements basis. They also ensure a wider eligibility of costs because they make it possible to cover more types of costs, thus enabling greater flexibility and facilitating project implementation. The FEI mechanism may potentially lead to improvement in the quality of projects through the due diligence involved in the assessment of a project by the private sector. Moreover, project promoters pay particular attention to project viability on the grounds of the obligation to repay (Schneidewind et al., 2013). The viability assessment of the projects is carried out in close connection with commercial conditions and thereby it does not distort the competition as the grant-based support may sometimes do. FEIs certainly promote a more entrepreneurial approach to spending European funds and, following that, the implementation of CP.

3.4 Principles of repayable financial instruments used for urban development

The use of financial instruments in CP follow the general rules which are applicable to this policy, that is, the logic and legal framework, including shared management and subsidiarity principles. Hence, they also contribute to pursuing the goals laid down under priority axes of the operational programme(s) prepared by the Member States and regions, and approved by the European Commission. This also means that they contribute to the achievement of the CP objectives. Regarding the implementation level, all the decisions related to implementation, financing and monitoring of performance of the specific instruments to be applied fall within the competence of the managing authority responsible for a particular operational programme (European Commission, 2012a). It is also up to the particular managing authority to decide whether it wants to implement the use of FEIs under its operational programme or not. The rules and regulations setting out the framework for the implementation of the financial instruments were specified in Article 44 of Regulation EC 1083/2006. According to those provisions, the EU funds can be used, as part of an operational programme, to finance expenditure in respect of an operation involving contributions to support financial engineering instruments for urban development funds, that is: *funds investing in public–private partnerships and other projects included in an integrated plan for sustainable urban development*. But when such operations are managed through holding funds (HFs) – that is, *funds set up to invest in several venture capital funds, guarantee funds, loan funds and urban development funds* – the managing authority is obligated to implement them through one or more of the following forms (Council, 2006b):

- the award of a public contract in accordance with applicable public procurement law;
- in other cases, where the agreement is not a public service contract within the meaning of public procurement law, the award of a grant, defined for this purpose as a direct financial contribution by way of a donation:
- to the EIB or to the European Investment Fund (EIF); or
- to a financial institution without a call for proposal, if this is pursuant to a national law compatible with the Treaty.

It should be added that the implementation of the FEIs under operational programmes was not strictly embedded in the legal documents. As Kłos (2018) argued, the legal regulations regarding financial engineering instruments were of a general nature in the 2007–2013 programming period. Most of the details, guidelines, recommendations and good practices were reflected in the notes of the Coordinating Committee of the Funds (COCOF).

Following the guidance notes on financial engineering instruments prepared by COCOF one can find explanations and interpretations of the legal rules which aimed to facilitate the implementation of FEIs under OPs. It was clearly stated that "operation" to be supported by FEIs, as provided for under Article 44 of Regulation EC 1083/2006, has to be interpreted as both the contribution from an operational programme to FEI, and the subsequent investment by that FEI in, or provision of loans or guarantees to, urban projects. A project or group of projects need to ensure the achievement of the goals of the priority axis of the OP to which it relates. In turn, the beneficiary within the meaning of the said Regulation is an entity, whether public or private, responsible for implementing operations, including FEI itself as it implements the operation through providing the assistance to urban projects (e. g. in the form of a loan). If a holding fund is used, it is the beneficiary too, since it initiates operations comprising contributions to support FEIs. If the managing authority decides to use a holding fund, it should make a selection according to two possible forms. The first of these is through the award of a public contract compliant with applicable public procurement law. The second possibility relies on awarding a grant in a direct manner to an institution which is not subject to public procurement rules. In case the managing authority decides to carry out the operation through a holding fund, where the EIB or EIF will act as holders, it is allowed to do so through the award of a contract directly to them (European Commission, 2012b).

The next step consists in selecting FEIs – here referred to as an urban development fund (UDF). No particular rules or legal structures were established for operations implementing FEIs. Therefore, the managing authority and the selected holding fund must assess and decide whether their contribution to a UDF is subject to public procurement law and works in accordance with any such applicable law. According to the COCOF (European Commission, 2012b) interpretation, financial resources allocated under OPs have to be disbursed in line with the applicable rules and regulations and, in what follows, any financial flows and transactions should be adequately recorded, monitored and audited. If these requirements are met, the managing authority and the holding fund have *ample freedom* to select legal structures and arrangements for FEIs (UDFs). Notwithstanding, the selection procedure should be transparent and based on specific and appropriate selection criteria linked to the objectives of the OP. Those criteria should be approved by the monitoring committee. All the relationships and in particular the legal structures of the functioning should be governed by way of agreements between the managing authority, the holding fund and the individual FEI (UDF).

Within the meaning of Article 44 of Regulation EC 1083/2006, an FEI (UDF) can support projects included in an "integrated plan for sustainable urban development" (IPSUD). However, the legal regulations for 2007–2013 did not specify a definition determining specific requirements thereof. The requirements should also be defined by the managing authorities. Some explanations helpful in this regard were included in Community strategic guidelines on cohesion. Pursuant to provisions of the Decision set out in section 2.1, IPSUD should have the following characteristics (European Commission, 2008b):
- a plan for a medium or long-term perspective,
- coherence of investments and of their environmental quality,
- a multidisciplinary or integrated approach,
- commitment and participation of the private sector in urban renewal,
- area-based actions,
- promotion of social inclusion,
- improvement of the quality of life (including the environment and housing),
- provision of services to citizens (e.g. development of new activities and job creation),
- focus on groups that are most in need, such as immigrants, young people and women,
- wide participation of citizens in both the planning and delivery of services.

Urban projects that are approved by a UDF for investment can be funded through equity, guarantees or loans. This means that such types of financial support, in whatever form, must be reimbursed in accordance with the conditions laid down while granting them. The repayment should be achieved either in the form of solely commercial returns or project revenues secured directly by investors (mostly from the public side) from other sources. Hence, the refund can be provided by either revenues obtained from the primary business activities of investors, or other revenues derived outside their main operations.

4 JESSICA initiative

4.1 Legal foundations

The JESSICA initiative is one of the financial engineering instruments used under the EU cohesion policy came into being in the 2007–2013 multiannual financial perspective. It was introduced, as an innovation, together with the JEREMIE initiative that focused on the development of enterprises. JESSICA was developed by the European Commission in cooperation with the EIB, which can act as a trust fund manager and which works in cooperation with the Council of Europe Development Bank (CEB). The initiative uses the resources of one of the structural funds – the European Regional Development Fund – in the form of revolving instruments (loans, guarantees), enabling, for example, the achievement of multiplier effects in relation to the actions implemented (Memorandum of Understanding, 2006).

This initiative was concentrated on the sustainable development of European cities. JESSICA aimed at addressing the problems arising from the uneven growth of cities and in that sense it has stressed (1) the importance and the role of the cities and (2) the need for public intervention in the form of urban policy in socio-economic development in Europe. At the same time JESSICA was proposed as a revolving instrument, which meant that allocations offered in the scope of this initiative might have been used multiple times. Increased access to the capital under this instrument, together with the returns left in the hands of regional authorities, were seen as an incentive for potential managing authorities to apply it in the operational programmes of the European Union cohesion policy. What is more, through a revolving system, EU funds are intended to be deployed on a more long-term and sustainable basis. Taking all this into consideration, JESSICA should not be assessed as a supplementary support programme, but rather as a systemic innovation in the plethora of EU initiatives and established operational programmes.

EU regulations
The JESSICA initiative is embedded in the EU structural funds system and falls within the scope of the EU structural funds regulations from the programming period 2007–2013. These are:

- Regulation EC 1083/2006 (General Regulation for the Structural Funds and the Cohesion Fund) (Council, 2006b),
- Regulation EC 1080/2006 (European Regional Development Fund Regulation) (European Parliament and Council, 2006),
- Regulation EC 1828/2006 (so-called implementing regulation) (European Commission, 2006a),
- Coordination Committee of the Funds notes.

The provisions of the above-mentioned regulations were already presented in Chapter 3 on the cohesion policy and urban policy. No separate regulation was dedicated at that time to the financial instruments to be used under the cohesion policy system, thus the JESSICA initiative is based on the legal acts related to the policy and funding. Nevertheless, special emphasis can be put on the last set of regulatory environments, namely the COCOF notes. COCOF itself operates on the basis of Article 103 of Regulation EC 1083/2006, which states that the Commission is assisted in applying the provisions of the regulation, by a *Coordination Committee of the Funds*. This committee provides guidance for practitioners, public authorities, beneficiaries or potential beneficiaries, and other bodies that are involved in the monitoring, control or implementation of the EU cohesion policy (DLA Piper, 2010, p. 6). According to the authors of the study presented to EIB (DLA Piper, 2010, p. 6), three guidance notes are of particular relevance for the JESSICA implementation, namely: two Guidance Notes on Financial Engineering from 2007 (European Commission, 2007) and 2008 (European Commission, 2008b) and the Guidance note on eligibility of energy efficiency and renewable energies interventions under the ERDF and the Cohesion Fund in the building sector including housing (European Commission, 2010). The first two Notes on Financial Engineering provide interpretation and explain the notions of operation and beneficiary, followed by specific issues concerning financial engineering techniques such as (DLA Piper, 2010, p. 6):
- selection of holding funds,
- selection of financial engineering instruments,
- selection of operations,
- management costs,
- major projects.

The second Guidance Note on Financial Engineering lists technical questions by the Member States followed by the European Commission's answers to these questions. In the third COCOF Note on eligibility of energy efficiency and renewable energies interventions under the Structural Funds, it was originally stated that this kind of support with the use of EU structural funds was not allowed in the so-called "old" Member States (EU-15), whereas, in the new Member States, support for energy improvements in housing was possible from the beginning but subject to certain conditions. Only after amending Regulation EC 397/2009 and inserting Article 7(1a) of Regulation EC 1080/2006, the European legislators opened the possibility of investments in energy efficiency and energy improvements in housing in all Member States (with some maximum amounts of funds to be dedicated for this kind of investment [DLA Piper, 2010, p. 14]).

Revolving character of JESSICA
The major principle of revolving instruments, including the JESSICA initiative, is that it is based on the use of financial engineering instruments such as loans, guarantees or equity. However, this did not mean that fund financing cannot be combined with grant funding. This joint venture might have been spent outside the urban development fund on unprofitable (sub-)projects. Taking into consideration the very nature of urban development projects and a pure market approach to funds, the sole use of revolving instruments in this regard is not taking place. The main assumption of JESSICA was to facilitate projects that would generate revenue, but their characteristics determine need for a longer-than-average time for redemption or occurrence of very high pre-financing costs. It is crucial to understand that the revolving nature of the JESSICA fund does not require projects to generate income on a profit-making basis immediately, but only calls for resources to be paid back into the fund (DLA Piper, 2010, p. 14). In that sense, this is the advantage of the use of this kind of financial engineering instrument by non-private entities, including public administration, because profitability can be achieved late in the "longer start-up periods for project investments". The requirement of revenue generation is also seen as an ex-ante discipline for the proper choice of the source of financing by potential beneficiaries. Nevertheless, when analysing the complex nature of urban projects, the JESSICA's design could also be assessed as a disadvantage, because only projects that can generate revenue are suitable for JESSICA, while the projects with low/zero profitability would rather be the subject of grant funding. It pushes again urban development funds that are responsible for project selection to incentivise beneficiaries to apply for funding under the JESSICA scheme (DLA Piper, 2010, pp. 6–9). Therefore, the selection criteria for the projects played a crucial role in the success of the JESSICA implementation. The selection of projects eligible for financing under the European Regional Development Fund was designed in the operational programmes on the basis of EU regulations on EU structural funds but the individual Member States were given "a margin of dis-

cretion in the development and implementation of a specific JESSICA fund architecture" (DLA Piper, 2010, p. 6).

4.2 Institutional system of JESSICA funding

The JESSICA initiative is characterised by a complex institutional structure (see Figure 7). The European Commission notifies the operational programmes at the national or regional level, in which the JESSICA initiative sources (under ERDF) are planned.

Holding fund
Under the provisions of the structural funds regulations, it is possible (but not mandatory) to use a *holding fund* to provide resources for investments in the individual urban development funds. This approach was advisable when several urban development funds were to be supplied from a single central pool. The holding fund can also be the source of expertise to urban fund managers, especially in the Member States who have been in the process of capital market evolution. It can also be set up in cooperation with the European Investment Bank. In Poland all regional managing authorities have decided to rely on the experience of the European Investment Bank (chosen as a beneficiary of the priority axes of the operational programme and a holding fund) with regard to FEIs. This movement also made it possible to release the managing authorities from launching the tender procedure for management of the holding fund. Cooperation between managing authorities and the EIB in this role was based on a funding agreement that laid down, for example, financial conditions, target investments, project monitoring and reporting obligations. Then the grant was awarded by managing authorities and the EIB took on the responsibilities of a beneficiary and fund manager (DLA Piper, 2010, p. 16).

Another gain (from the interest-generation point of view) is that the holding fund structure provides an opportunity for pooling different funding with other public and private resources to create a larger supply of capital for beneficiaries. What is more, different experts representing financial institutions provide a pool of competences to project beneficiaries (DLA Piper, 2010, p. 19). They may learn from both private and public partners and manage the urban project in an optimal way. Nevertheless it was also up to the managing authorities together with the fund manager to decide on the investment strategy.

From a legal perspective, too, an autonomous legal form of a holding fund was not necessary but separate accounts must be kept within the financial institution that plays the role of this fund (DLA Piper, 2010, p. 16).

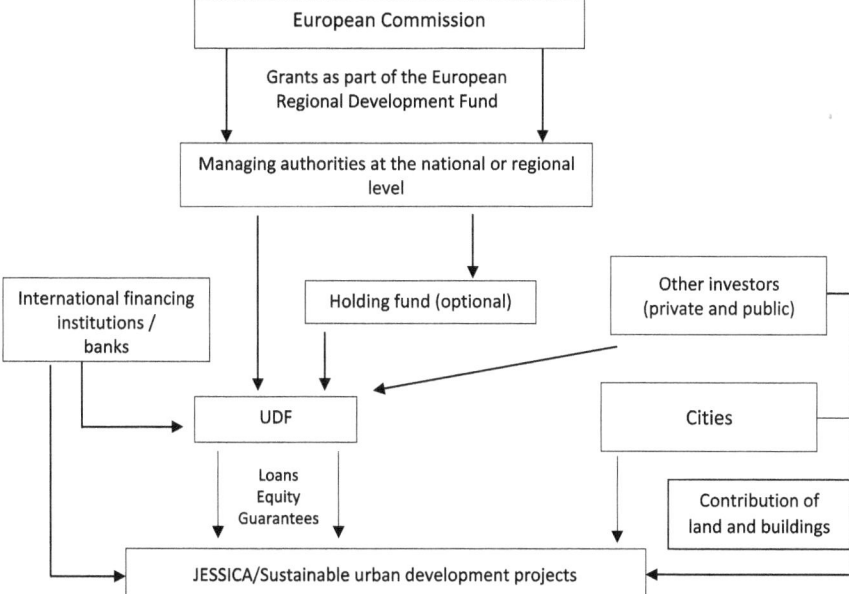

Figure 7: The JESSICA institutional system in the years 2007–2013
Source: adapted from (EIB, 2008)

Urban development fund

EU regulations state that the UDF must be designed and structured before any kind of assistance can be transferred to individual projects and their beneficiaries. The UDF is responsible for setting a proper selection and implementation architecture for the projects, where application of both the European and national/local laws is taking place. From the legal point of view, the projects are bound by EU and national regulations indirectly through agreements signed with the fund itself, while in the case of the UDF, EU regulations are binding in a direct way (DLA Piper, 2010, p. 6). What is also important, in addition to the directly applicable European requirements, one must take into account the applicability of the provisions of national budgetary laws, unless they are contrary to EU law. This applies in particular to eligibility of expenditure, the requirements for which, under Article 56(4) of Regulation EC 1083/2006, must be laid down by the Member States (DLA Piper, 2010, p. 17).

JESSICA allows for the participation of private and public partners at both fund and project levels and promotes a public–private partnership approach. This understanding of the initiative architecture makes it possible for the integration of private capital at various phases of the implementation process and at different institutional levels. This might potentially have increased the capital inflow and thus sustainability of the funds used under JESSICA. The decision on the structure and operation of the fund is left to the fund itself. There was also no specific legal form stipulated to the UDF in the regulation. The choice of legal form and the specific structure of a JESSICA fund depends on the way in which the fund is to be technically structured.

Before setting up the fund there are several aspects that need to be decided because of the potential consequences and to meet the aims of the JESSICA initiative established by the European decision-makers. These are, for example (DLA Piper, 2010, p. 17):

- The inclusion of private investors in a UDF may bring many advantages in relation to the fund structure and the use of private sector know-how. In this solution there is also the risk of possible conflicts of interest among the shareholders that need to be resolved as early as possible.
- In the case of a purely public-driven UDF (with one or more public actors) the conflict of interest is relatively low, but there is a danger of diluting the synergies with the private sector.
- In the case of the participation of public bodies and/or their subsidiaries participating in PPP and projects through a UDF, aside from the requirements of the structural funds, the legal environment depends on shareholder structure, legal form, corporate governance and the type and size of the investment.
- Private sector participation in a UDF together with a public institution generally requires a tender procedure if such participation is connected directly with a public contract. This creates the situation of competition among private investors that are the potential shareholders of the UDF.

An urban development fund must be organised as an independent legal entity or at least a separate block of finance within an existing financial institution. Separate accounts ensure that JESSICA must be clearly distinct from other assets of the financial institution or body. It is possible to model and modify the structure or composition of the fund over its life, for instance in terms of the proportions of funding from complementary financing. However, the maximum contribution of ERDF funding (depending on the co-financing rate – 75% or 50% for the years

2007–2013) and the programming of the operational programmes must be respected and ensured for JESSICA eligible projects. What has to be borne in mind at the designing phase of a UDF is long-term ERDF philosophy and the duration of operational programmes that are programmed for a given period of time.

In terms of competence allocation, a UDF can be set up at different territorial levels, namely: nationally, regionally or locally/municipally. What matters in the proper choice is (DLA Piper, 2010, p. 18):
- the material and geographical scope of the fund company to be formed,
- the definition of the level of commitment of private capital (to UDF/ projects),
- the acquisition and inclusion of private partners (depending on the definition of investment level).

There are also different options or models for making the necessary contributions into UDFs that are determined by including participants in the funds. This offers the possibility of including in the funds participants who can provide tangible assets necessary for furthering projects, but who do not have the necessary financial resources. This requires (DLA Piper, 2010, p. 18):
- the definition of fund assets with reference to partners and specific area of investment,
- the choice of financial means/sources – e.g. subsidy programmes, equity or mezzanine capital,
- the examination of the contribution of tangible assets, in particular land and buildings (see Figure 7).

Private sector involvement in the JESSICA fund can also take the form of outside capital. However, it should be borne in mind that UDFs *may not* invest in the creation of venture capital, loan and guarantee funds (second subparagraph of Article 46(1) of Regulation EC 1828/2006), but only directly in the financing of projects (DLA Piper, 2010, p. 19). Urban development funds are required to prepare in concert with the holding fund its investment strategy and business plan. Summing up, the main elements include (EIB, 2012a, pp. 53–55):
- Investment strategy. This outlines the investment objectives of the UDF, summarises the portfolio of potential urban projects, including the methodology of selection, and provides preliminary detail on expected income receipts and capital receipts, first and second round investment principles and exit strategies. This section also includes an application of the state-aid-rules.

- Investment period. This reflects the proposed life span of a given UDF, which informs the timescales for investment, income receipts, capital receipts, the scope for recycling in subsequent investments and exit strategy.
- National co-financing. This presents the form of contributions (financial/in-kind), verification of the contributions and any expected "swapping" of contributions at the urban project level.
- Additional public and private co-investment.
- Financial forecasts. These outline the initial financial estimates for the UDF based on urban project information (including the projected income and capital receipts) and other costs and fees for the operation of the UDF; financial model used, the nature of investments (loans, equity, guarantees), and processes for credit scoring, investment drawdown and investment repayment.
- Legal and ownership structure of the UDF and its rationale.
- Governance structure. This presents the governance and management structure including the key functions for investment portfolio management, fund management, overall programme oversight and how these functions need to work in concert with one another including any checks and balances.
- Management costs and management fees that outline the proposed level of fees payable to a UDF, including fee structure and calculations.
- Other operating and control procedures such as procedures for monitoring, auditing and reporting required to ensure regulatory compliance and regular assessment of urban project progress. It also includes other necessary activities such as marketing, risk management and stakeholder engagement.
- Winding-up provisions and re-utilisation of resources that discusses plans for first and follow-on investments, as well as exit strategies. The components may vary depending on the type of UDF applicant.

4.3 Rules on the eligibility of project expenditure

The rules of eligibility for an urban project to be selected under the JESSICA initiative and decided on by the UDF are solely based on the European regulation on structural funds. Several articles are of major importance for ERDF JESSICA expenditure:

1. As regards Regulation EC 1080/2006 (DLA Piper, 2010, pp. 12–13):
- Articles 4 and 5 describe the different permissible areas of investment, depending on the objective of the Cohesion Policy that is applicable to the operational programme (Convergence or regional competitiveness and employment). The requirements adopted on that basis in the existing operational

programmes are thus relevant to the use of the ERDF under the JESSICA initiative.
- Article 7 of the Regulation, which lays down rules on expenditure and excludes certain categories of expenditure from ERDF support.
- Article 8 extends the scope of Articles 4 and 5 with regard to "Sustainable urban development", with some general exemptions stating that the operational programme already negotiated for the 2007–2013 programming period can be modified only subject to the conditions laid down in Article 33 of Regulation EC 1083/2006.

2. As regards Regulation EC 1828/2006 (Implementing regulation), Articles 43, 44, 45 and 46 of Section 8 – Financial engineering instruments, which implement Regulation EC 1083/2006 in relation to funds, are of crucial importance with regards to JESSICA funding because of reference to governing the organisation and the utilisation of the financing elements (management costs, business plan and use of revenue). There are also specific requirements for holding funds and urban development funds. The applicable operating conditions include (DLA Piper, 2010, pp. 12–13):
- revolving use of resources beyond the end of the programming period for the benefit of urban development projects or in support of SMEs (Article 78(7) of Regulation EC 1083/2006);
- the use of recycled resources in the region(s) covered by the operational programme (European Commission, 2008b, p. 4);
- the definition that states that the fund and not the enterprise is the beneficiary. Thus, the resources can be invested in a fund without proof of previous expenditure. Payments into the fund are treated as "expenditure and do not need to be settled until the end of the programming period (the expenditure reimbursement principle does not apply at fund level)". What is more, a profitable interim investment from ERDF funding is also possible. This means that and secures the advantage that interest can be generated in the fund itself and capital growth can thus be achieved;
- normal banking duties in relation to reporting and proof of ERDF use at the level of the supported enterprises at project level.

4.4 Ex-ante analyses of the implementation of JESSICA in Poland

It is generally assumed that the JESSICA initiative should bring a number of benefits, as can be summarised by the above-mentioned regulatory conditions (Musiałkowska & Idczak, 2016):
- Generating profits through projects implemented using financial engineering instruments, thus making them more profitable for investors; it is also a more permanent alternative compared to traditional support in the form of grants.
- Occurrence of leverage – by combining structural funds with other existing sources of funding; the JESSICA initiative contributes to increase the pool of resources and facilitate support for more projects than in the case of repayable funds.
- The initiative is to provide flexibility in structural terms regarding the usage of funds (in the form of equity, debt or guaranteed investments, which can be adapted to the specific needs of the countries and regions).
- Gaining know-how – JESSICA is to allow the structural funds managing authorities and urban authorities to benefit from the aid of the private and banking sector, which ultimately aims to facilitate the acquisition of further investments in the coming years, and provide technical and financial performance in the implementation phase of the project and during its management.
- JESSICA can be a catalyst for establishing partnerships between countries, regions, cities, the EIB, CEB and other banks, and investors, in order to solve the problems of urban areas.
- The initiative emphasises the so-called social aspect of the projects, estimated based on the advantage of positive externalities of an urban project (the so-called social elements) over the commercial part of an investment.
- Projects will potentially represent greater complexity than under the grant system and be more varied (e.g. shopping malls, business incubators, office space, dormitories, hotels, underground parking, etc.).

Before the institutional setting of the JESSICA initiative was constituted in Poland, there were several aspects analysed ex-ante with regard to initiative implementation and decision-making on the forms of the holding/urban development funds together with project selection criteria.

Firstly, nine groups of potential stakeholders (beneficiaries and project participants) in the JESSICA initiative were identified (Arup, 2009, p. 104):

- Group 1 – Polish and international banks and commercial financial institutions (including the Polish development bank – Bank Gospodarstwa Krajowego – BGK),
- Group 2 – international financial institutions (including the EIB and CEB),
- Group 3 – public administration (including local and regional authorities/ urban and regional self-governments),
- Group 4 – national agencies and other public institutions (such as the National Fund for Environment Protection, urban housing funds and housing associations),
- Group 5 – investment funds (private equity, other investment funds),
- Group 6 – managers of real estate funds,
- Group 7 – real estate developers,
- Group 8 – other interested entities,
- Group 9 – non-financial institutions supporting the processes of urban regeneration and development (e. g. the Institute of Urban and Regional Development).

Analysis of the expectations held by JESSICA stakeholders led to formulation of the following conclusions (Arup, 2009, pp. 104–106):
- Financial institutions preferred involvement at the level of individual projects due to the unknown character and nature of UDFs. This implied that the size and value of the project is an important factor that had an impact on the involvement in a given enterprise.
- Guarantee and loan funds were already focused on specific types of projects and beneficiaries and offered quite an attractive source of financing in comparison to these in commercial/private banks. Thus, the scope of JESSICA interventions was assessed as potentially overlapping with the scope of projects financed from above-mentioned sources. On the other hand JESSICA might have been perceived as an additional source of capital and finance for projects that cannot be financed from other sources. Also the quite narrow specialisation of guarantee and loan funds created a chance for JESSICA to become a potentially interesting source for the investors. The main requirement (see Chapter 3.4) for JESSICA projects was to comply with IPSUD. What is more, JESSICA funding could have served as an alternative to the beneficiaries if the conditions were more attractive than in other funds. The competitiveness of JESSICA was based on the share of public/private capital in the fund. The bigger the public share of resources in the holding/urban development fund, the more appealing the funding conditions in comparison to commercial funding should be.

- The main actors in the system that were better prepared to play the role of JESSICA funding managers (HF/UDF) were banks and professional funds. The participation of development agencies or other public entities would require changes in their statutes, which seemed to be difficult to implement.

Another important aspect that needed to be analysed, besides the assessment of demand for resources, was business plan and investment strategy, size and capital mobilised, of both holding fund and urban development funds (EIB, 2012a).

Potential size of the holding fund and urban development funds
In the case of both the HF and UDF the main determinants are the amount of money to be designated under the regional operational programmes and the potential resources of national authorities: the Ministry of Finance and regional self-governments. National co-funding could have increased the available amounts of money by an additional 25–50%. However, due to the identified financial needs to be addressed under the regeneration processes, even additional funding does not permit meeting the needs of the cities. Moreover, the increase in shares held in the funds by private investors and institutions was too complicated at the time due to (Arup, 2009, p. 121):
- problems related to state-aid regulations that refer to joint for-profit use of public and private capital,
- an increase in complexity of the decision-making procedures with regard to the designation of JESSICA resources, size of the projects and investment risk assessment procedures (which is crucial for banks),
- conflicts of interests with regard to banks that could have acted as HF/UDF shareholders and the financing institutions for JESSICA beneficiaries at the same time,
- the increased exposure of a UDF to credit risk and bank investment policy in the case of a given bank's participation as a UDF financing institution.

Therefore, the majority of HF/UDF could have been increased mainly through public financing. It was estimated that the additional pool of funding would not exceed by more than 50% the amount designated under the regional operational programmes.

Potential capital mobilised for the implementation of the JESSICA projects
Key parameters that have an impact on the amount of capital involved in the regeneration investments of JESSICA projects are (Arup, 2009, pp. 121–122):

- percentage share of the UDF in financing the costs of JESSICA projects (the bigger the share, the lower the number of projects financed)
- project profitability (the higher the profitability, the bigger the interest of private investors and credit institutions, thus – the lower need for co-financing by UDF).

In the case of grants, the co-financing of eligible costs varies between 50% and 80% but the HF/UDF is to decide on their maximum level of project co-financing. This implies the necessity/lack of necessity to apply for (public or private) funding other than JESSICA funding.

UDFs need to decide the amount available for JESSICA projects. In the case of the projects that are attractive for investors it was estimated that a UDF can designate approximately 10% of the investment value. If we assume that the developers and commercial financial institutions bear the majority of costs, and the public sector will contribute with land or buildings, it would be possible to implement projects of value ten times higher than the primary amount collected by the UDF.

In the case of projects of lower commercial potential, the UDF share in the project would be higher. The public sector (cities) would also need to contribute to the investment. If the UDF share is equal to 50% of the investment inputs, there would be a possibility to implement projects of value two times higher than the primary amount collected by the UDF. As a result, the JESSICA impact on sustainability of financing would be much smaller and not much higher than in the case of the grant system.

Still, in the countries that are characterised by a huge capital gap (e.g. Poland), the effect of JESSICA funding might be an important element in addressing societal and economic challenges.

4.5 Implementation of JESSICA funding in Poland

In the years 2007–2013, the JESSICA initiative, was applied in 11 EU countries, including Poland (European Commission, 2011b). In Poland only five regions – Mazowieckie, Pomorskie, Śląskie, Wielkopolskie and Zachodniopomorskie – decided to implement JESSICA under their regional operational programmes. Following the ex-ante analyses and studies it was eventually agreed that the European Investment Bank would be a beneficiary of the measures of regional operational programmes and perform the function of the holding fund that co-operated with the specialised urban development funds (namely, two development banks: Bank Gospodarstwa Krajowego – BGK, and Bank Ochrony Środowiska – BOŚ, and a private bank: Bank Zachodni WBK S.A. – BZWBK S.A.) responsible for selection of the projects (Musiałkowska & Idczak, 2020, p. 179). Details related to this are presented in Figure 8 and Table 3. The main institutional actors came from the development banking sector and one from the private banking sector. The involvement of other private investors and institutions in UDFs was limited/not applicable due to procedural complications related to legal constraints in regards to state-aid, public–private partnerships and mixing for-profit use of the joint funding for the JESSICA projects. Thus, public capital dominated in the shares of both HF and UDFs in Poland.

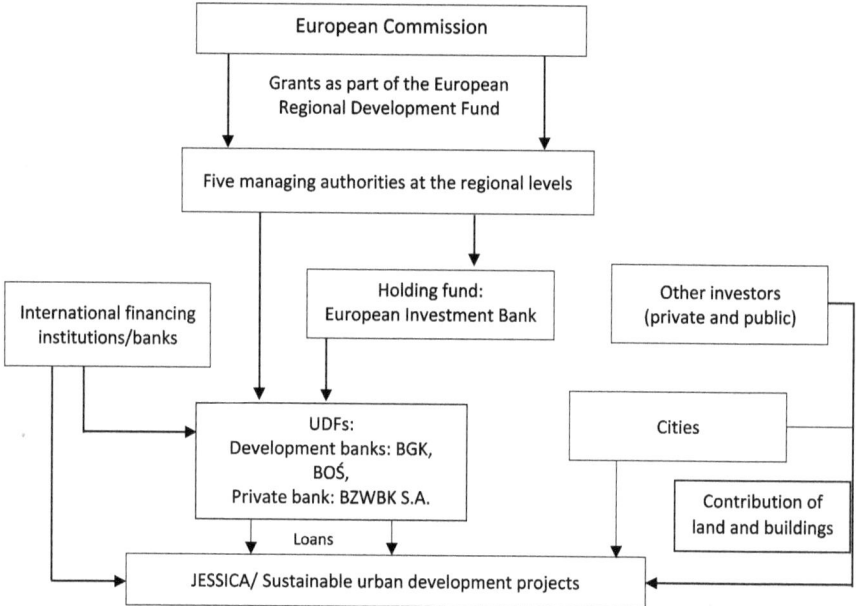

Figure 8: The institutional system of JESSICA in Poland in the years 2007–2013
Source: the authors' own elaboration

According to the investment strategies and Regional Operational Programmes (ROPs) structure, JESSICA, in general, supported projects in many areas, such as: urban infrastructure (including for transport, water and sewage systems or power), heritage or places relevant to the culture (contributing to the development of tourism or other permanent use), development of brownfield sites (including cleaning and decontamination of the areas), creation of new commercial premises for small and medium-sized enterprises, development of information technology and research and development works, expansion of university buildings and improving energy efficiency (Musiałkowska & Idczak, 2016). The areas reflected the measures and priority axes of the regional operational programmes (see Table 3). Almost all types of legal persons enumerated in Polish law were eligible to apply for funds. The initiative was implemented under nine measures in five regional operational programmes that reflected the possible scopes of the eligible projects. In two regions – Pomorskie and Śląskie – there was only one measure related, in general, to the regeneration of degraded urban areas. In the Zachodniopomorskie region, two measures were designed for operations of regeneration: first, of the metropolitan area of the city of Szczecin, and in the second measure – of other cities of the region. The remaining two regions – Mazowieckie and Wielkopolskie – planned additional measures focused on the environment (Mazowieckie) and support to the business environment or regional innovation system (both regions) (see Table 3). In total the allocation of 265.5 million EUR was used for the initiative for all 161 projects implemented in the country up to 2015 (according to the "n+2" rule). The JESSICA allocation was distributed via a loan system only through the above-mentioned UDFs, which increased the possibility of reuse of the allocated amount (see Figure 9). No equity or guarantees were applied.

The project selection was the task of the UDFs according to the criteria set in place. In the first years of JESSICA implementation, interest in the call for proposals was relatively low due to the fact that meeting all criteria seemed to be barely possible for some of the beneficiaries. The main barrier was the delimitation of degenerated urban areas where the projects could have been located (Musiałkowska and Idczak, 2016). After slight modification and the acceptance of the larger areas for the project to be implemented the number of projects increased.

Since 2009 (when the first Memorandum of Understanding on JESSICA was signed with the Wielkopolskie region) 161 projects were implemented up to 2015. The majority of projects were implemented in the Pomorskie region – 45 projects – and in the Wielkopolskie region – 40. The Zachodniopomorskie region implemented the lowest number of projects (19) (see Figure 9 and Table 3). Nevertheless this region, with the lowest number of projects, was the best performing in terms of fulfilment of criteria of the regeneration projects. More details on this will be given in Chapter 5.

What was missing in the scheme was the active participation of important actors such as cities in the process of planning and designing the selection criteria in this first pilot JESSICA initiative in Poland. Although managing authorities were allowed to incorporate cities into the distribution system of European funds, they did not do that. Cities were seen in applying for JESSICA funding in the same way as all other beneficiaries. Their role was limited to the development of IPSUD and the designation of areas with the highest concentration of

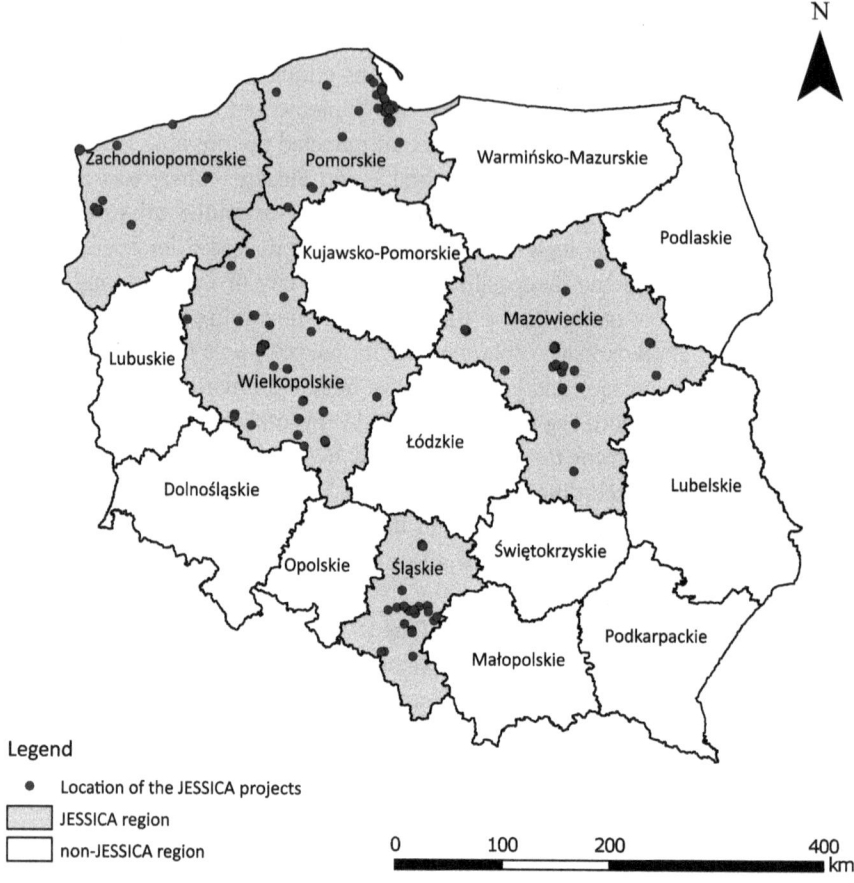

Figure 9: JESSICA regions and the locations of JESSICA projects in Poland
Source: the authors' own elaboration

negative phenomena (the most disadvantaged urban areas). Since cities were not directly involved in the JESSICA implementation, it would then appear that the projects granted were not based on an approach that took into consideration the integrated development of urban areas.[15] All the eligible types of beneficiaries were entitled to apply for JESSICA funding, provided that the projects were located in the disadvantaged areas. Cities as the main players taking full responsibil-

---

[15] It should be added that the legal framework providing a more territorial approach to urban development and urban regeneration came into force in Poland only at the end of 2015. (For more see Idczak & Musiałkowska, 2021).

Table 3: JESSICA in the Polish regional operational programmes for the years 2007–2013

Region	Regional Operational Programme (ROP): measure	Objective of the measure	Beneficiary – holding fund (HF)	Urban development fund (UDF)	JESSICA allocation per measure (EUR)	No. of JESSICA projects
Mazowieckie	"Mazovia" ROP for the years 2007–2013:		EIB	Bank Gospodarstwa Krajowego	49.4 m	31
	1.6 Support of the business network at the regional level	Development of business networks;				
	4.3 Air protection, energy	Improvement of air quality. Ensuring energy security; increase of the use of renewable energy.				
	5.2 Regeneration of cities	Renewal of degraded urban areas.				
Pomorskie	"Pomerania" ROP for the years 2007–2013:		EIB	Bank Gospodarstwa Krajowego	56.8 m	45
	3.3 Infrastructure of the development of the cities – non-grant aid: (JESSICA initiative)	Development of urban and metropolitan functions that aim at an increase in the socio-economic potential of cities				
Śląskie	"Silesia" ROP for the years 2007–2013:		EIB	BOŚ	60.0 m	26
	6.2.3 Regeneration – JESSICA	Multi-function use of degraded urban areas				
Wielkopolskie	Wielkopolska ROP for the years 2007–2013:		EIB	Bank Gospodarstwa Krajowego	66.3 m	40
	4.1 Urban regeneration					

Table 3: JESSICA in the Polish regional operational programmes for the years 2007–2013 (Continued)

Region	Regional Operational Programme (ROP): measure	Objective of the measure	Beneficiary – holding fund (HF)	Urban development fund (UDF)	JESSICA allocation per measure (EUR)	No. of JESSICA projects
	1.4 Support of the activities related to Regional Innovation Strategy	Increase in the socio-economic potential of supra-local and local centres of growth; Strengthening of regional innovation system				
Zachodniopomorskie	Zachodniopomorskie ROP for the years 2007–2013: 5.5.2 Regeneration – JESSICA initiative 6.6.2 JESSICA initiative at metropolitan area	Regeneration of degraded urban areas	EIB	BOŚ BZWBK S.A.	33.0 m	19
5 regions	9 measures	–	1	3	265.5 m	161

Source: (Musiałkowska & Idczak, 2020, p. 179)

ity for urban issues were not adequately considered for their role by managing authorities. This significantly negated the aims of JESSICA to achieve greater added value by making more integrated and coherent urban investments. Moreover, not taking into account cities as major players in the JESSICA institutional framework is also not in accordance with the model of the integrated approach to urban regeneration applicable at the European level. The model clearly puts cities first in decision-making on urban development and gives them a decisive role in the implementation of urban policy and, in particular, urban regeneration measures. In fact, the JESSICA institutional framework lacked a very crucial actor responsible for the creation of the strategic framework supporting long-term sustainable urban development.

5 JESSICA initiative and sustainable urban development – empirical evidence from Poland

5.1 Rationale of the research and objectives

The fundamental assumption of the JESSICA initiative was to support projects included in integrated plans for sustainable urban development. The task defined in this way includes combining the objectives of public intervention focused on sustainable urban development with a renewable financial model that brings together various sources of financing municipal investments (Nadler & Nadler, 2018). The revolving financing model assumes, in principle, the long-term profitability of projects, which in turn entails the need to propose such project activities that will respond to the identified market demand and introduce the desired products or services. However, taking into account the specific needs of urban areas, as well as the objectives of urban and EU cohesion policy as well as the organisation and operation of financial engineering instruments, JESSICA from the very beginning seemed to be a very ambitious undertaking and a big challenge for both managing authorities and project promoters themselves. To put it more precisely, its aim was to develop an effective process for supporting urban development and to enhance and accelerate a potential for new investments in urban areas. This means that in principle only projects that generate return flows are eligible for funding offered by this instrument. The repayment should be achieved in a form of either solely commercial returns or project revenues secured directly by investors from other sources.

The problem as described above represented a great challenge for cohesion policy on the grounds of its novelty as a non-grant-based funding alternative to support sustainable urban development, thus promoting a new culture of financial support and circulation of public money. But it also posed an intriguing challenge to carry out an investigation in order to determine whether JESSICA is capable of actually achieving the goals pursued. This is all the more important given that at the early stage of our research process only a few studies dealt with the problematic aspects of JESSICA. Most of them indicated some shortcomings and achievements that are far from the expected goals. For instance, Bode (2015, pp. 174–178), in his legal analysis of repayable instruments, pointed to some weaknesses in the assessment procedure of projects, with the consequence that they may not address actual market needs and have little real impact on

Piotr Idczak, Ida Musiałkowska

the ground. He also drew attention to a relatively low real leverage rate of the private sector and a consequently disappointing multiplier effect. Fotino (2014, pp. 245–251) underlined the novelty of JESSICA which, in conjunction with a lack of expertise and existing "grant-framework culture", leads to uncertainty especially in the public sector as regards the use of financial revolving instruments and creation of PPP. Dąbrowski (2014, 2015), in turn, argues that the major barriers for the wider use of repayable instruments arise when it comes to cooperation between the public authorities and private entities. As a result, the implementations of urban projects leads often to tensions, misunderstandings and clashes of interest. Musiałkowska and Idczak (2016), in their exploratory study on JESSICA, noted that key decisions on project selection are made by financial institutions, whose operating objectives may differ from the objectives of the EU cohesion policy and city authorities, which may mean that the benefits assumed by the designers of JESSICA at the EU level are being achieved only partially. In a follow-up investigation, Musiałkowska and Idczak (2018) found that projects implemented under the JESSICA initiative respected the overall spirit of this instrument in a very diverse way. The projects were characterised by a widely varying scope of operations and executed by different types of project promoters in terms of their legal status. Some of the projects did not ensure repayment of the loan based on self-financing capacity, and some of them did not even provide any revenues, which downscaled significantly the repayable nature of JESSICA financing. A study on this topic carried out by Nadler and Nadler (2018) confirmed many of the previous findings and additionally outlined several reasons for the main difficulties encountered including, among others, incapacity of private financial institutions to risk sharing, relatively high implementation and administrative costs and low financing at the project level.

Therefore, drawing upon the theoretical background and evidence provided so far, seven operational objectives were formulated that refer to the implementation level of JESSICA. The first objective of this study is to examine to what extent the JESSICA projects meet the fundamental requirements originally set out in the JESSICA initiative. Therefore, taking into consideration the above-outlined perspective of the research subject, the following questions were addressed:
- How many projects have received revenues from primary business activities, and which of them have gained revenues derived outside their main operations?
- What types of project promoters in term of their legal form applied for funding and implemented the JESSICA projects?
- Do the operation scopes of the projects influence the degree of the achievement of the JESSICA aims?

5.1 Rationale of the research and objectives — 137

- Which of the factors significantly contribute to achieving capacities to generate own revenues by the JESSICA projects?
- How does the project capacity to generate own revenues vary spatially in particular regions?
- Did the JESSICA projects contribute to generating positive market effects perceived through the lens of the direct effects of projects in the form of creating new types of activities, offering new products or services, and creating new jobs?
- What kinds of factors contributed to the occurrence of positive market effects to the greatest extent?
- Did the JESSICA projects have a social component(s) that created positive social impacts viewed through the prism of the projects' direct effects taking the form of enhancing integration among persons, improving their health and the overall level of safety, delivering facilities for people with disabilities, increasing people's access to culture, education and training, information, sport and recreation etc.?
- What kind of factors significantly contributed to the production of positive social impacts?
- And finally, which projects meet the JESSICA requirements to the greatest possible extent?

Our focus on these question was also motivated by the observation that the operation scopes of many of the JESSICA projects in many cases were relatively narrow, indicating that their multidimensional impacts on urban areas, in particular the deprived ones, could be rather weak. Therefore, the next question arose whether JESSICA funding through the JESSICA projects contributes significantly to sustainable urban development. As a matter of fact, this question was already discussed in the earlier mentioned studies, which pointed to some existing gaps and shortcomings. However, they concentrated the main research effort on the novelty of this recyclable funding and the JESSICA functioning in the context of its legal and institutional framework. Hence, there is a need to examine projects implemented with the use of JESSICA funds against the goals of urban sustainability. This will provide further evidence for the debate on the specific nature of revolving funds used to accelerate investments in urban areas. The original contribution of this study, in contradiction with earlier findings, is to assess the JESSICA projects implemented in Poland with regard to the assumption of the JESSICA funding model. Thus, the next two objectives of the study are:
- the second one: to build a methodological approach for assessing the extent to which projects implemented under the JESSICA initiative have contributed

to achieving its fundamental assumptions as a new tool for supporting urban development, and its objectives to be initially adopted;
- the third one: to evaluate the results of JESSICA through the conceptual lens of sustainable urban development.

These objectives do not exhaust the scope of all the urban policy issues it recognises as important when dealing with urban development. As already known, diseconomy forces affect urban areas sufficiently enough to form a pattern of spatially unbalanced urban growth. It is also known that these agglomeration diseconomies can be tackled through place-adjusted public interventions addressing the tendencies towards urban inequalities. From this perspective, what this does imply is that the territorial dimensions of urban development cannot be ignored. Furthermore, it should be seen as an indispensable element of urban development requiring that particular attention must be paid to the impact of programmes and projects in terms of promoting spatially balanced, harmonious and sustainable development. Such an approach should work towards ensuring a more cohesive territory through diminishing socio-economic territorial inequalities, encouraging environmental sustainability, enhancing the territorial governance processes and, essentially, strengthening a polycentric urban system. It follows that urban regeneration actions must provide an optimal trade-off between people-, sector-, and area-based interventions with a view to maintaining the original character of a place, on the one hand, and carrying out the restructuring process aimed at addressing a variety of problems in deprived areas, on the other. This, however, requires horizontal, vertical and territorial integration, otherwise implementation of urban measures may remain effectively irrelevant.

Thus, the question arises whether these projects have contributed to improving territorial cohesion in urban areas. This study seeks to fill this gap in the context of the integrated approach which requires the close coordination of measures promoting good territorial governance to ensure sustainable urban development. Therefore, the fourth objective of the research is to examine the territorial impacts of JESSICA projects through providing scientific evidence on the significance of the outcomes and changes brought about by those projects in urban areas. To do so, a critical analysis of JESSICA project impacts from the territorial perspective needs to be conducted to obtain insights that are especially relevant for supporting sustainable urban development.

UE cohesion policy embodies a place-based approach in which policy measures and financial resources are tailored to specific places, and at the same time support balanced socio-economic growth and territorial cohesion. In this context, as the European Commission (2008a) argued, urban problems should be addressed through implementing territorial cohesive policies, such as avoiding diseconomies of agglomerations, shunning urban sprawl, combating urban decay and social exclusion, etc. But apart from the importance of the metropolitan areas in this process, following the reasoning of Medeiros and Rauhut (2020), second-tier cities have a key role in achieving territorial cohesion within a country, and should also be beneficiaries of financial support triggering new investments through wise policy-making. Therefore, on account of the fact that the decisive criterion to obtain a JESSICA loan was the project's capacity to ensure the repayability of JESSICA funding, it may be assumed that: (i) a spatial factor is inadequately or not at all taken into account in spending JESSICA funding at the regional level, (ii) JESSICA funding is mostly allocated to projects characterised by high financial and/or economic profitability, which may presumably imply that, (iii) the main beneficiaries of this kind of repayable assistance are the strongest regional growth centres, namely, the largest cities. Such reasoning can be justified in particular in the light of findings delivered by several studies (Churski, Borowczak, & Perdał, 2015; Churski & Perdał, 2016; Murzyn, 2018; Smętkowski, 2011) which have suggested that the financial support from EU funds in Poland is focused on major economic development nodes created by leading cities. Therefore, by addressing these questions, there is a need to broaden current knowledge of the spatial allocation of EU funds with an emphasis on the repayable financial means provided by the JESSICA initiative. For this reason, three additional objectives are included:

- The fifth one: to explore the spatial allocations of JESSICA funding across cities within particular JESSICA regions. Though there is a "natural" tendency towards accumulation of the EU funds around key urban centres, we set out to ascertain to what extent smaller cities may also benefit from this instrument.
- The sixth one: to attempt to determine whether the city size matters in terms of the project's capacity to ensure the repayability of JESSICA funding. In a study investigating the JESSICA initiative, Idczak and Musiałkowska (2019) reported that the highest capacities to generate revenues on the basis of their primary business activities and in such a way to as ensure the repayment of the JESSICA loan are found in those projects of a high value and executed by private entities. Nevertheless, the main limitation in their study is that they did not make an attempt to take the city size into account.
- The seventh one: to conduct a unique analysis by applying a methodology that uses a geoprocessing tool to cope with the relatively small number of cases of JESSICA projects at regional level. The advantages of such a solution is that it allows further in-depth information on the spatial dependencies on

the allocation of JESSICA funding to be obtained, and consequently it complements the gaps identified in previous studies.

By doing so, this study bridges a noticeable gap in the available literature and expands the scope of research on financial engineering instruments used to support urban development.

5.2 Data collection and preparation

The subject of the research on the JESSICA initiative was defined very broadly and raises many different aspects related to both the assessment of the implementation of this instrument and the evaluation of the achieved outcomes and impacts. This task required the collection of data that were not available in public databases. Hence, the study makes use of two separate data sources, one for assessing JESSICA projects and depicting how their implementation operates, and the other to identify impacts of JESSICA projects on urban areas. As regards the former, we use a personally compiled database of all JESSICA projects implemented in Poland during the 2007–2015 period. The essential part of the data originates from the Marshal Offices of all regions implementing the JESSICA initiative and institutions acting as managers of the urban development funds. Since the data obtained in this way were of a general nature and did not exhaust the needs of the study, additional records were obtained from other sources. For instance, data on beneficiary entities were matched with the National Court Register database in order to gain additional information on their legal form. Moreover, the data on the location of projects were acquired as a result of an in-depth analysis of commonly available descriptions of all JESSICA projects, including information widely available on the Internet. This in turn made it possible to undertake among others geocoding and thus to determine the latitude and longitude coordinates of projects. Secondary sources, in particular multiple online resources, were also used to find missing information. An important source supplementing the records was also information obtained in the course of field studies, and the result so achieved was additional detailed information and photographic material. The remaining data come from the examination of other documentary sources, such as project descriptions, policy reports and evaluation reports, but also were obtained by the participatory observation method and interviews. Consequently, it was possible to carry out a triangulation, which allowed more complete and comprehensive descriptions of the analysed phenomena to be obtained. It should be also added that the conclusions obtained by the participatory observation method in the JESSICA project implementation process and interviews with people involved in this process had a significant share in the creation of the research material. The source material collected in this way was properly edited, processed and entered into the database in the form of statistical variables.

As for the second data source on the JESSICA achievements and impacts, it was based on the judgements of experts. As is well known, the main challenges that achievement and impact assessment has to face is the difficulty of measuring the effects of intervention. We address this problem through linking expert knowledge and judgements about the impact with the data from our database describing the characteristics of JESSICA projects. There were two separate expert judgements – one on the territorial impact assessment and the other on the evaluation of the JESSICA results within the conceptual context of sustainable urban development. By this route, we gathered reliable and robust information which serves as input for the analysis and facilitates the interpretation of the output indicators of both the territorial impact assessment and evaluation of the JESSICA results in the light of the sustainable urban development concept. A complete account of the evidence from these two surveys constitutes an integral part of our database.

Overall, the above description indicates that there are two different types of data, the first of which includes data in quantitative form, and the other which contains results in non-quantitative form being a function of researchers' insights and impressions. This brings to light the fact that two research approaches need to be applied – i.e. the quantitative approach and the qualitative approach – in order to achieve the objective set out.

5.3 Methods and research design

The JESSICA initiative involved support for the development of urban areas in their economic, social, environmental, institutional and governance dimensions through an innovative revolving mechanism and strategic framework. Projects granted by JESSICA had to be incorporated into an integrated plan for sustainable urban development. It follows that those projects formed part of the system of interconnected interventions aimed at improving the socio-economic, environmental and physical conditions of urban areas. Thus, an important distinguishing characteristic of the JESSICA projects was their complex nature that was manifested by multi-dimensionality of both project activities and results. Since the projects themselves are multifaceted, as are their results, their investigation requires multifaceted responses to deal with the research problems. Therefore, to meet the objectives identified at the beginning of this section, we undertook a four-pronged approach[16].

First approach, addressing the fundamental requirements of JESSICA
The aim of this part of the research is to examine the capacities of projects: (1) to generate revenues obtained from primary business activities of investors,[17] (2) to give rise to positive market effects in terms of new jobs, products or services, (3) to create positive social impacts with regard to social integration and participation in public and civic life. To begin with, we identified how many projects have received revenues from primary business activities, and which of them have gained revenues derived outside their main operations. We wanted to expound whether the capacities of the JESSICA projects to generate own revenues vary by certain attributes and factors that may affect the performance of the JESSICA initiative. First, we aimed to examine if there is any statistical dependency between the project capacity to generate own revenues and the amount of JESSICA funding or the value of JESSICA projects. Furthermore, we considered the legal form of the beneficiary as an important factor that may also have an impact on the project capacity to generate own revenues and also other effects under study. Generally, the beneficiaries represent 20 different types of legal forms. Therefore, for the purpose of statistical calculations, we grouped them first into two main categories: (1) public entities – acting in the widely defined social and public interest and (2) private entities – operating for profit. In the next step, we extracted within each category those types of beneficiaries that largely outnumbered the other types. We decided to investigate as a separate legal form those of entities that have company status. The same procedure was used to take a local government authority as a separate legal form as well. The rationale behind this is the fact that they represent the legal forms of the two largest groups of beneficiaries. Another factor taken into consideration in the study

---

[16] This section to a certain extent makes use of the research designs proposed previously in the following studies (Idczak & Mrozik, 2021; Idczak, Mrozik, & Musiałkowska, 2021; Idczak, Musiałkowska, & Mrozik, 2019b; Idczak & Musiałkowska, 2019, 2021; Musiałkowska & Idczak, 2020).
[17] Throughout this study the term "revenue-generating project" stands for cash in-flows directly paid by users for the goods or services provided by particular projects. This means that the projects had to achieve neither an adequate level of profitability nor even an operational margin. Such an assumption can be justified on the grounds of the promotion of economic and social cohesion by correcting urban imbalances. Hence, the insufficient level of revenues in some projects can be offset by subventions that are paid in the form of other operating revenues by public institutions due to the occurrence of an important public interest.

was location. Due to the relatively small number of projects in our study population (161), location was analysed in dichotomous terms, that is, whether the projects were implemented in the capital cities of the regions or in areas situated outside the capital cities.[18] Additionally, the analysis covered two other factors, namely region and urban development fund. By this route, we wanted to find out whether these factors could influence the capacities of the projects to generate the desired effects.

Second, we examined the dependence existing between all of the variables included in the study. Since the assessment of the statistical significance relies here upon comparing different groups of measures (numerical and categorical data), we applied the *Wilcoxon rank sum test* with continuity correction. It is a non-parametric test and can be used to compare two independent groups of samples.[19]

In order to explain whether the JESSICA projects are characterised by the capacity to generate revenues from their primary business activities, we used a logistic regression that allows us to estimate the probability of the binary response variables (Y_r, Y_m, Y_s)[20] based on predictor variables (X) (Lever, Krzywinski, & Altman, 2016). The model in simple form is the following:

---

[18] For statistical purposes the variable "location" was defined here in a dichotomous category – a project located in the capital city of the region, and outside the capital city. Notwithstanding, it has to be added that the term "capital city" used in the study refers, as a rule, to the capital city of the particular region, with the exception, however of Pomorskie region and Śląskie region, where, due to their specificity and agglomerative linkages, one continuous urban area covers more than the only one main city. Thus, in Pomorskie region the term "capital city" comprises three cities: Gdańsk, Gdynia and Sopot, that is, the so called Tri-city, and in Śląskie region applies to the Upper Silesian conurbation including the cities: Chorzów, Dąbrowa Górnicza, Gliwice, Katowice, Ruda Śląska, Sosnowiec, Świętochłowice and Zabrze.
[19] It is assumed that it tests with the null hypothesis that the distribution of given measurements in population X is the same as that in Y – to put this more precisely, the median difference between the first and the second measurement groups amounts to zero. If the medians of two populations differs, it points to a difference in the shapes of two distributions.
[20] The operational scope of projects implemented with the framework of the European funds is generally complex, which means that they have a multifaceted impact on the environment. This multifaceted impact means that the examined effects may be difficult to compare. To deal with this, a multi-criteria method was adopted, which makes it possible to measure the degree of the achievements of the effects by means of the objective function defined by many criteria. This approach is often used to evaluate complex and incomparable projects, where it is not enough, and often even impossible, to use one measure based on scalar optimisation taking into account only one criterion. In the research procedure, a binary rating scale was adopted, where "1" meant that the desired effect occurred, and "0" – otherwise. The evaluation was carried out for all JESSICA projects. The integer values were assigned to particular projects in the following manner: *binary response variable* Y_r – "1" – a project ensured cash in-flows directly paid by users

$$Y_r = \log\left(\frac{p(X)}{1-p(X)}\right) = \beta_0 + \beta_1 X_1 + \beta_2 X_2 + \ldots + \beta_X X_X \quad (1)$$

$$Y_m = \log\left(\frac{p(X)}{1-p(X)}\right) = \beta_0 + \beta_1 X_1 + \beta_2 X_2 + \ldots + \beta_X X_X \quad (2)$$

$$Y_s = \log\left(\frac{p(X)}{1-p(X)}\right) = \beta_0 + \beta_1 X_1 + \beta_2 X_2 + \ldots + \beta_X X_X \quad (3)$$

where the odds ratio is defined by the function of the probability of success, that is, of having capacity: to generate own revenues ($Y_r = 1$), to give rise to positive markets effects ($Y_m = 1$) and to create positive social impacts ($Y_s = 1$), which is given by the fact that a particular project is a revenue-generating, market-effect-generating and social-impact-creating project, and the probability of failure otherwise. β_0 is the fixed component and is an integral part of the model, while β_1, β_2, ... β_X are regression coefficients associated with particular independent variables and must be estimated with the use of the maximum likelihood. X_1, X_2, ... X_X stand for p predictors and are respectively: *type of the beneficiary; company status; local government authority status (LGA)* etc.

Finally, because we used multiple predictor variables in the regression models we also wanted to find out which variable is the most influential in predicting the binary response variables (Y_r, Y_m, Y_s). This was done by applying ANOVA analysis that assesses potential differences in a ratio-scale dependent variables by categorical independent variables. All calculations were done in the R statistical package (R Core Team, 2018).

Second approach, addressing JESSICA against the goals of urban sustainability

Sustainable urban development is seen as a response to global trends and challenges related to urbanisation. Since JESSICA was set out to deal with this issue in a sustainable fund model, there is a need to examine its results from a broader

---

for the goods or services as a result of its operations, "0" – did not; *binary response variable Y_m* – "1" – an implementation of a project resulted in generating new activities, offering new products or services, and creating new jobs, etc., "0" – did not; *binary response variable Y_s* – "1" – a project contributed to enhancing the integration among persons, improving their health and the overall level of safety, delivering facilities for people with disabilities, increasing people's access to culture, education and training, information, sport and recreation etc., "0" – did not.

perspective, i.e. through the conceptual lens of sustainable urban development. The question of JESSICA has been primarily discussed in the context of complexity and multi-functional impacts occurring in urban areas, therefore the research focuses on *multivariate analysis* (MVA) techniques. No single assessment can evaluate all of the kinds of JESSICA results we value for the improvement of urban areas, nor can a single measure (variable) meet all of the objectives held by JESSICA promoters, stakeholders and policy-makers. Therefore, it is important to envision a multivariate approach to assessment, in which different criteria are used as a basis for formulating evaluative questions through the full range of evaluation issues (OECD, 2008). The criteria should be such that they make it possible to judge whether the desired level of performance has been met or not, in light of the objectives and assumptions set.

As a result of conceptual work, five interrelated, but distinct, evaluation dimensions of JESSICA projects were formulated: financial, economic, social, spatial and horizontal (for more see Musiałkowska & Idczak, 2020). These dimensions lay down the main priority aspects of the assessment that characterise, in principle, the conditions to be fulfilled by individual projects. However, each of the dimensions are still reflected by multi-scale representation and cannot be measured precisely by a single indicator. This implies the need for determining some sub-components and, subsequently, selecting individual indicators that clearly reflect their relative importance and the complexity of the overall composite (OECD, 2008). Thus, in the next step we specified within particular dimensions the individual indicators that were selected in a way that takes into account existing linkages between them and indicating their desirability in relation to the relevance of the specificity of the single dimension. The assessment dimensions, and the individual indicators describing them, are displayed in Figure 10. All in all, these dimensions, as well as individual indicators deriving from a conceptual base, create a construct that provides relevant items to operationalise the concept of the assessment of the JESSICA projects.

Admittedly, most of the individual indicators cannot be measured directly or are still represented by multi-dimensionality. They have the nature of latent variables that can be indirectly measured by means of variables, which, in turn, can be perfectly observed and measured. Means of variables, here called just variables, contain information that reflect the approximate characteristic of an individual indicator. It should be pointed out that MVA techniques facilitate the transfer of data, including qualitative (soft) data, from surveys into the assessment process (Walesiak & Bąk, 1997). Therefore, we decided to measure individual indicators (latent variables) indirectly through the use of variables that were derived from a survey. To put it simply, each indictor was described by a single variable expressed in the form of a question. The responses to the questions con-

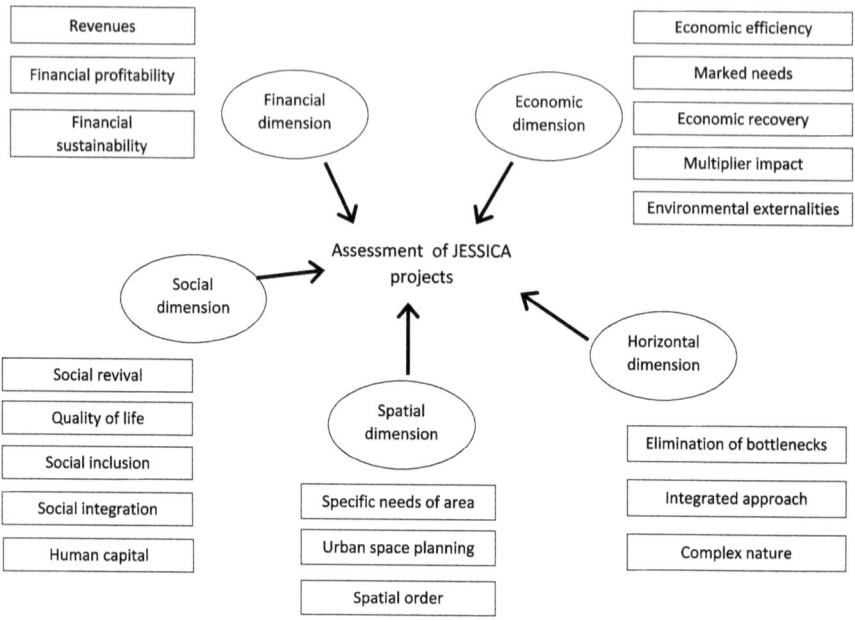

Figure 10: Operationalisation of the assessment of the JESSICA projects
Source: the authors' own elaboration

sisted of choosing a proper integer value as follows: 0 – "no"; 1 – "no/yes"; 2 – "yes". The assessment equals "0" when requirements defined through the individual question were not absolutely met by the particular projects, and "2" otherwise. The in-between assessment designated as "1" related to a situation in which it was not possible to assess the projects accurately and entirely.[21] The approach based on MVA, as outlined above, allows for assessing JESSICA projects by means of the objective function defined by many criteria.

We decided to invite four experts, specialised in European funds, urban planning and sustainable urban development, to participate in a survey.[22] This

---

21 The use of the three-point scale of assessment was dictated by an intention to obtain results that may be expressed in binary form, i.e. meet or do not meet. However, narrowing the possible responses to the only two opposing categories would have deprived respondents of the possibility to manifest reasonable doubts, if the sufficiently precise assessment was not possible. Therefore, an intermediate grade was also implemented.
22 The experts came from academia and municipal departments dealing with regeneration. To ensure impartiality, none of the experts were involved in the implementation of the JESSICA projects. The experts assessed all 161 projects against detailed model criteria. It is worth men-

means that the variables used in the study provide information stemming from a process that represents a shared perception of a reality, which, in this case, relates to a given state of affairs reflecting individual projects. In order to avoid explaining separately particular variables describing complex (dependent) phenomena (projects), there was a need to demonstrate the global relation of complex explanatory (independent) features to other given complex phenomena/projects (viewed as a uniform whole). To do this meant applying composite indicators that aggregate multidimensional undertakings into simplified concepts and make their comparability possible.

The main point of the construction of a composite indicator is to put together, in a meaningful way, different dimensions included in the study. This implied the use of a weighting method to aggregate information. In order to give variables appropriate weight, we applied a *principal component analysis* (PCA) (Bollen, Glanville, & Stecklov, 2007, pp. 19–22). PCA has often been adopted to obtain composite indicators (Jolliffe, 2002). Moreover, PCA methods explain the highest variation in the dataset. They use the smallest possible number of factors that reflect the latent "statistical" dimension (factors) of the dataset (M. Kaczmarek, 2016; Mori, Tanaka, & Tarumi, 1998; Walesiak & Bąk, 1997). By doing so, the values of the weights derive from statistical models, and this approach is deemed non-arbitrary. Applying PCA was preceeded by the estimation of the correlation between latent variables. To this end, we used *polychoric correlation*, which measures the correlation between two continuous latent variables that have a bivariate normal distribution.[23] Additionally, it is important to emphasise that, when calculating the factor loadings, we applied the *maximum likelihood method* to receive the most appropriate estimators for the factor loadings (Olsson, 1979).

Finally, we wanted to identify among all projects, those (in term of their scopes of activities dedicated to particular urban areas) which best reflect the JESSICA goals. This implies the identification of similar groups of projects in

---

tioning that the group of potential experts capable of providing in-depth evaluation of JESSICA in Poland, with regard to the assessment approach proposed in the study, is quite limited. Moreover, the number of experts invited to the survey, in our opinion, meets the rules of the approach proposed by Christopoulos (2009) relating to expert interviewing/surveying, and those experts can legitimately be considered relevant for our research purposes. In view of the above, we believe that the information collected in this way ensures the reliability of data and the validity of research results based on them. For further details see Dorussen, Lenz, and Blavoukos (2005). Nonetheless, bearing this in mind the results from such analyses should be treated with caution.
23 This method is frequently applied when analysing items on surveys that often use rating scales with a small number of response options. (For more see Kolenikov & Angeles, 2009; Uebersax, 2015).

terms of the scale of features specific for the five-dimension-assessment model. To this end, cluster analysis was applied, which groups data objects based on the information found in the data. As a distance measure, the *Euclidian distance method* was used, and then clustering was done with the *Genie linkage algorithm*. This new hierarchical clustering linkage criterion overcomes the limitations of traditional clustering algorithms that are sensitive to outliers. It mostly outclasses the Ward or average linkage in terms of the clustering quality (Gagolewski, Bartoszuk, & Cena, 2016; Gagolewski, Cena, & Bartoszuk, 2016). Concurrently, we assigned the support areas of JESSICA that derive from the legal basis (European Commission, 2013) to the particular projects on the grounds of the project descriptions, which defined the scope of activities being implemented.

Third approach, addressing the territorial impacts of the JESSICA projects
The aims of this approach are, first, to map JESSICA projects with a view to depicting their overall spatial relationships and, second, to identify the territorial impacts of JESSICA projects on urban areas. While achieving the first aim comes down to the graphical presentation of data, the second one is based on the judgements of experts. As is well known, the main challenge that territorial impact assessment has to face is the difficulty of measuring the effects of intervention. We address this problem through linking expert knowledge and judgements about the impact with the data from our database describing the characteristics of JESSICA projects. By doing so, we gathered reliable and robust information which serves as input for the impact analysis and facilitates the interpretation of the output indicators of the impact assessment. A complete account of the survey evidence is provided in Appendix A in the supplemental data online (Idczak, 2020).

In order to extract meaningful information on the territorial impacts of JESSICA projects on urban areas, we used the territorial impact assessment methodology (TIA). This methodology has been devised to be applied in the EU to enable the identification and evaluation of actual or potential territorial impacts in relation to concrete projects, programmes or policies at national, regional and local levels (ESPON, 2012). The analysis includes all nine JESSICA projects implemented in the city of Poznań. The main criterion for the choice of the city for the purpose of this study was simple – first, Poznań was a city with a relatively high number of JESSCA projects out of all the JESSICA regions; second, it was possible to gather sufficient information and data on projects; third, there was a chance to select and mobilise experts needed for qualitative judgements.

In the study, the assessment was based on the conceptual framework proposed by Medeiros (2014, pp. 50 – 101), known as TARGET_TIA. A major advantage of this approach is that it provides more robust TIA procedures and techniques. To put it more precisely, TARGET_TIA uses a wider and more holistic set of data and is distinguished by the adaptability to each geographical scale. It allows for assessing the ex-post impacts of a given project in a given territory and for being tailor-made to a specific evaluation context. Therefore, in order to properly assess the territorial impacts of the JESSICA project on an urban area, we used TIA dimensions and components designed for urban areas, i.e. economic, social, environmental, governance and spatial planning (Medeiros, 2014, pp. 102–104). It is also necessary to add that the methodology introduced here refers to TARGET_TIA, however, it was modified by being limited to the use of a participatory and qualitative TIA approach.[24] For the purpose of analysis, 14 subject domain experts were invited, from the fields of spatial and urban planning, urban regeneration, architecture, socio-economic geography and economics. The rules for the selection of independent experts covered not only their knowledge and professional experience of the research subject under study, but also their ability to conduct an objective, correct fact-finding and intuitive-logical analysis of the impact of JESSICA projects on urban areas with ordinal assessments, so as to obtain quantitative assessment of experts' judgements that cannot be directly measured. An important assumption underpinning the selection of the experts was their deep understanding of the wider context of the various regeneration projects pursued in the city so as to take into consideration the synergies and complementarities induced by a whole variety of regeneration initiatives. To this end, a questionnaire was drawn up and sent to all of the experts. The questionnaire was designed in such a way that the particular components of the urban area TARGET_TIA dimensions were described in the form of closed ended questions. They structured the possible answers by allowing responses which fit into TRAGET_TIA criteria determining the degree of impact. In addition, all the experts invited to the survey were provided with descriptions of JESSICA projects, including their initial assumptions and final achievements, so that they were able to carefully analyse and properly assess their impacts. In the end, ten experts returned the completed questionnaires. Bearing all this in mind, one may argue that the study provides a sufficient array of information stemming from a process that represents a shared perception of a reality, which, in this case, relates to a given state of affairs reflecting impacts of individual JESSICA projects.

---

[24] A major problem with quantitative information is that it is difficult to separate impacts caused by the assessed projects from those induced by many other projects, in particular when the number of JESSICA projects under study is relatively low.

Fourth approach, addressing the spatial distribution of the JESSICA funding
When deciding on which procedure to apply for this analysis two main aspects were relevant. The methods must be able to properly handle a relatively small population of JESSICA projects and reveal whether the city size is of significance for the project's capacity to ensure the repayability of JESSICA funding. Therefore, following this study's line of reasoning, we used two different methods. First, to analyse the spatial relationships of JESSICA projects we employed the directional distribution method (*standard deviational ellipse – SDE*). Second, it was decided that the best procedure for the second aspect of the investigation was to show the characteristics of JESSICA projects with regard to the city size by mapping the aesthetics in a certain plot to the specific variables in our dataset. The former method makes it possible, upon a prior mapping of projects, to provide visual insights into the data that due to many reasons may not otherwise be apparent. SDE is widely exerted in many research fields, mainly to explore the geographical distribution of some phenomena and thereby to detect a relationship to particular characteristics that are of interest to the investigation. As a spatial statistics method, it can be used to uncover accurately the economic characteristics of spatial distribution. Consequently, it may be conducive to promote the policy formulation in response to the identified dependencies (Wang, Shi, & Miao, 2015).

Overall, SDE reflects the characteristics of the entirety of the spatial distribution of the particular elements under investigation. To put it more precisely, it shows an average location, dispersion (concentration), and orientation of a specific data set (points) in a relatively simple and clear manner (Yuill, 1971). In this case, SDE was chosen to gain insights into the spatial distribution of JESSICA projects, using geographic coordinates (the longitude – x_i, and the latitude – y_i) with the weight of the value of JESSICA projects and the value of JESSICA loans. Drawing on Yang and Grigorescu's work (2017), the computation formulas presented below are expressed as follows (separately for each of the regions):

$$\begin{array}{c}\textit{Average location}\\ \textit{(mean centre)}\end{array} \quad \bar{x}_w = \frac{\sum_{i=1}^{n} w_i x_i}{\sum_{i=1}^{n} w_i}, \quad \bar{y}_w = \frac{\sum_{i=1}^{n} w_i y_i}{\sum_{i=1}^{n} w_i} \quad (4)$$

$$\tan \theta = \frac{\left(\sum_{i=1}^{n} w_i^2 \tilde{x}_i^2 - \sum_{i=1}^{n} w_i^2 \tilde{y}_i^2\right) +}{\sum_{i=1}^{n} w_i^2 \tilde{x}_i^2 \tilde{y}_i^2}$$

Azimuth angle	$\dfrac{+\sqrt{\left(\sum_{i=1}^{n} w_i^2 \tilde{x}_i^2 - \sum_{i=1}^{n} w_i^2 \tilde{y}_i^2\right)^2 + 4\sum_{i=1}^{n} w_i^2 \tilde{x}_i^2 \tilde{y}_i^2}}{\sum_{i=1}^{n} w_i^2 \tilde{x}_i^2 \tilde{y}_i^2}$	(5)
Standard deviational distance of x	$\sigma_x = \sqrt{\dfrac{\sum_{i=1}^{n}(w_i x_i - w_i x_i)}{\sum_{i=1}^{n} w_i x_i}}$	(6)
Standard deviational distance of y	$\sigma_y = \sqrt{\dfrac{\sum_{i=1}^{n}(w_i \tilde{x}_i \cos\theta - w_i \tilde{y}_i \sin\theta)^2}{\sum_{i=1}^{n} w_i^2}}$	(7)
Eccentricity	$e = \dfrac{\sqrt{a^2 - b^2}}{a}$	(8)

where x_i and y_i are the geographic coordinate data (respectively longitude and latitude), the value w_i refers to the quantity of the phenomenon being measured at the i th point, and here it represents the value of JESSICA projects and the value of JESSICA loans. Finally, i means the JESSICA project. As regards the eccentricity, a is the length of the semi-major axis and b is the length of the semi-minor axis, $a \geq b$. The study uses SDE method to carry out a spatial analysis for JESSICA projects in each region separately. The calculation was performed using the *ArcGIS* software.

Since the findings take the form of elliptical polygons, an overall understanding of their properties is a critical requirement to being able to analyse the results. Hence, Table 4 demonstrates the three properties that, as applied to or by an ellipse, may be used to facilitate the interpretation of the findings.

Table 4: Properties of an ellipse for the purpose of the overall interpretations*

	Average location (mean centre)	Dispersion (concentration)	Orientation (shape)
Interpretation	The closer relative position of the ellipse's mean centre to the region's centroid (barycenter), the more equal the distribution the point set across the region's space, and vice versa	A very small ellipse relative to the study region means that the point set is concentrated or clustered. Conversely, a relatively large ellipse points to a wide distribution (dispersion) of data in the region	The lower the ellipse's eccentricity, the more equal the distribution of the point set, and vice versa. Since the shape of the study region may affect the shape and orientation of a point set and its ellipse, this fact must also be taken into consideration

* As a result of calculation, the rotated axes that generate the ellipses (the major axis showing the direction of maximum dispersion of the point set and the minor showing that of the minimum dispersion) are not equal. The shape of an ellipse is measured by its eccentricity (i.e. the flatness of the ellipse) whose ratio ranges from zero when the major and minor axes are equal (ellipse = circle, this means an equal distribution) to one when the minor axis is zero (ellipse = line, which defines the locus of all points).
Source: authors' own elaboration based on Yuill (1971)

Turning now to the second method that was applied to reveal the dependence between the city size and the allocation of JESSICA funding as well as the project's capacity to ensure the repayability of the JESSICA loan, we constructed a faceted scatterplot with all the variables involved. To this end, we used exploration tools available in an *R* environment. The three variables – (1) value of the JESSICA projects and value of the JESSICA funding (loan), (2) class of the city size,[25] (3) the project's capacity to ensure the repayability of JESSICA funding[26] – were mapped to visual properties (aesthet-

---

[25] All cities that were recipients of JESSICA projects were classified into four classes depending on their populations. The population figures provided by Statistics Poland are based on the data from 2010 because this year can be considered as the starting year for the practical implementation of the JESSICA initiative. The classification of cities was based on the conceptual framework proposed by Runge (2012, p. 84). However, it was slightly modified so as to add one class more suggested in the Concept of the National Spatial Planning 2030 (CNSP, 2012). As a result, the city classes are as follows: small cities (I) – less than 20,000 population; medium-sized cities (II) – from 20,000 to less than 100,000 population; large cities (III) – from 100,000 to less than 300,000 population; extra-large cities (IV) – over 300,000.
[26] The term "repayability" refers throughout this study to the term "revenue-generating project" as defined by Musiałkowska and Idczak (2018, p. 146). This is predicated upon the assumption

ics) of the geometric objects (geoms) in a five-facet scatterplot. The particular facets display the subset of data for each of the JESSICA regions.

5.4 Results, analysis and discussions

Results on the fundamental requirements of JESSICA

As mentioned above, JESSICA projects should have a long-term viability and demonstrate a high level of self-financing. However, as Table 5 shows, nearly one in every three projects implemented under the JESSICA initiative in Poland does not provide any financial profitability but also no revenues. Against this background, Zachodniopomorskie region stands out notably as a region where all projects feature the capacity to generate revenues on the basis of their primary business activities. In turn, at the bottom of the ranking is Pomorskie region in which more than a half of projects (53.33%) do not demonstrate the creation of any revenues. In all remaining regions, this relationship remains at the level that is close to the general average. What is surprising is the fact that the framework of the JESSICA initiative did not provide here for the desired scale of long-term viability. It is worth noting that, indeed, in many projects (32.3%, Table 5) the repayment of the loan was not made from sales revenues but was secured by investors from other sources. Taking into account the meaning applied to the definition of "revenue-generating projects" (see footnote 17), it is likely that the number of non-profitable projects is even higher.

---

that most projects generating revenues on the basis of their primary business activities are able to ensure the repayment of the JESSICA loan, while non-revenue-generating projects are required to guarantee reimbursement in the form of other operating revenue secured directly by investors from other sources. Due to non-availability of the full project's financial data, this variable has a form of a binary variable with integer values assigned as follows: 1 – "the project's capacity to ensure the repayability of JESSICA funding", and 0 – otherwise.

Table 5: Number of JESSICA projects implemented in 2007–2015 according to their capacity to generate revenues

Region	Revenue-generating capacity YES		NO		Market effects YES		NO		Social impacts YES		NO		Total
Mazowieckie	23	*74.2*	8	*25.8*	22	*71.0*	9	*29.0*	11	*35.5*	20	*64.5*	31
Pomorskie	21	*46.7*	24	*53.3*	19	*42.2*	26	*57.8*	17	*37.8*	28	*62.2*	45
Śląskie	20	*76.9*	6	*23.1*	21	*80.8*	5	*19.2*	19	*73.1*	7	*26.9*	26
Wielkopolskie	26	*65.0*	14	*35.0*	31	*77.5*	9	*22.5*	26	*65.0*	14	*35.0*	40
Zachodniopomorskie	19	*100.0*	0	*0.0*	19	*100.0*	9	*0.0*	15	*78.9*	4	*21.1*	19
Total	109	*67.7*	52	*32.3*	112	*69.6*	49	*30.4*	88	*54.7*	73	*45.3*	161

Numbers in italics are percentages
Source: the authors' own elaboration

JESSICA funding should also respond to problems present in the market's deficiency in inner-city areas. The aim of this kind of revolving financing was to support the projects of various stakeholders in order to compensate for market failures in the disadvantaged urban areas. Thus, JESSICA projects should contribute to reducing imbalances in urban areas by providing specific types of goods or services that match the challenges responding to social and market needs, particularly in terms of labour market, business activity and social demand. Further analysis of the data presented in Table 5 shows that most of the projects (112 out of 161) generated a positive market effect, expressed through the emergence of new jobs, new types of activities or services. It is notable that the spatial distribution of the projects meeting the "market effect" criteria is similar to the spatial pattern drawn by projects capable of generating own revenues. Again, Zachodniopomorskie region topped the ranking, having 100% market-oriented projects, while in the Pomorskie region, only 42.2% of the projects had a clear focus on creating new products or services. Not surprisingly, these two variables show a strong correlation with each other. A completely different picture is presented by data showing the third variable under study. Only a little more than every second project (54.7%) turned out to be good enough for ensuring comprehensive actions in the dysfunctional areas so as to ensure the restoration of social functions and strengthen social integration. The main idea behind JESSICA was to enable the social and economic objectives of urban area development to be accomplished with efficiency, achieving simultaneously economic and financial viability. It follows that the objectives of social resurgence are applicable in addition to those laid down by a project's financial performance. Projects should not only promote social integration but also contribute to enhancing the social and professional activity of residents as well as their growing participation in public and civic life. The latter includes all measures targeting those persons who are (or feel) marginalised and excluded, and it is oriented to bring them back into the area's social life and to the conventionally recognised mainstream society. While in Zachodniopomorskie and Śląskie three out of every four projects resulted in a sustained social change through implementing various community-related activities, a relatively low number of projects in the Pomorskie and Mazowieckie regions had a considerable role in promoting the social component compared to other regions. This intriguing observation threw up many questions in need of further investigation.

In order to provide an additional explanation in the research, further analysis is focused on reasons that may be helpful in clarifying why some of the JESSICA projects did not fully achieve JESSICA's aims. In order to do so, the next step of the analysis relies upon examining the results achieved so far within the operational scopes of the projects. To conduct this examination, therefore, the particular projects were assigned, based on the project descriptions, to the JESSICA support areas derived from the legal basis (European Commission, 2013), which defined the scope of activities being implemented. It was decided that the best procedure for this investigation was to monitor dependencies between the examined variables and the support areas describing the scopes of the project activities by mapping the aesthetics to them and their presentation. The faceted scatterplot in Figure 11 compares the breakdown of all the variables involved – i.e. revenue-generating capacity, market effects and social impacts – with the JESSICA projects' support areas. Inspection of the charts reveals that the projects that did not generate revenues and that did not give rise to market effects and social impacts were those focused on "energy efficiency" and to some extent also "urban infrastructure" (blue dots on the chart). Most of these projects are located just in two regions, namely Pomorskie and Mazowieckie.

These rather surprising results can be accounted for by the fact that these projects cover as projects promoting mainly housing cooperatives and housing communities. The projects aimed to implement "energy efficiency improvements" – which consisted of, among other things, the modernisation of boiler plants, replacement of heating networks and improvement of the thermal insulation of buildings – and, for instance, the modernisation of car parking and other infrastructural elements of residential estates. Those projects have undoubtedly made substantial contributions to achieving savings in heat and energy consumption, and thus improving the environment and perhaps achieving the objective of social cohesion in a wider perspective. Nonetheless, these kinds of projects do not provide sales revenues and thereby do not ensure any operational margin, and as a consequence the projects are financially unsustainable.

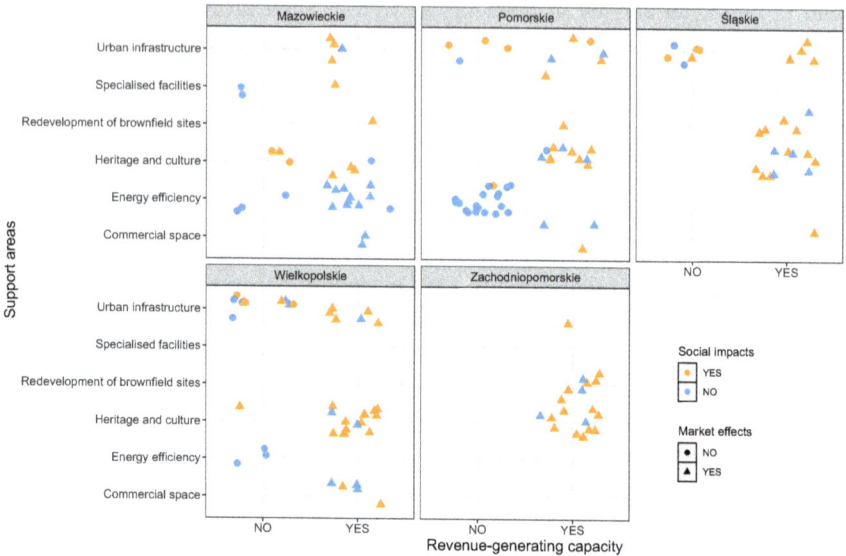

Figure 11: Mutual dependencies of the involved variables
Source: the authors' own elaboration

Moreover, they did not contribute to the generation of positive direct market effects in terms of new jobs or products or services, and did not have significant social impacts that could address social integration. It should be added that in many aspects these projects may be advantageous for a society as a whole. Nevertheless, as Breuer and Brueser (2013) argued, such types of projects usually concern problems for which the reasons of unwanted development are not market failures. Thus, it does not seem to be worth funding them from a market failure point of view. Conversely, the projects that best match the JESSICA assumptions (orange triangles on the chart) – i.e. generated revenues and initiated positive market effects as well as social impacts – are those classified in the following areas: culture and heritage, redevelopment of brownfields sites, and to some extent also urban infrastructure.

The main goal of the subsequent analysis is to identify what factor(s) contributed mostly to achieving the main assumptions of the JESSICA initiative. As stated before, the research was carried out in order to examine the capacities of projects: (1) to generate revenues obtained from primary business activities of investors, (2) to give rise to positive market effects in terms of new jobs, products or services, and (3) to have positive social impacts with regard to social integration and participation in public and civic life. To be more precise, we want to find out whether these capacities of projects vary for instance in the amount of JES-

SICA funding or in the value of JESSICA projects. Moreover, we intend to reveal if there are other important factors such as legal forms of beneficiaries, project locations, UDFs etc., that may affect the project capacities to generate desired outcomes and thereby could reflect an effect on the performance of the JESSICA initiative. For this reason the study now turns to investigate the relationship between the above-mentioned project capacities and other variables to find the statistical dependences. To do so, we used the *Wilcoxon rank sum test*.

The results of the *Wilcoxon rank sum test* are displayed in Table 6. What clearly emerges from this table is the existence of the significant differences between the examined groups of variables. We can conclude that the variable "project capacities to generate revenues" is significantly different when it comes to almost all variables, except for "location" where the results show that the medians of both variables are almost equal with $W = 2839.5$ and $p\text{-value} = 0.9832$. Furthermore, results also highlight a relatively strong dependence between the variable Y_1 and the value of the JESSICA project, which was confirmed by the output of calculations: $W = 765$, $p\text{-value} = 7.555e\text{-}14$. The same procedure was conducted regarding the statistical link between, on the one hand, the variable Y_2 (positive market effects) and the other selected variables, and on the other, the variable Y_3 (social impacts) and also the selected variables. We found that there are no significant differences between Y_2 and Y_3 and the location, while with regard to other variables a strong dependence is visible. The most surprising aspect of the data is in the considerable independency between the location and the examined variables. Therefore, it was decided to check the statistical link between the location and three variables – i.e. the value of a JESSICA project, the value of a JESSICA loan and the revenue-generating capacity of a project. It can be seen that the test showed evidence with *p-values* equal to, respectively, *0.9959, 0.8755* and *0.9832*, which means that the distributions of the location and the three variables differ significantly.[27] In brief, the most marked observation to emerge from the data analysis conducted so far is that the location, admittedly understood in dichotomous terms, seems not to be a relevant factor in the assessment of the JESSICA initiative. This could also point to a

---

[27] In addition to that, we checked the statistical dependency between the variables "the value of the JESSICA projects" and "support area" as they are not binary variables. Based on the results of the *Kruskal-Wallis rank sum test: chi-square* = 53.551, degrees of freedom = 5, *p-value* = 2.592e-10, it can be concluded that the differences in the distributions of these two variables are statistically significant. Furthermore, a post-hoc *Dunn's multiple comparison test* was used to pinpoint which specific support areas differ significantly from the others. From the output of the *Dunn's test*, we know that the biggest differences in terms of project value are between "energy efficiency" and other support areas.

relatively equal spatial distribution of JESSICA funding within particular JESSICA regions.

Table 6: Identification of differences based on the Wilcoxon rank sum test

Y	Comparison of the two distributions	W	p-value
Y_1	value of the JESSICA project	765	7.555e-14
	value of the JESSICA loan	981	2.128e-11
	type of beneficiary	3798	3.588e-05
	project location	2839.5	0.9832
	companies	1076	2.194e-13
	local government authorities	3243	0.04849
Y_2	JESSICA region	1873	0.001033
	project location	2936.5	0.4121
	value of the JESSICA project	472	2.2e-16
	value of the JESSICA loan	618	5.768e-15
	type of beneficiary	3479	0.001367
	revenue-generating capacity	395.5	2.2e-16
	type of activity	1113	4.511e-12
	support area	2392	0.1809
Y_3	JESSICA region	2080.5	8.128e-05
	project location	3518.5	0.2269
	value of the JESSICA project	1960	2.14e-05
	type of beneficiary	2800.5	0.09776
	revenue-generating capacity	2292.5	0.0001167
	type of activity	2919.5	0.252
	support area	1677.5	6.793e-08
	positive market effect	2102.5	2.3e-06
Y_4	value of the JESSICA project	3193	0.9959
	value of the JESSICA loan	3241.5	0.8755
	revenue-generating capacity	3200.5	0.9832

Note: Y_1, Y_2, Y_3, Y_4 denote, respectively: project capacities to generate revenues, positive market effects generated by a project, social impacts caused by a project, project location. The table presents comparisons of the only selected variables. Significance levels – statistically significant at the $p<0.05$ level.
Source: the authors' own elaboration

A further interesting aspect of the analysis refers to the examination of the relationship between our dummy dependent variables (Y_r, Y_m, Y_s) and other variables that influence (explain) whether or not the JESSICA projects have the capacity to generate the desired effects. The final set of explanatory variables (X) used in the estimation includes, for instance: *type of beneficiary; company status; region;*

value of the JESSICA project; support area etc. The detailed set of considered variables are shown in Table 7.

Table 7 presents the coefficient estimates and other information that result from fitting our logistic regression models in order to predict the probability of having capacities to generate revenues (equation 1), positive market effects (equation 2) and social impacts (equation 3). According to these results, it can be seen that only two variables suggest a statistically significant relationship in relation to our response variable Y_r, that is, *Company status – YES* and *Value of the JESSICA project*. When looking at the estimates, one can observe that the coefficients are positive and amount to $\beta_{Company\ status}$ = 3.49289 and $\beta_{Value\ of\ the\ JESSICA\ project}$ = 0.87224. This indicates that an increase in both variables is associated with an increase in the probability of having capacities to generate revenues by the projects. The findings indicate that the odds ratio that a project has the capacity to generate revenues is 3.5 times higher for projects which were implemented by entities having the company status compared to other entities having different legal status. In turn, in the case of the second significant variable – *value of the JESSICA project*, which is a continuous predictor – the estimate can be interpreted as: for every one unit (log scale) increase in the value of the JESSICA project the odds ratio of the projects having capacities to generate revenues increases by 87%. Results in graphical form are shown in Figures 12 and 13. Thus, it can be generally concluded that the projects with the highest capacity for producing revenues on the basis of their primary business activities are those of high value and implemented by investors with the company status. One possible explanation for this is that large projects run by companies encompass a wide range of actions that are strictly geared to achieving the required profit. These kinds of investments target actions necessary to achieve the project objectives but also to generate return on investment, which covers both investment and operating costs, and makes a profit. It is also found that there is no significant relationship between regions, urban development funds and the project capacities to generate revenues.

A predictive analysis of the second response variable Y_m (Table 7) indicates that only two explanatory variables have a significant impact on the generation of positive market effects by the JESSICA projects, i.e. *Value of the JESSICA project* and *Revenue-generating capacity – YES* (results are significant at the $p<0.05$ level). When analysing carefully the level of the model estimate values, it should be noted that the coefficients have positive values and amount respectively $\beta_{Value\ of\ the\ JESSICA\ project}$ = 1.4524, and $\beta_{Revenue-generating\ capacity}$ – YES = 5.3909. This means that an increase in the value of the factors described by both variables is associated with an increase in the probability of generating positive market effects by projects. In the case of the first variable, i.e. a continuous variable, this predictor indicates that one unit increase in the value of the project, will increase the odds of generating positive market effects by 145%. On the other hand, in relation to projects characterised by the capacity to generate revenues, the chance of generating positive market effects is more than five times higher compared to projects that do not have this capacity (Figure 14). These results prove that the projects that contribute relatively most to generating positive market effects are those characterised by a relatively high value and, at the same time, the capacity to generate revenues on their own. The explanations for these dependencies should be sought basically in the fact that large projects are implemented mainly by private entities and cover a wide range of activities making it possible to achieve a required profitability. These investments, as a rule, focus on activities aimed not only at achieving the objectives of the project, but also at generating a return on investment that allows one to cover both operating and investment costs and achieve the expected profit level. Hence, the key factor for the success of this type of undertaking is to run specific activities offering only those goods or services for which there is currently demand on the market. On the one hand, such projects will respond adequately to market needs, and on the other, they will create real opportunities for the development of new types of activities in a particular location.

The logit model of the dependent variable Y_s estimating the log odds of social impacts shows slightly different results than the two previous ones. From the output presented in Table 7, it can be seen that only four predictors belonging to the nominal independent variable "support area" are significantly associated to the outcome. These include: energy efficiency, heritage and culture, redevelopment of brownfield sites, urban infrastructure, of which the first and the last ones are statistically significant at the $p<0.10$ level. Three coefficient estimates of these variable are positive: $\beta_{\text{support area - heritage and culture}} = 1.77201$; $\beta_{\text{support area - redevelopment of brownfield sites}} = 1.77397$; $\beta_{\text{support area - urban infrastructure}} = 1.74086$, while one describing the "energy efficiency" is negative: $\beta_{\text{support area - energy efficiency}} = -2.38090$. The logistic regression results mean that the fact that the project scopes are characterised by three support areas – heritage and culture, redevelopment of brownfield sites and urban infrastructure – is associated with an increase in the probability of generating positive social impacts by 1.76 times on average. Conversely, the coefficient estimate for the variable "energy efficiency" indicates that if a project concerns the "energy efficiency" area, it will be associated with a decreased probability of generating positive social impacts by a project by more than two times (Figure 15). This result has further strengthened the earlier observation that "energy efficiency" projects drive resource efficiency and can also frequently generate direct cost savings, but do not contribute significantly to stimulating social integration and activity. This finding also confirms that "energy efficiency" projects do not provide actions of the required comprehensiveness to be an efficient response (granted by public recyclable money) to the complex nature of problems affecting some urban areas and their communities.

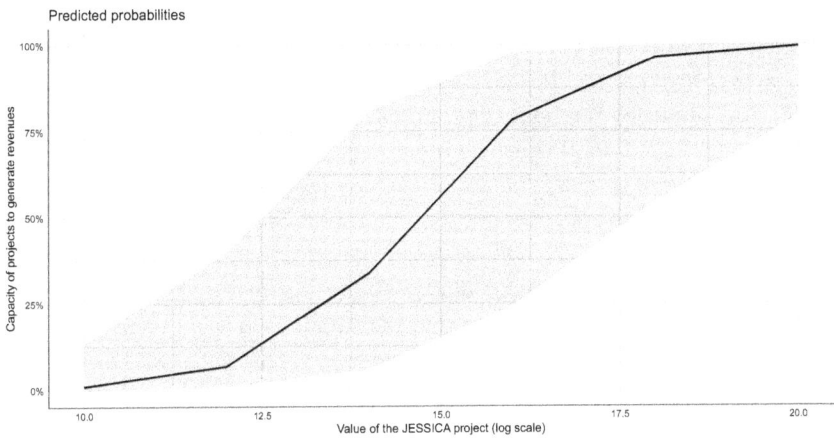

Figure 12: Effect display for the predictors of the project capacity to generate revenues
Source: the authors' own elaboration

A closer look at the other predictors reveals that they became insignificant in explaining the probability of having the capacities required by projects to generate the effects under study. The p-values associated with most of these variables are very high, indicating that there is no statistically significant association between these explanatory variables and our response variables (Y_r, Y_m, Y_s). However, the positive value of the coefficient estimate for the *type of the beneficiary – public*, by way of illustration, points out that public entities are more likely to implement projects generating revenues than the private ones. The same also refers to the *LGA status – YES*, where an increase in LGA status is associated with an increase in the probability of generating revenues. In turn, in the case of the Y_m model, its regression coefficient for Region – Zachodniopomorskie is 15.4571. This indicates that JESSICA projects implemented in this region are characterised by a 15-times-higher probability of generating positive market effects than projects implemented in other regions. On the contrary, projects implemented in Pomorskie region feature a 2.4-times-lower probability of generating positive market effects. This result may be explained by the fact that a relatively high number of the "energy efficiency" projects were implemented in Pomorskie as compared to other regions. A striking result to emerge from the data related to Y_s model is that projects having positive market effects are associated with an increase in the odds of generating positive social impacts by 94%. Given that these findings are based on an insignificant association between variables, the results from this part of the analysis should thus be treated with the utmost caution (for more see Wasserstein & Lazar, 2016).

After fitting the logistic regression models to a set of data, it is also reasonable to verify how well the proposed model fits the observed data. We used the *Nagelkerke pseudo-R^2* and *Hosmer-Lemeshow test* to assess the goodness of fit for the Y_r, Y_m, Y_s models. The level of pseudo-R^2 coefficients amount to respectively 65.61%, 87.19% and 48.23%, which represents a good or very good fit. In addition, verification of goodness of fit of the binary regression models was also confirmed with the *Hosmer-Lemeshow test*. The results indicate no significance (respectively: *p-value* = 0.6339; 0.8878; 0.5262), and for this test, no significance is desired. Binary logistic regression models fit the data reasonable well. The same conclusion can be drawn with regard to the comparison of differences between the values of null deviance and model deviance. As highlighted in the notes to Table 7, the values of the residual deviances are lower than the null deviances, which points to a very good fit as well.

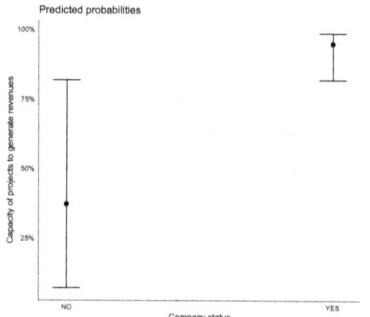

Figure 13: Interaction effect of the company status on the project capacity to generate revenues
Source: the authors' own elaboration

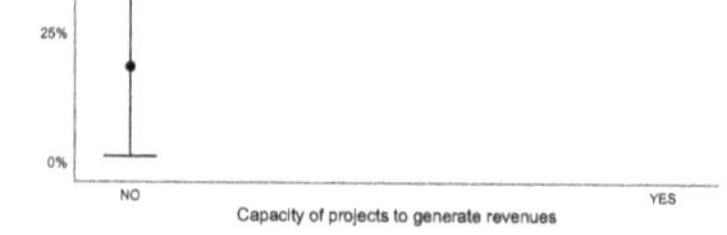

Figure 14: Interaction effect of the project capacity to generate revenues on positive market effects
Source: the authors' own elaboration

The results of ANOVA are presented in Table 8. These results are consistent with those of the logistic regression, i.e. they indicate that as regards: Y_r model – the projects implemented by companies and possessing a high value are significantly associated with capacities to generate revenues; Y_m model – the projects having revenue-generating capacity and a high value are significantly associated with capacities to generate positive market effects; Y_s model – the projects implemented within the support areas of heritage and culture, redevelopment of

Table 7: Coefficients of logistic regression for the JESSICA projects implemented in Poland

Term	Estimate	Std. error	Statistic	p.value	Deviance Residuals					Goodness-of-fit tests	
					Min	1Q	Median	3Q	Max	Nagelkerke's R squared	Hosmer-Lemeshow test
Y_r – Project capacities to generate revenues												
Intercept	-14.04977	3.64180	-3.858	0.000114 ***							
Type of beneficiary – public	0.93195	0.99125	0.940	0.347125							
Company status – YES	3.49289	1.01945	3.426	0.000612 ***							
LGA status – YES	0.51902	0.69037	0.752	0.452173							
Region – Pomorskie	-0.67245	0.93601	-0.718	0.472498	-2.2990	-0.2367	0.1455	0.4391	1.7985	Pseudo-R^2 0.6561281	X-squared = 6.1186, df = 8, p-value = 0.6339
Region – Śląskie	-0.09454	1.31065	-0.072	0.942498							
Region – Wielkopolskie	-0.86111	0.72293	-1.191	0.233596							
Region – Zachodniopomorskie	15.67709	1708.991	0.009	0.992681							
UDF – BOŚ S.A.	0.25502	1.05065	0.240	0.808221							
UDF – BZ WBK	1.60222	2488.579	0.001	0.999486							
Value of the JESSICA project (log)	0.87224	0.24836	3.505	0.000457 ***							
Y_m – Positive market effects												
Intercept	-24.3804	7.2390	-3.368	0.000757 ***							
Region – Pomorskie	-1.4153	1.1574	-1.223	0.221381	-2.1725	-0.0259	0.02851	0.15641	2.42813	Pseudo-R^2 0.8719507	X-squared = 3.6432, df = 8, p-value = 0.8878
Region – Śląskie	1.4145	1.4764	0.958	0.338030							
Region – Wielkopolskie	1.7741	1.2752	1.391	0.164151							

Table 7: Coefficients of logistic regression for the JESSICA projects implemented in Poland (Continued)

Term	Estimate	Std. error	Statistic	p.value	Deviance Residuals					Goodness-of-fit tests	
					Min	1Q	Median	3Q	Max	Nagelkerke's R squared	Hosmer-Lemeshow test
Region – Zachodniopomorskie	15.4571	2216.821	0.007	0.994437							
Value of the JESSICA project (log)	1.4524	0.4669	3.111	0.001864 **							
Type of beneficiary – public	-0.1467	0.9165	-0.160	0.872784							
Revenue-generating capacity – YES	5.3909	1.2280	4.390	1.13e-05 ***							
Y_s – Social impacts											
Intercept	-2.18887	2.69106	-0.813	0.4160	-1.8220	-0.3016	0.6723	0.7171	2.7735	Pseudo-R^2 0.4823878	X-squared = 7.0973, df = 8, p-value = 0.5262
Region – Pomorskie	0.07471	0.67944	0.110	0.9124							
Region – Śląskie	0.15242	0.72955	0.209	0.8345							
Region – Wielkopolskie	0.17096	0.68018	0.251	0.8015							
Region – Zachodniopomorskie	0.19431	0.83970	0.231	0.8170							
Value of the JESSICA project (log)	0.04822	0.17748	0.272	0.7859							
Revenue-generating capacity – YES	-0.19178	0.83094	-0.231	0.8175							
Support area – energy efficiency	-2.38090	1.26961	-1.875	0.0608 .							
Support area – heritage and culture	1.77201	0.72710	2.437	0.0148 *							

Table 7: Coefficients of logistic regression for the JESSICA projects implemented in Poland *(Continued)*

Term	Estimate	Std. error	Statistic	p.value	Deviance Residuals					Goodness-of-fit tests	
					Min	1Q	Median	3Q	Max	Nagelkerke's R squared	Hosmer-Lemeshow test
Support area – redevelopment of brownfield sites	1.77397	1.00389	1.767	0.0772 .							
Support area – specialised facilities	0.99558	1.31990	0.754	0.4507							
Support area – urban infrastructure	1.74086	0.79088	2.201	0.0277 *							
Positive market effects – YES	0.93882	0.85791	1.094	0.2738							

Significance levels: " . " statistically significant at the p<0.10 level; * statistically significant at the p<0.05 level; ** statistically significant at the p<0.01 level, *** statistically significant at the p<0.001 level.

For Y_t – null deviance: 202.57 on 160 degrees of freedom; residual deviance: 100.45 on 150 degrees of freedom; number of Fisher Scoring iterations: 17. For Y_m – null deviance: 197.870 on 160 degrees of freedom; residual deviance: 42.732 on 152 degrees of freedom; number of Fisher Scoring iterations: 19. For Y_s – null deviance: 221.79 or 160 degrees of freedom; residual deviance: 149.76 on 148 degrees of freedom; number of Fisher Scoring iterations: 6.

Source: the authors' own elaboration

brownfield sites and urban infrastructure are significantly associated with capacities to generate positive social impacts. The last column of this table shows relative importance (contribution percentages) from all possible orderings of the predictors. It can be seen that *value of the JESSICA project* and *company status* in Y_r model, with the former slightly ahead of the latter, are the most important factors influencing the project capacity to generate revenues. In turn, *revenue-generating capacity* and *value of the JESSICA project* are the most influential factors in Y_m model, while *support area* is a dominant factor in the generation of social impacts in Y_s model.

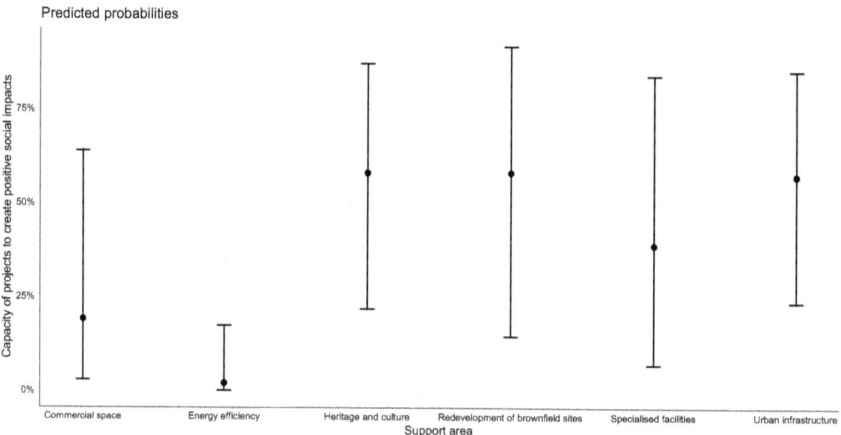

Figure 15: Effect display for the predictors of the project capacity to create social impacts
Source: the authors' own elaboration

Table 8: Results of ANOVA for the JESSICA projects implemented in Poland

Term	Statistic	df	p.value	p
Y_r – Project capacities to generate revenues				
Type of beneficiary	0.937036711	1	3.330411e-01	2.618790
Company status	15.10277906	1	1.018133e-04	42.208605
LGA status	0.570658147	1	4.499975e-01	1.594851
JESSICA region	3.766258716	4	4.385624e-01	10.525780
UDF	0.058653823	2	9.710989e-01	0.163923
Value of the JESSICA project (log)	15.34589352	1	8.951528e-05	42.888051
Y_m – Positive market effects				
Region	7.80652746	4	9.892803e-02	10.41202638

Table 8: Results of ANOVA for the JESSICA projects implemented in Poland *(Continued)*

Term	Statistic	df	p.value	p
Value of the JESSICA project (log)	15.94887591	1	6.507641e-05	21.27195701
Type of beneficiary	0.02558575	1	8.729162e-01	0.03412523
Revenue-generating capacity	51.19507396	1	8.362822e-13	68.28189138
Y_s – Social impacts				
Region	0.08748096	4	9.990708e-01	0.2423251
Value of the JESSICA project (log)	0.07406228	1	7.855114e-01	0.2051549
Revenue-generating capacity	0.05404501	1	8.161685e-01	0.1497064
Support area	34.64359519	5	1.772277e-06	95.9638681
Market effect	1.24148224	1	2.651856e-01	3.4389456

Source: the authors' own elaboration.

In short, the empirical analyses undertaken here suggest that the most desirable projects from the JESSICA perspectives are those of high total value and implemented by companies. These types of projects are characterised by relatively large capacities to generate revenues resulting from their primary business activities. Moreover, many of them, mostly enacted by private entities, demonstrate strong capabilities to achieve a fair commercial return on investment. This means that those projects were not only able to ensure the repayment of the JESSICA loan on their own but were also able to overcome market failures through introducing or restoring market activities in deprived urban areas. Furthermore, projects characterised by a high value contribute to the greatest extent to generating revenues and positive market effects, and, in addition, if they relate to support areas, such as heritage and culture, redevelopment of brownfield sites and urban infrastructure, to causing positive social effects. Thus, these projects best meet the assumptions of the JESSICA initiative.

Results on JESSICA against the goals of urban sustainability

As outlined in the theoretical framework, the JESSICA initiative focuses on supporting sustainable urban development through a revolving financial mechanism.[28] This entails designing undertakings that, on the one hand, ensure a strong and long-term viability, while on the other, activate all relevant stakeholders to play a critical role in selecting and implementing operations that have to be regenerative for cities. In a nutshell, JESSICA has been seen as a tool that con-

---
[28] This unit benefits partly from Musiałkowska and Idczak (2020).

veys the model of urban sustainability based on financial engineering in a real city world. However, Figure 16 reveals that the overall assessment of projects implemented with the support of JEESICA varies considerably according to both the five evaluation dimensions and the individual indicators. What is surprising is that even the financial dimension, originally foreseen as a key part of this instrument, was not assessed particularly positively. This suggests that a certain number of projects have not been financially sustainable, at either the investment or the operational stage. A closer look at this dimension and its performance reveals that none of the indicators have reached the maximum achievable result. This also relates to "financial sustainability", which serves as some kind of financial collateral to balance project cash flows, including, and especially, the security for the repayment of JESSICA loans. As such, it should be seen as a necessary condition for being a JESSICA beneficiary. A reasonable explanation for this result may be that, according to experts, some projects have been completely lacking in profitability. In other words, some beneficiaries were not able to secure the loan repayment not only from their primary activities, but also from any other activities due to the non-commercial nature of those activities. Therefore, the coverage of lifelong operating costs and the reimbursement of the JESSICA loan had to be ensured by some external bodies, such as governing authorities.[29]

As far as the economic dimension is concerned, most prominence is given to the two indicators that almost obtained the maximum result: "economic efficiency" and "market needs". These findings imply that, in principle, all projects were perfectly matched to the current needs and made a significant contribution to welfare by providing benefits for citizens. The three other indicators, in contrast, point to an average level of satisfaction with the economic impact of a project in particular urban areas. Considerably poor effects are especially observed when it comes to the creation of a new chain reaction and, through that, stimulation of the local economy.

The weakest characteristics assessed seem to be those related to the social dimension. Apart from "quality of life", which received the highest score and shows a substantial impact on projects in this aspect, the other indicators are evaluated below expectations. The relatively large share of inconclusive responses, and wider scope of negative responses than positive ones, may prove that projects have exceptionally little impact (not to say negligible) in shaping social development in the face of the complex set of challenges described in IPFSUD.

---

29 This could partly include, for instance, public educational entities that, in Poland, are governed by self-governing units or other public legal persons.

5.4 Results, analysis and discussions — 169

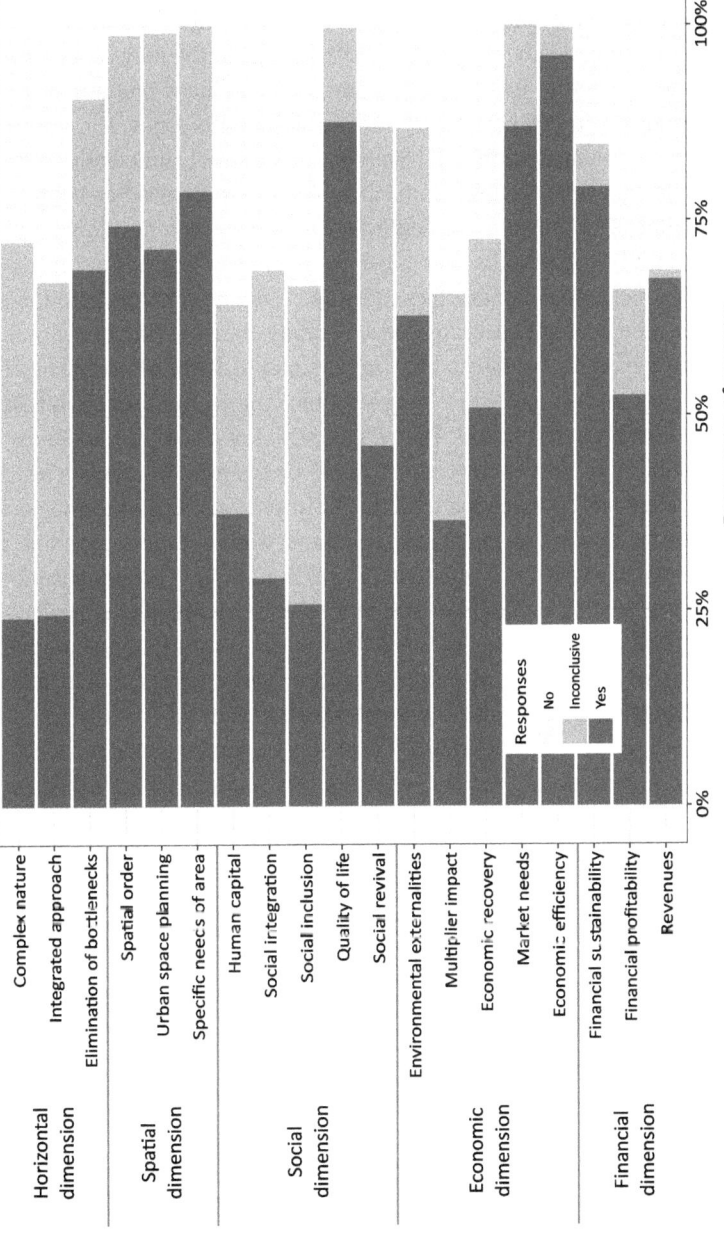

Figure 16: Assessment of the JESSICA dimensions by projects implemented in Poland in 2007–2015 (results of the survey)
Source: the authors' own elaboration

Regarding the spatial dimension, the results highlight that projects in principle, were quite well prepared and adequately fulfil the requirements described in strategic and planning documents. In turn with respect to the horizontal dimensions, one may notice that the results provide a predominant proportion of inconclusive responses in comparison with the other possible ones. These results indicate that the implementation of JESSICA projects has not sufficiently respected the principles of an integrated approach, which are recognised as being of a particular challenge in the enhancement of sustainable urban development.

The most striking observation to emerge from the data analysis at this point is that many projects are not characterised by operating profitability (profit margin), and that their real added value derives mainly from specific benefits that the investment generates for the society (understood in terms of economic efficiency). These are mostly projects for which financing in the form of JESSICA loans did not constitute public aid. They are deprived of a commercial element, and the profitability condition has been replaced by the project promoter's creditworthiness. Moreover, the actions undertaken in projects related to the social dimension often had a complementary nature and were not an appropriate response to the real needs of the inhabitants. The actions in their scope concentrated mainly on issues such as the improvement of security through the installation of video monitoring or the reduction of social exclusion by adapting buildings/ facilities to the needs of persons with disabilities. These effects should not be questioned. However, they result from legal regulations or generally applicable standards, which means that they would probably be implemented anyway.

As was discussed in the theoretical section, not all projects are expected to accomplish fully the individual assumptions of the JESSICA model to support sustainable investments in urban areas. Nonetheless, their activities should be adjusted to local needs as much as possible and pursue the goals of sustainable urban development. This is of primary importance. In order to assess the extent to which projects implemented under the JESSICA initiative have contributed to achieving its fundamental assumptions, we need the overall picture of projects pointing to all aspects covered by the five dimensions. Therefore, following this line of argument, we applied a principal component analysis to determine the weight that was subsequently used to construct a composite indicator. It turned out that the variables are quite well represented by a single component (factor). The eigenvalue of this component amounted to 6.964, which accounts for 0.367 of the total variance in the dataset. This was deemed sufficient to explain the highest possible variation in the variable set. Thus, the variable loadings of the component were considered as optimal weights because no other set of weights could produce a set of components that are more successful in explaining the variation in the analysed variables. Finally, we constructed a composite indicator as an average value of data from four independent respondents.[30] The results, normalised to 100, are illustrated in Figure 17.

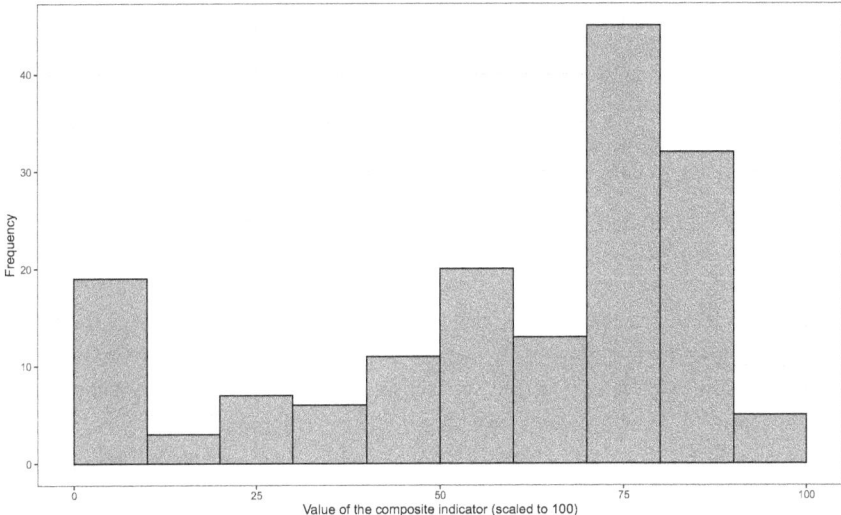

Figure 17: Histogram of the composite indicator
Source: the authors' own elaboration

What clearly emerges from Figure 17 is a wide variety of JESSICA projects in terms of the value of the composite indicator. There are few projects that perfectly comply with JESSICA goals focused on sustainable urban development. Half of all projects meet the assumptions of this financial engineering instrument at a very high level, and make a significant contribution to achieving urban sustainability. Nevertheless, there are also a certain number of projects that were judged as partly unsatisfactory or unsatisfactory. This may be due to their scope of activities, which were often limited to one type of operation and did not include components rendering positive externalities for urban citizens.

In order to provide additional depth to the research, further analysis was conducted at the regional level to compare results between particular regions. As illustrated in Figure 18, there is a wide variety of JESSICA projects in terms of the value of the composite indicator. There are few projects that perfectly comply with the JESSICA objectives that are focused on sustainable urban develop-

---

30 Such calculation was possible due to a strong correlation between the four individual composite indicators (0.89 on average).

ment. Indeed, some projects were evaluated as partly unsatisfactory or even unsatisfactory.[31] This may be due to the scope of activities, which were often limited to one type of operation and did not include components rendering positive externalities for urban citizens.

Figure 18 presents the distribution of the value of the composite indicator in all Polish regions that implemented the JESSICA initiative. Such comparison makes it possible to point out differences between the regions examined. The Kruskal-Wallis test proved that the differences are statistically significant: *chi-squared = 112.08, df = 4, p-value < 2.2e-16*. Furthermore, in order to pinpoint which specific regions differ significantly from the others, we applied the Dunn's test of multiple comparisons. By doing so, we obtained evidence that the best performer in terms of the composite indicator value is the Zachodniopomorskie region. This region is also characterised by the high value of the majority of its implemented projects. In turn, the worst performing region is Pomorskie, which, among others, includes many projects of a substantially lower value. The analysis of the graph provides also a critical conclusion that the higher the value of the JESSICA project, the higher the value the composite indicator obtained in the assessment procedure. The remaining three regions in the area of analysis conducted so far rest in the middle of the scale.

Figure 18 also shows a positive relation between the composite indicator and value of the JESSICA project and two other variables, namely, the type of project and the type of beneficiary. With regard to the Kruskal-Wallis test, we found that at the general level there are significant differences between the examined groups: type of projects v. composite indicator – *chi-squared = 95.137, df = 1, p-value < 2.2e-16*; legal form of the beneficiary v. composite indicator – *chi-squared = 48.789, df = 6, p-value = 8.219e-09*. The results are also visible at the regional level and are interesting in two ways. First, both the type of project as well as the legal form of the beneficiary matter in determining the value of the composite indicator. Second, if the individual project was a revenue-generating project or the project was implemented by a private entity, the value of the composite indicator is higher. Thus, the projects which best reflect the priorities of the JESSICA initiative are those that were executed by private entities and which possess the capacities to generate revenues. The best projects in terms of this study are marked in the graph by the green triangles. If one takes into account all of the variables analysed, the conclusion that can be drawn is that

---

31 Expert evaluation was conducted as a part of the project and presented in Musiałkowska and Idczak (2020).

the most appropriate projects to be considered for JESSICA support are those of a high value and developed by private entities.

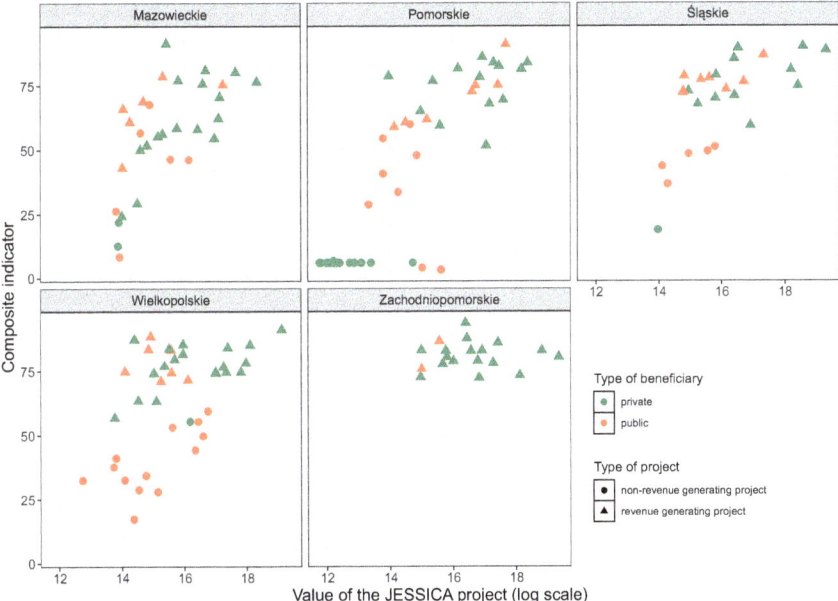

Figure 18: Composite indicator in Polish regions by type of project and type of beneficiary
Source: the authors' own elaboration

The analysis conducted so far does not reveal what kind of projects, in terms of their scopes of activities, best reflect the main conditions of the JESSICA initiative. In order to identify these projects, we applied a cluster analysis. The analysis of the results of the agglomerative hierarchical clustering summarised in the dendrogram highlights that among all the JESSICA projects examined on the basis of the composite indicator a few clusters (groups of similar projects) are found. As regards the dendrogram showing Genie-based linkage criterion, there are three main groups of observations that are similar in terms of the examined five-dimension assessment model (Figure 19).[32] As a result, we obtained a vector containing the cluster number of each group, where the biggest is the cluster number 1, including 87 projects, the cluster number 2, which covers 24 projects, and the cluster number 3, 50 projects.

---

[32] We assumed that the increasing level of dissimilarity is noticeable from the linkage distance above 1.3 that was the most appropriate cut-off height to form clusters.

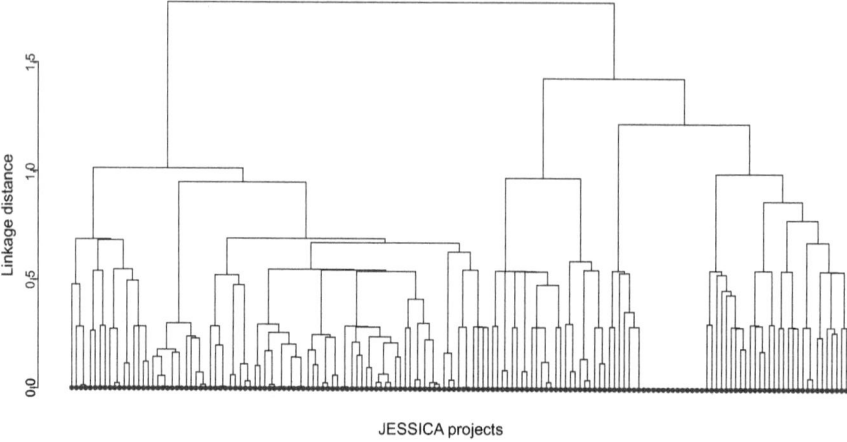

Figure 19: Dendrogram for the Genie linkage algorithm of the composite indicator
Source: the authors' own elaboration

The results of the agglomerative hierarchical clustering provide information only on several groups of projects that are similar in the light of the characteristics investigated. However, in order to identify the types of projects that, according to the assumption of this study, may reach the objectives defined by JESSICA and would be ancillary to it, an in-depth analysis of the data is required. The general rule determining the scope of projects to be implemented within the framework of financial engineering instruments derives from Article 44 of the General Regulation. It requires that these kinds of instruments can support operations (projects) through the provision of repayable investments, which are included in an integrated plan for sustainable urban development, and promote in particular activities such as: strengthening economic growth, rehabilitation of the physical environment, brownfield redevelopment, the preservation and development of natural and cultural heritage etc. (European Commission, 2013). Therefore, at the next stage of the analysis, the particular JESSICA support areas were attributed to the projects based on the project descriptions, gathered by the authors in our own database, which specify the scope and the detail of the tasks to be executed. By this route, we were able to identify which of the clusters are dominated by a certain type of support area. Table 9 displays the characteristics of projects grouped in the clusters from the perspective of the support areas that were promoted by the JESSICA initiative. Furthermore, in order to confront the new typology of the projects with the project capacities to repay the JESSICA loan, we extended the table by adding one variable, namely "(non-)revenue-generating projects" – which reveals whether the use of the project outputs is subject to charges borne directly by the users. As can be seen, in the biggest cluster the projects referring to the heritage or cultural sites of cities play the most important role (more than half of all the projects classified by cluster 1). The second place was occupied almost equally by projects focused on urban infrastructure (16) and the redevelopment of brownfield sites (14). Cluster 2, which is the smallest in terms of the number of projects, covers projects related to four different JESSICA support areas. The second largest cluster of projects (cluster 3) includes the remaining projects that are also scattered over the four JESSICA areas. However, the projects implemented within the area of "energy efficiency improvements" represent not less than 60% of all the projects from this cluster. One in three projects in this cluster was related to the first support area, "urban infrastructure". Interestingly, the largest numbers of projects were accumulated in cluster 1, which at the same time put together projects from almost all support areas, excluding only one: "energy efficiency improvements" (present in two other clusters).

At this point it is important to emphasise that cluster 1 encompasses almost all the projects that stand out as revenue-generating projects, except for only one. By contrast, the largest numbers of non-revenue-generating projects were gathered in cluster 3 (38 out of 44). Unsurprisingly, all of the projects (from cluster 3) dealing with urban infrastructure did not generate revenues. A satisfactory explanation for this may be that they were implemented by public institutions, and are related to the provision of public services, which on principle may be partly free of charge. However, the unexpectedly high number of "energy efficiency improvements" projects is undoubtedly due to the single kind of operations (or a very narrow scope of operations) implemented. The scopes of these projects were aimed mostly at upgrading the energy efficiency of buildings or establishing new or modernising existing heat sources and heating installations. This was done in many cases by private entities in their own interests. The truth of the matter is that such investments allow the generation of significant savings in the area of operational processes and enhance economic efficiency, but as such do not ensure a broader impact that is required by the JESSICA framework. The findings make it possible to draw a conclusion that the projects covered by cluster 1, indeed, may ensure the repayment of the JEESICA loan based on the self-financing capacity. On the contrary, however, this cannot be stated as far as the "energy efficiency improvements" projects are concerned. It is important to stress that the composite indicators reflect here the final result of all the characteristics defined in the study and expressed by individual indicators. It is also noteworthy that these data have to be analysed in conjunction with the results of the cluster analysis presented in Figures 20 and 21. Both figures report the value of the composite indicator and the value of the JESSICA

Table 9: Characteristics of clusters of projects by the JESSICA support areas

Support areas	Cluster 1		Cluster 2		Cluster 3		Total
	NofP	R/N-R	NofP	R/N-R	NofP	R/N-R	
Urban infrastructure, including transport, water/waste water, energy	16	16/0	8	4/4	16	0/16	40
Heritage or cultural sites – for tourism or other sustainable uses	47	46/1	6	4/2	2	1/1	55
Redevelopment of brownfield sites, including site clearance and decontamination	14	14/0	0	0/0	0	0/0	14
Creation of new commercial floor space for SMEs, IT and/or R&D sectors	8	8/0	3	3/0	0	0/0	11
University buildings, including medical, biotech and other specialised facilities	2	2/0	0	0/0	2	0/2	4
Energy efficiency improvements	0	0/0	7	6/1	30	5/25	37
Total	87	86/1	24	17/7	50	6/44	161

Note: NofP – number of projects, R/N-R – revenue-generating projects/non-revenue-generating projects
Source: the authors' own elaboration

project for all clusters investigated in the study. Note immediately that cluster 1 covers projects featuring overall higher levels of the value of both the composite indicator and the value of the JESSICA project. In turn, the other clusters comprise projects which are characterised respectively by lower values of both variables, whereas projects concentrated around cluster 2 are distinguished by significantly higher levels of both variables in comparison with cluster 3. What clearly emerges from the graphs is that all the projects in cluster 1 perfectly comply with the JESSICA assumptions as a revolving instrument and thereby contribute to achieving its fundamental goals focused on supporting sustainable urban development. The allocation of projects for the other clusters indicates without any doubt that their impacts on urban areas may be considerably lower, and they may not fulfil the conditions of JESSICA with the required due diligence. However, the single most conspicuous observation to emerge from the data comparison is that the projects of higher value grouped in cluster 1, and simultaneously ranked highest in terms of the composite indicator, best reflect the JESSICA priorities as well as meet its financial obligations.

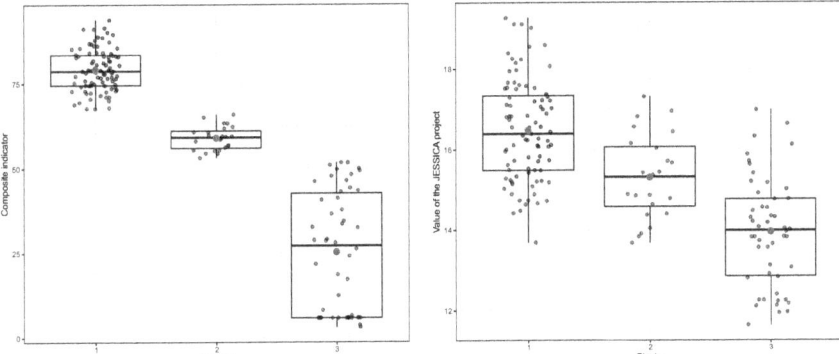

Figure 20: Clusters by the composite indicator
Source: the authors' own elaboration

Figure 21: Clusters by the value of the JESSICA projects
Source: the authors' own elaboration

When combined with information in the field of the support areas promoted by the JESSICA initiative, it can be observed that the best projects are those which are related to heritage or cultural sites, including operations for tourism or other sustainable uses, while the worst are projects dedicated to energy efficiency improvements, as noted, grouped respectively in cluster 1 and cluster 3. The group of best-performing projects besides the heritage-oriented ones comprises also the projects related to urban infrastructure, the redevelopment of brownfield sites as well as the creation of office spaces for SMEs, IT and/or R&D sectors. All of them clearly stand out due to their high composite indicator level. Undoubtedly, they respect the spirit of JESSICA in the best way. The majority of projects are featured by the occurrence of a commercial element. This means that they provide a desirable level of financial profitability that generates a return on investment, which in turn ensures the repayment of the JESSICA loan. Their main characteristic is the nature of their infrastructural investments. The scope of these projects is very wide and includes, among others: shopping centres, entertainment centres, restaurants, business incubators, technology incubators, office spaces, warehouses, hotels, car parks, city marketplaces, sports facilities, rehabilitation or medical treatment centres, new systems of energy generation. Many of the projects combine not only the redevelopment of brownfield sites in connection with the restructuring of production but also the preservation and development of the historical and cultural heritage. They also include measures to promote local employment, entrepreneurship, innovation and the knowledge economy, and last but not least, community development. It is clear that these projects scored highly and that their high value, apart from the commercial components, consists of a relatively broad spectrum of various services including social, cultural and others available to the public. Therefore, as a result of running a wide business activity within the projects, their promoters can also achieve an accurate level of profitability that guarantees both a return on investment as well as the availability of social and cultural aspects.

As far as projects that are rated low are concerned (the results in Figure 20 and 21 and in Table 9), it can be seen that they are in general either deprived of a commercial component, and the profitability condition has been replaced by the project promoter's creditworthiness, and/or their scopes are limited to the single kind of operations which do not enable the complete fulfilment of the requirements of the JESSICA initiative. For this reason these projects are not seen as a complex set of activities to overcome existing market failures. Many actions undertaken in the projects related to the social dimension often had a complementary nature and they were not an appropriate response to the real needs of the inhabitants. For instance, they focused mainly on creating a pitch to play football, volleyball, basketball, a tennis court, a children's playground, a set of fitness equipment in the open air along with technical facilities etc. This includes also projects on "energy efficiency improvements", which were mostly implemented by the housing cooperatives and housing communities. The effects achieved by the beneficiaries of these projects should not be questioned. However, by their nature they seem to be inconsistent with the JESSICA funding model.

As argued at the beginning of this section, the level of the composite indicator differs between regions and varies by the type of beneficiary. The spatial dimension of the composite indicator was illustrated in Figure 22. The differences are statistically significant, which was proven by a chi-squared test: *chi-squared = 37.04, df = 8, p-value = 1.13e-05*. The Zachodniopomorskie region is the best performing because almost all projects were grouped in cluster 1, which is proof of the positive effects of the actions carried out. The Śląskie region ranks second, and the Wielkopolskie region, third. The highest number of projects that are assessed as low, that is, those covered by cluster 3, is in the Pomorskie region. The Mazowieckie region features a comparable number of projects classified in particular clusters.

An interesting insight can be obtained by looking at the relation between the value of the composite indicator and the type of beneficiary (Figure 23). Cluster 1 was dominated by projects implemented by private entities. In turn, the public entities are scattered among the three clusters, whereby the largest number of projects implemented by them is found in cluster 3. The result of the chi-squared test reveals that these differences are statistically significant: *chi-squared = 7.896, df = 2, p-value = 0.01929*.

5.4 Results, analysis and discussions — 179

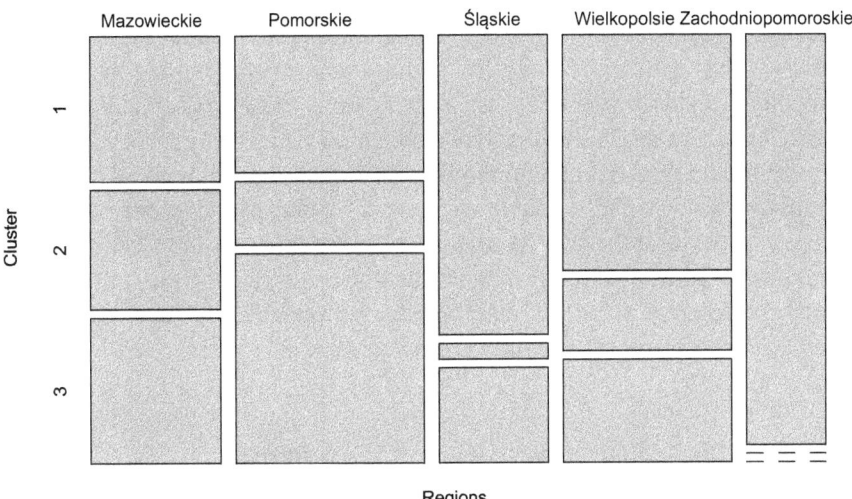

Figure 22: Distribution of clusters of projects in regions
Source: the authors' own elaboration

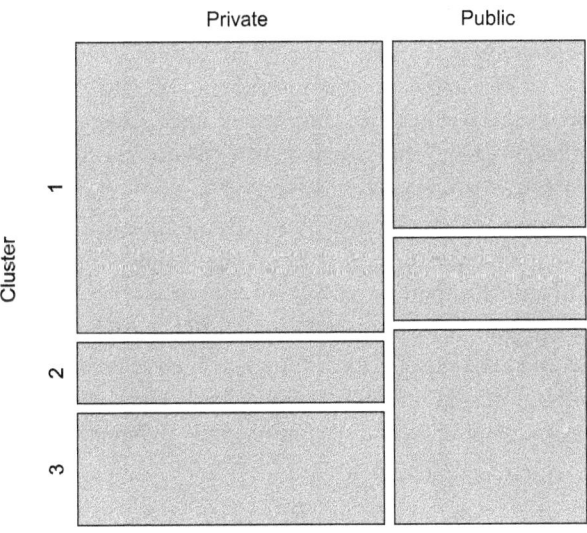

Figure 23: Distribution of clusters of projects according to type of beneficiary
Source: the authors' own elaboration

Bearing in mind the aforementioned evidence, it can be argued that the projects whose profile best matches the assumptions of the JESSICA instrument are those which consist in a culture and heritage renovation, followed by the redevelopment of the brownfield sites. What is more, those projects are executed mostly by private entities and feature a high total value. This may be interpreted as meaning that these kind of projects often include a wide range of diversified business activities offering a large spectrum of services or goods, and in so doing they can provide, at the same time, positive externalities for the local citizens in line with the integrated urban development plans. Consistent with our expectations, these projects reflect the most both the repayment of the JESSICA loan and the complexity of sustainable urban development.

Results on the territorial impacts of the JESSICA projects

This section presents the key findings from the assessment of the territorial impact of JESSICA on urban areas in Poznań in the light of economic, social, environmental, governance and spatial planning-related dimensions.[33] Prior to analysing the data, it is important to investigate the location of projects within the urban area of the city. Interestingly, as is apparent from Figure 24, eight out of nine JESSICA projects are located in the area of the city centre (Śródmieście). This is of particular importance because the Urban Regeneration Programme for the city of Poznań identifies Śródmieście as a specific area of concern due to "a particular concentration of socio-economic problems of its citizens" (URPofP, 2013, p. 32). It suffers high levels of unemployment and poverty, a high crime rate as well as low levels of entrepreneurial activity (these are presented in Figure 24 as criteria of urban deprivations). Śródmieście has become a deprived urban area which hinders investment activity and development. However, JESSICA projects could be implemented in accordance with the guidelines applicable at that time in dysfunctional urban areas delimited by at least one regeneration criterion. In practice, this means that in Poznań JESSICA projects were allowed to be executed in an area covered by criterion 1 as illustrated in Figure 24. Despite this, almost all projects that received JESSICA loans are placed in the area featuring the highest levels of concentration of negative phenomena.[34] In

---

[33] This unit is largely based on the findings provided by Idczak and Mrozik (2021).
[34] It should be added that the location of a project in a problem area designated by regeneration criteria was an essential condition for obtaining a JESSICA loan. The decisive criterion, however, was the project's capacity to ensure the repayability of JESSICA funding. For more see Idczak and Musiałkowska (2019).

this context, all JESSICA projects should be undoubtedly viewed in a positive light.

Regarding assessment of the territorial impact of JESSICA projects, Figure 25 shows that not all projects fully comply with the territorial cohesion approach to counteract multiple urban deprivation. What is interesting about the data in Figure 26 is that two projects clearly stand out among others in terms of the value of the territorial impacts indicator (TIM). These are a parking lot (project 2) and a hotel (project 4) located in the Śródka district. At first glance, such a result might come as a surprise. However, closer inspection of the data shows that these projects were rated highly in all assessment dimensions. A reasonable explanation for this outcome is that these projects, through their comprehensiveness, were able to fill the existing socio-economic gap and overcome the existent market failures, and consequently effectively meet the special needs of particular locations. For instance, project 2 resulted in the creation of, on the one hand, a four-level underground car park which led to the improvement of the parking system in the city centre, and on the other, modern infrastructure for commercial office activities intended for public and private entities but most of all for civic organisations. The project's added value brought about the formation of the new functions notably as regards the historical value of Kolegiacki Square (it was just a car park earlier) and innumerable social effects attained as a result of charity and support foundations based in the building. Project 4, in turn, relied on the reconstruction and adaptation of an old tenement house to hotel functions. It is important to remark that this undertaking was placed right on the historic market square of the Śródka district[35]. In fact, renewal of this building not only allowed the preservation of the historic urban tissue of this district and, through the improvement of public spaces, formation of an architecturally harmonious whole, but also resulted in the introduction of new functions creating favourable conditions for growth. In addition, the project included a strong social component, which, having regard to Śródka's needs, have had the utmost importance. Concretely, a new restaurant was established in the building that operates as a social cooperative. The restaurant staff consists of people who have returned to the labour market after taking part in social and professional reintegration programmes. Thus, it promotes social inclusion and provides a real chance to improve people's lives. The results obtained from the analysis of TIM can be compared in Figure 26.

---

[35] It is necessary here to clarify exactly that the Śródka, although it is the oldest district of the city, for a long time was one of the most deprived area in Poznan. It was a zone riddled with poor housing, blighted by unemployment and socially excluded from other more prosperous districts.

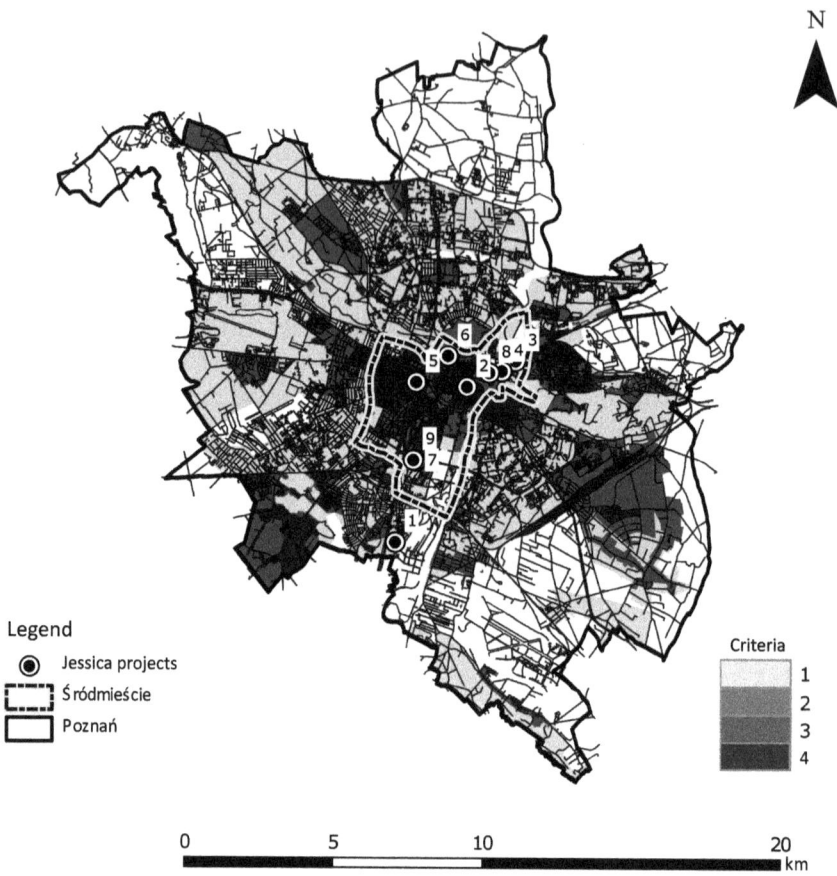

Figure 24: Location of JESSICA project in Poznań
Source: the authors' own elaboration

As far as the other JESSICA projects are concerned, Figure 26 reveals that their TIM values do not deviate from the average level of all projects. Nevertheless, one important observation should be made regarding their potential impacts values (PIP), which in all cases are significantly higher than TIM values. One might simply even say that the territorial impacts of JESSICA projects measured through the lens of PIP provide a satisfactory level of desired added value in deprived urban areas in Poznań. PIP, however, does not take into account the policy intensity (PI) and urban sensibility (US). Admittedly, while PI does not affect the PIP values, US alters them significantly here such that the TIM values differ remarkably as a result. In this respect it appears clear that the scopes of those projects do not fully comply with the diagnosed requirements and needs of par-

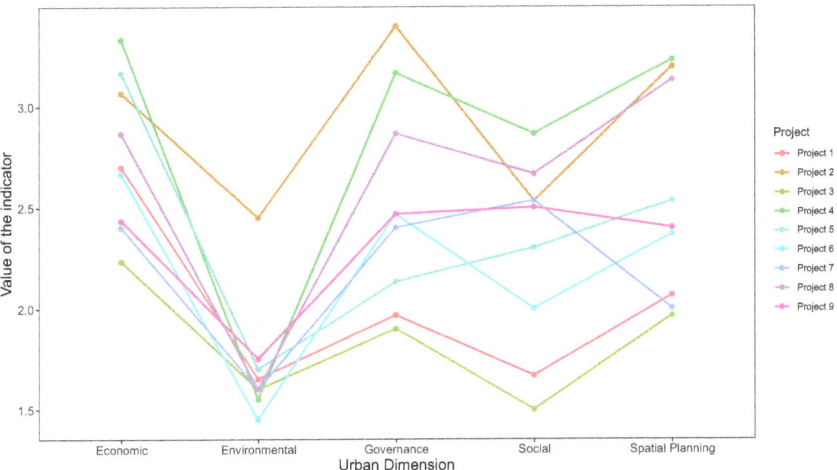

Figure 25: Sub-indicators in the assessment of the territorial impact of JESSICA projects implemented in Poznań
Source: the authors' own elaboration

ticular urban areas. It does not mean that those projects are inappropriate and do not respond inherently to the main challenges facing the particular deprived urban areas. Especially, since all of them have had an important role in overcoming structural barriers and stimulating social, cultural and business activities in their locations. But the projects rated lower do not entirely meet the essential assumptions of the integrated territorial approach, in the strictest sense of this term. By way of illustration, "Galeria Tumska" in the Cathedral Island enabled the renovation of the antique building and the creation of a restaurant and centre of cultural life, the "Bałtyk" building provided a modern office and relaxation spaces as well as a publicly available "bay of art" courtyard made in the formerly underused areas, the Medical Centre HCP Sp. z o.o. expanded the scope of the health services (some of them were previously unavailable) by means of the modernisation and extension of its building. The reason for the unsatisfactory territorial impacts of these projects becomes clear when looking at their US values. The lower US values imply that the activities under these projects' scopes, according to the experts' judgement, are not as relevant as they could be to the specific needs of the particular urban areas. Although the projects, throughout their economic and non-economic activities, create local benefits or help spread the benefits accruing from them, they do not take full advantage of the territorial approach which underlines a deep anchorage in the specificity of a given territory. Hence, the contributions of these projects to mitigating social,

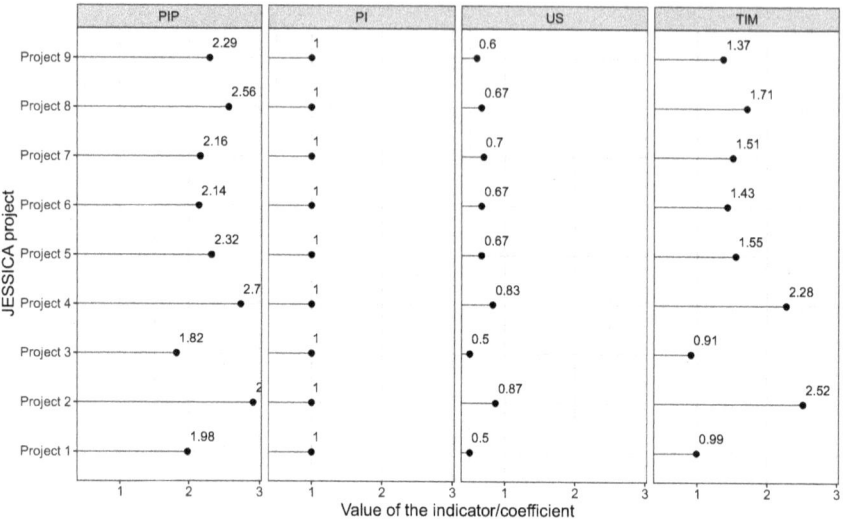

Figure 26: Indicators in the assessment of the territorial impact of JESSICA projects implemented in Poznań
Note: The chart includes the averaged results of the judgement made by ten experts. PIP means Potential Impact of a Project. It was calculated as a geometric mean of the five dimension indicators. TIM denotes Territorial Impacts of a Project. It is a result of the multiplication of PIP by the PI and US indicators. PI stands for the importance of the particular measures in development policy and the amount of money used. Since the regenerative projects are very important in current urban policy, the value of PIP was defined arbitrarily. US means the relevance and territorial development needs, in other words, whether the given area needs such changes as those introduced by a project.
The particular projects are: 1 – Development of the Poznań Industry and Technology Park – stage II; 2 – Construction of a parking lot and commercial office building at Za Bramką street in Poznań; 3 – Regeneration of the degraded area at Małachowskiego street and the construction of the Office Centre "Podwale"; 4 – Reconstruction, extension and superstructure and use change of a tenement to service and guesthouse in the Poznań's Śródka district; 5 – Construction of a commercial office building "Bałtyk" in Poznań along with regeneration of an adjacent area and development of public space; 6 – Adaptation of the former "Polonez" hotel to the new socio-economic functions; 7 – Extension and modernisation of the Medical Centre HCP Sp. z o.o.; 8 – "Galeria Tumska" in Poznań – restaurant and centre of cultural life of the Cathedral Island in the antique interiors of the eighteen-century canonry; 9 – Extension and modernisation of the Medical Centre HCP Sp. z o.o. through the establishment of a Centre for Mental Health.
Source: the authors' own elaboration

economic and environmental harm may not be totally effective, and some diagnosed problems of individual areas may remain unresolved and could hamper the balanced implementation of the entire urban regeneration programme.

By contrast, Figure 26 also reports two projects that were assessed well below the average level, namely, the Poznań Industry and Technology Park (project 1) and the Office Centre "Podwale" (project 3). Both projects aimed at stimulating the emergence of new businesses, the former, located outside Śródmieście, also by way of incubating. As shown, their relatively low TIM values arise not only from the medium levels of UP indicators but also from the lower level of the sub-indicators describing particular urban dimensions. They poorly reflect the specific needs of their location and, conversely, their contribution to resolving the social problems and environmental issues was also judged as unsatisfactory. This means that projects focused mostly on boosting only the creation of new business have a significantly lesser impact on deprived urban areas and thus do not effectively address the challenges of these less-favoured areas.

With all this in mind, these results make it possible to conclude that the territorial impacts of JESSICA projects were generally positive and only two projects were rated as low. It also means that all of the analysed projects have contributed to enhancing the territorial cohesion of the urban areas of the city of Poznań. Nonetheless, their impacts are considerably diversified. The main reason for these relatively interesting results is that some of them were not sufficiently well-tailored to the specific needs of the particular urban areas. A possible explanation for this might be the fact that one of the decisive criteria for granting JESSICA loans is repayability. Thus, the Urban Development Bank, who is an official body responsible for distributing JESSICA funds, may be more willing to provide a JESSICA loan to such projects that display higher profitability and repayment security than those with well-designed scopes of activities.

Results on the spatial distribution of the JESSICA funding
This section presents the key empirical findings stemming from the study, consisting of the following[36]: (1) discovering spatial dependencies through SDE as a GIS technique for delineating the geographical distribution trend of the features of interest under study; (2) examining the spatial allocation of JESSICA funding across the Polish cities with a view to investigate whether this kind of funding supported the implementation of the urban projects in cities of differing sizes in the five regions.

As noted, SDE can be calculated on the basis of the locations of the features or some attribute values associated with the features. To put it simply, by draw-

---

36 This unit is based on the study delivered previously by Idczak, Mrozik, and Musiałkowska (2021).

ing the features on a map one may get orientation, however, by computing SDE one may receive a clear trend. Figure 27 shows the location of JESSICA projects in Poland as well as the standard deviational ellipse calculated for three aspects: location of JESSICA projects, their total value and the value of the JESSICA loan granted to particular projects. First, it highlights that JESSICA projects are scattered across the JESSICA regions, that is, are placed in regions' different cities, and not only their capital cities. However, the direction of the project dispersion points to an unequal distribution of them in a regional space – in all cases the ellipses are located neither centrally in the particular regions nor are their shapes circular. Moreover, a similar conclusion is provided by the analysis of the ellipses' areas. In all cases, the areas enclosed by the ellipses actually occupy smaller areas compared to the total surface of the particular JESSICA regions, indicating that the projects are thinly spread. Notwithstanding this, the overall spatial patterns of projects revealed that the most uniform distribution of them can be found in the Mazowieckie and Wielkopolskie regions. As can be seen from Table 10, the azimuth (respectively 103.75° and 150.12°) reflects the trend directions, making it possible to see that the distribution of projects to a certain extent mirrors the shape of the regional boundaries, whereas the spatial dispersion of projects is more even in Wielkopolskie region than in Mazowieckie region. Furthermore, this spatial pattern is noticeably illustrated by the concentration index whose value at the level of approximately 65% in both regions proves a relatively wide distribution.

Conversely, in two other regions, namely Pomorskie and Śląskie, JESSICA projects are more concentrated in one locality than they are in other regions. The areas enclosed by ellipses in both regions are considerably smaller than their territories, and if so, the smaller the area of the ellipse is, the denser the distribution of JESSICA projects appears. In the case of Pomorskie region, this fact is further confirmed by the concentration index (82%) showing the overwhelming majority of points occurring within the ellipse. These results may be explained by the fact that those regions are distinguished by special agglomerative linkages which means that one continuous urban area covers more than only one city, that is, the so-called Tri-city in Pomorskie, and in Śląskie region the cities being part of the Upper Silesian conurbation. It is also noticeable that a relatively low level of project dispersion was also detected in Zachodniopomorskie region, which coincides most likely with the fact that 14 out of 19 projects were clustered in two cities – Szczecin and Świnoujście.

Furthermore, the most striking results to emerge from the data are the strong relationship between the value of JESSICA projects and the value of JESSICA loans, and the relatively comparable distribution of these two attributes with the locations of JESSICA projects across particular regions. This, on the one

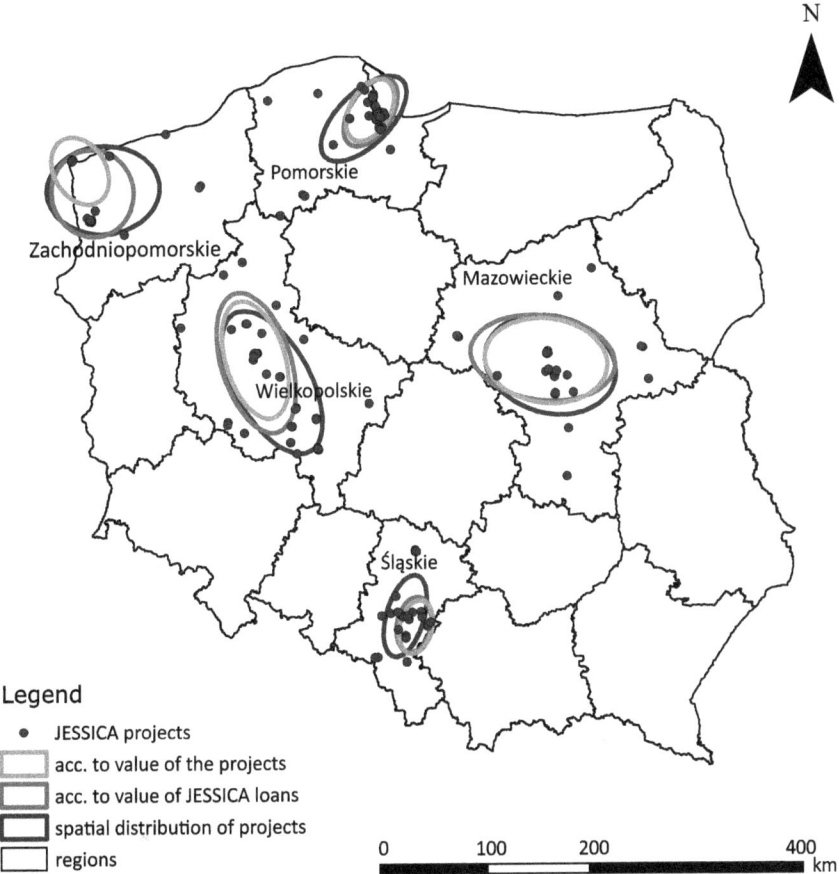

Figure 27: SDE for the spatial spread of the JESSICA projects in Poland
Source: the authors' own elaboration

hand, indicates the strong correlations between the value of JESSICA projects and the value of JESSICA loans,[37] but on the other, shows that there are no significant differences between these two attributes and the locations of JESSICA projects. However, what is also interesting about the data in Figure 27 and Table 10 is the difference in the distribution of projects in terms of their value and the value of JESSICA loans in Zachodniopomorskie region. The ellipse enclosing the projects in respect of the value of JESSICA loans has the azimuth

---

[37] The correlation coefficient between those two variables reaches .775, and is significant at p < .01.

of 157.16° and eccentricity index of 0.27. The former means that the JESSICA allocation was widely scattered, while the latter indicates a more circular distribution. The projects analysed by the same indices in terms of their values seem to be more linearly distributed. To conclude this part of the analysis, it can be suggested that the allocation of JESSICA funding across particular regions does not significantly differ from the location of JESSICA projects. These findings coincide with those of Idczak, Musiałkowska and Mrozik (2019b, pp. 212–213) which reveal that JESSICA projects in terms of their value and the size of the JESSICA loan do not vary by their location.

Table 10: SDE parameters of JESSICA projects in five regions

Region	Ellipse	Ellipse centre		Area (km²)	Azimuth° (orientation)	Eccentricity	Concentration (%)
		Major axis (km)	Minor axis (km)				
Maz	SDEofP	62.01	43.88	8548.46	103.75	0.71	64.52
	SDEofP-JL	67.80	38.29	8154.97	97.42	0.83	64.52
	SDEofP-JV	57.34	38.23	6885.64	97.20	0.75	64.52
Pom	SDEofP	49.83	24.23	3792.39	46.96	0.87	82.22
	SDEofP-JL	34.62	19.25	2093.67	34.89	0.83	80.00
	SDEofP-JV	30.68	18.70	1801.57	31.64	0.79	80.00
Slas	SDEofP	38.20	17.48	2097.26	16.97	0.89	61.54
	SDEofP-JL	25.57	15.73	1263.12	12.16	0.79	53.85
	SDEofP-JV	24.58	15.12	1167.33	14.57	0.79	46.15
Wiel	SDEofP	71.88	35.14	7934.76	150.12	0.87	65.00
	SDEofP-JL	65.89	32.59	6744.92	162.03	0.87	40.00
	SDEofP-JV	55.16	27.58	4779.47	162.22	0.87	40.00

Table 10: SDE parameters of JESSICA projects in five regions *(Continued)*

Region	Ellipse	Ellipse centre		Area (km²)	Azimuth° (orientation)	Eccentricity	Concentration (%)
		Major axis (km)	Minor axis (km)				
Zach	SDEofP	52.82	39.95	6629.11	86.62	0.65	78.95
	SDEofP-JL	39.61	38.18	4750.43	157.16	0.27	78.95
	SDEofP-JV	32.75	24.01	2470.31	147.28	0.68	31.58

Note: *Maz, Pom, Slas, Wiel and Zach* denote the names of the JESSICA regions respectively: Mazowieckie, Pomorskie, Śląskie, Wielkopolskie, Zachodniopomorskie. *SDEofP, SDEofP-JL and SDEofP-JV* mean respectively SDE of the JESSICA projects, SDE of the JESSICA projects weighted by the value of the JESSICA loan, SDE of the JESSICA projects weighted by their total values. *Concentration* index was calculated as the ratio of points (projects) within the ellipse compared to the entire population of projects expressed in particular regions.
Source: the authors' own elaboration

For the sake of completeness, the investigation was expanded to gain a deeper insight into the spatial dependencies of JESSICA funding allocation with regard to the metropolitan areas of the regional capital cities (MA). Such a breakdown is justified because, as argued by Smętkowski, Jałowiecki and Gorzelak (2009) and Śleszyński (2013), these areas, on the one hand, consisting of the major city (densely inhabited urban core) and its adjacent lower-density areas, form spatially and functionally linked zones based on people's daily movements, while on the other, their peripheral surroundings often suffer adverse changes by reason of the polycentric development. Thus, cities located within MA may have higher capacities to absorb funding due to their strong socio-economic ties than those laying outside. From Figures 28–32 we can see that this statement might be reasonable. At first glance, one can observe that the higher number of JESSICA projects were located within MA than those which are outside them. What emerges from the data is that two-thirds of the JESSICA projects are situated in the interior of MA. The only region in which the number of projects located outside MA (22 out of 40) exceeds the number of projects placed internally is the Wielkopolskie region. Similar relatively high levels of unequal distribution are shown in terms of the allocation of JESSICA funding between inside versus outside MA-located projects. Nearly 70% of the total JESSICA funding was directed towards urban projects implemented in cities covered by MA. In this context, the Pomorskie region stands out against the other regions as 93% of JESSICA assistance was intended there for supporting the implementation of urban projects located within MA. Overall, urban projects in cities encompassed by the economic and functional extent of MA, as expected, received the greater part of the JESSICA assistance.

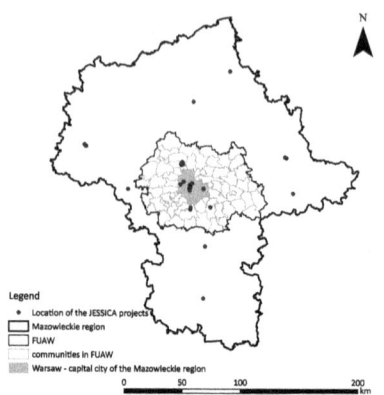

Figure 28: Location of the JESSICA projects in Mazowieckie in the context of MA*
Source: the authors' own elaboration

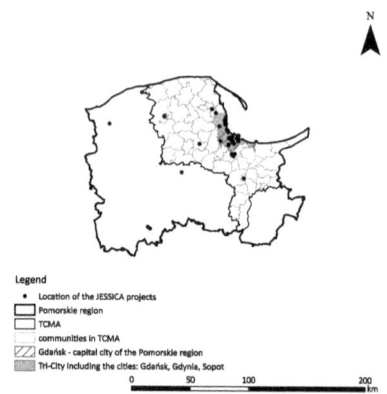

Figure 29: Location of the JESSICA projects in Pomorskie in the context of MA*
Source: the authors' own elaboration

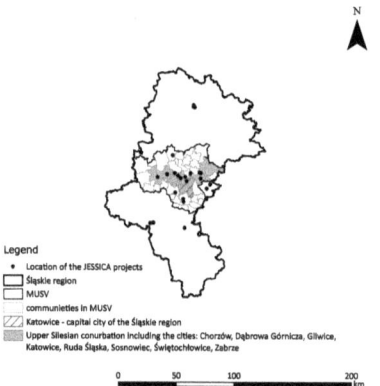

Figure 30: Location of the JESSICA projects in Śląskie in the context of MA*
Source: the authors' own elaboration

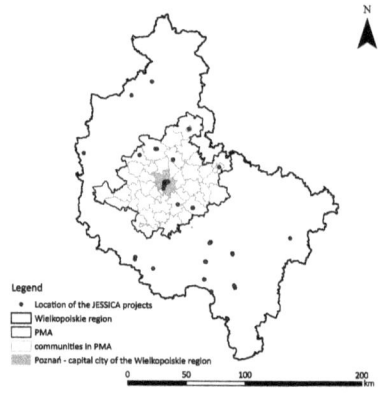

Figure 31: Location of the JESSICA projects in Wielkopolskie in the context of MA*
Source: the authors' own elaboration

The analytical work carried out so far has provided evidence on the spatial dependencies of the projects and JESSICA funding, but has not shown any information about the distribution of JESSICA funding among Polish cities. Therefore, we move on now to determine whether the size of the city is of significance for the allocation of the JESSICA funding, and also for the project's capacity to ensure repayability of the JESSICA loan. Figure 33 illustrates the distribution pattern of

JESSICA funding across cities located within JESSICA regions. It is evident that the vast majority of the JESSICA funds reached the small number of cities in particular regions. To put this more in detail, Figure 34 pinpoints exactly all the mutual dependencies of the features being investigated. This figure is quite revealing in several ways. First, it shows that the JESSICA projects have been situated in all types of cities regardless of their size. Thus, the recipients of JESSICA funding are large, medium-sized and small cities. Second, the size of the city does not appear to be a relevant factor in examining the value of the JESSICA loan. In other words, in small cities projects supported by both the high and low value of the loans, and vice versa, were implemented. Third, there is no linear relationship between the city's size and the project's capacity to ensure repayability of the JESSICA loan. This means that the capacities for generating revenues on the basis of the primary business activities, thus ensuring repayability of the JESSICA loan, occur in all kinds of cities. Likewise, the type of beneficiary does not show any significant relations between variables with the visible exception of the Zachodniopomorskie region where the majority of projects were implemented by private entities.

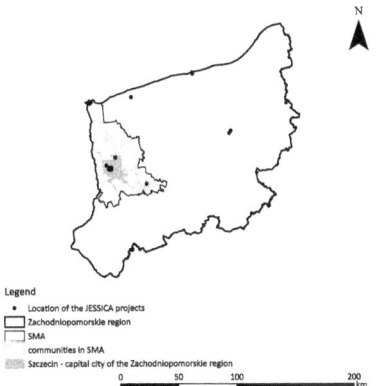

Figure 32: Location of the JESSICA projects in Zachodniopomorskie in the context of MA*
Source: the authors' own elaboration
* Metropolitan areas were designated on the basis of the delineation provided for in the regional spatial managements plans. They are as follows: Urban Functional Area of the City of Warsaw in the Mazowieckie region (FUAW, 2018), Tri-City Metropolitan Area (Gdańsk-Gdynia-Sopot) in the Pomorskie region (TCMA, 2016), Metropolis of the Upper Silesian Valley in the Śląskie region (MUSV, 2017), Poznań Metropolitan Area in the Wielkopolskie region (PMA, 2019), Szczecin Metropolitan Area in the Zachodniopomorskie region (SMA, 2020).

To provide further insights into the analysis, Table 11 presents the percentage of the value of the JESSICA funding granted to projects in particular cities. Closer

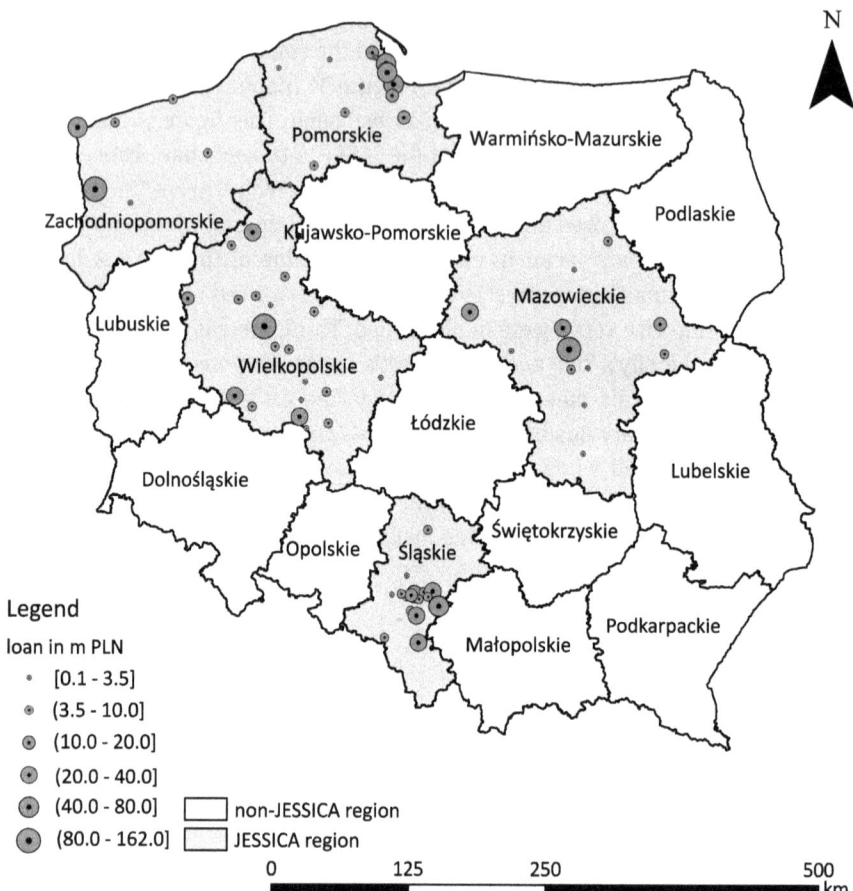

Figure 33: Distribution of JESSICA funding across Polish cities
Source: the authors' own elaboration

inspection of the table shows that almost half (47.5%) of the JESSICA funds was transferred to small and medium-sized cities. Half of the JESSICA funding was granted to support 83 projects (out of 161) implemented in small and medium-sized cities. However, the figures demonstrate a somewhat more diverse picture of these relationships at the regional level. Despite this, the findings clearly reveal that JESSICA funding was spread across cities of a different size, and not only concentrated in the largest ones.

Overall, the results are somewhat counterintuitive. Although it cannot be said that the projects and JESSICA funds were spread evenly throughout the five regions, it is noteworthy that this type of EU support was not only absorbed

Table 11: Distribution of the JESSICA projects and funding among Polish cities*

City class	Mazowieckie		Pomorskie		Śląskie		Wielkopolskie		Zachodniopomorskie		Total	
	P-JF	N-P	P-JF	N-P	P-JF	N-P	P-JF	N-P	P-JF	N-P	P-JF	N-P
Extra-large cities	43.0	11	28.6	17	1.9	1	48.6	9	53.8	8	33.8	46
Large cities	21.6	5	24.1	12	45.9	15	0.0	0	0.0	0	18.7	32
Medium-sized cities	25.5	10	45.7	13	52.2	10	34.7	18	39.3	8	40.0	59
Small cities	9.9	5	1.6	3	0.0	0	16.7	13	7.0	3	7.5	24
Total	100.0	31	100.0	45	100.0	26	100.0	40	100.0	19	100.0	161

* P-JF means the percentage of total JESSICA allocation; N-P denotes the number of JESSICA projects.
Source: the authors' own elaboration

into the JESSICA projects implemented in the largest cities. About half of the total JESSICA assistance was passed on to beneficiaries that executed projects in small and medium-sized cities. More generally, it can thus be argued that the allocation of JESSICA funds in the spatial dimension seems to be dispersed and not only major regional cities were supported by JESSICA funds but also other cities. This outcome, in turn, contrasts with previous results reported by Churski, Borowczak, and Perdał (2015, pp. 188–192) who found that the funds under cohesion policy (grants) are mainly absorbed by the strongest urban centres. Admittedly, the allocation of JESSICA funding was not conditional on any territorialised criteria and its territorial pattern of distribution follows from an interest expressed by beneficiaries, as confirmed by the interviewees.[38]

---

[38] Interviews with experts, 25 June 2013, 15 October 2013, 8 May 2014, 23 May 2016. Interviews with beneficiaries, 26 June 2013, 9 July 2013, 23 May 2016. Interviews with representatives of cities, 19 June 2013, 7 November 2014, 2 March 2017. Note that in order to ensure the anonymity of interview data, places where interviews were held will not be disclosed throughout this study. The reason for this is that there were cities where only one project was implemented. Thus, the disclosure of places could bring about the identification of interviewees, mainly the JESSICA beneficiaries.

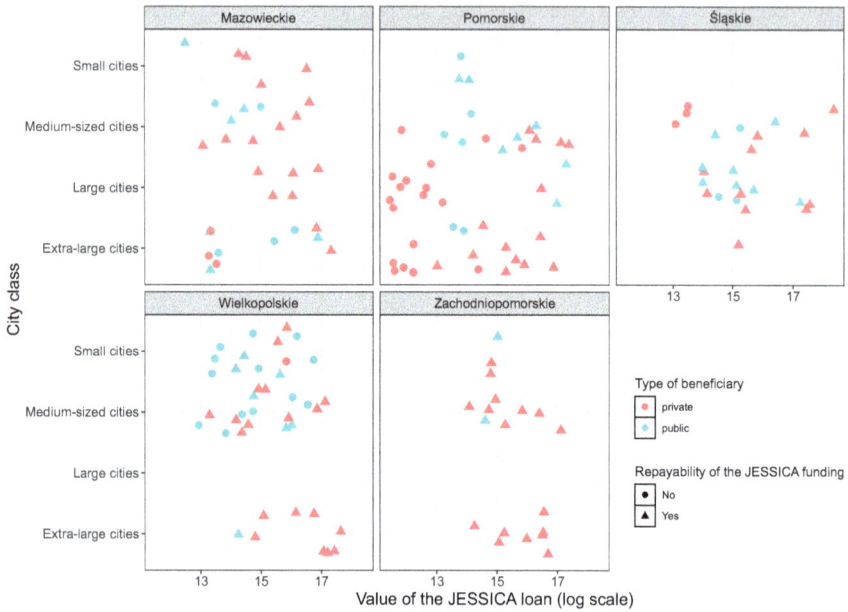

Figure 34: Mutual dependencies of the city's size and the value of the JESSICA loan
Source: the authors' own elaboration

5.5 Synthesis and assessment: lessons and added value

The most obvious finding to emerge from this study is that every third JESSICA project pursued mainly by public entities did not provide any revenues and did not generate any desired market effects. Just over half of the projects contributed to creating positive social impacts. Further, slightly more than a half of all beneficiaries classified as public entities implemented non-revenue-generating projects. Promoters of these projects had to cover their own repayment needs from sources other than sales revenues which, in turn, reduced notably the repayable nature of JESSICA financing. A vast majority of the projects that made it possible to achieve the expected socio-economic effects concerned, in particular, such investment areas as cultural heritage, redevelopment of brownfield sites and urban infrastructure. The greatest number of projects characterised by not providing an intended stimulus for local communities were those implemented basically within two support areas: energy efficiency and urban infrastructure. The scope of these projects was relatively narrow and as far as the first area of support is concerned, it was mainly focused on improving the energy efficiency of residential buildings or public utility facilities. Those projects consist, in particular, in the modernisation or improvement of physical and technical characteristics of residential infrastructure, and their main "net value added" is created primarily as a result of the reduction of operational costs due to savings engendered by the rise of energy efficiency. By contrast, some projects in the area of urban infrastructure, which resulted in positive social impacts but, in the light of the adopted assumptions, did not bring the desired market effects and repayability, mainly consisted in the improvement of public infrastructure, thus increasing urban and architectural values and the sense of security in city public spaces. These were mainly investments involving the construction or modernisation of playgrounds, recreational parks, outdoor gyms, school or residential playgrounds, parking lots, etc. Indeed, these projects are non-revenue-generating projects and bring rather weak market effects, if any at all, but provide public goods and services in a cost-effective manner which is essential for sustainable urban development.

The study also identified the factors affecting the capacities of the JESSICA projects to generate revenues, produce positive market effects and create positive social impacts. The empirical results can be summarised as follows. As regards revenue generation, the capacity of projects to generate own revenues is higher when, first, they are implemented by companies, and second, they are characterised by a higher value (total cost of a project). As regards bringing positive market effects, the overwhelming factor that has the greatest impact on the occurrence of the desired market effects is the profitability of the project, i.e. the provision of products or services in exchange for a specific cash equivalent. This feature, as expected, constitutes a necessary condition in the case of investment projects implemented by private entities. In the case of public projects focused on the provision of public goods, the generation of revenues does not have to translate into profitability of the project (often even at the operating level), but it is certainly a derivative of the market activity. The second feature that also turned out to be statistically significant is the value of the JESSICA project – the higher the value, the greater the probability for market effects. As regards the social impacts, the most expected effects related to this matter were delivered by projects financed within three support areas: heritage and culture, redevelopment of brownfield sites and urban infrastructure. All in all, findings emerging from the empirical analysis suggest that the most appropriate projects to be considered for JESSICA support are those of a high value and implemented by companies. Those kinds of projects covering often diverse business activities and offering a comprehensive range of services or goods are not only able, by nature, to generate profits and ensure the repayment of the loan based on their self-financing capacity, but can also provide, at the same time, positive externalities for the local citizens in line with the integrated urban development plans. Moreover, the projects characterised by high value and pursued by entities having the company status involve private capital and consequently do generate capital back-flows. In this sense, they contribute to the leverage effects and thereby raise the role of JESSICA as a powerful instrument aimed at addressing existing market failures.

Returning to the issue of energy efficiency projects and "non-market" urban projects, it should be noted that many of them are not only non-profit operating but also do not generate any revenues. The so-called economic component covered by their operational scope is mainly due to the specific benefits that the investment produces for society. In the case of public investments, these were projects in which financing in the form of a JESSICA loan did not constitute state aid (schools, kindergartens, playgrounds etc.). Private investments, in turn, were carried out mainly by and for the benefit of housing cooperatives or communities (residential buildings). They are inherently devoid of a business element, and the profitability condition required to repay the JESSICA loan was replaced by the investor's creditworthiness. Adopting such a solution was possible only in the case of important and socially desirable projects. The scale of the type of loan was relatively large, which translated into a large number of non-market projects. Admittedly, these investments allow the generation of significant savings at the operating level and increased economic efficiency, but as such they do not provide the broader impact required by the JESSICA framework. These conclusions are in line with the results of research conducted by Breuer and Brueser (2013), who prove that such projects should not always be viewed in terms of market failures and thus supported by public funding. However, this does not mean that those non-market projects should not be perceived as producing positive effects. Many of them had a significant impact on the structural changes in deprived urban areas and contributed to stimulating their development. However, due to their specific nature, such projects do not always fit into the JESSICA funding model. They do not integrate multiple stakeholders and create partnerships for the development of specific urban areas. As a result, the JESSICA loan becomes a conventional credit or a loan (granted under better financing conditions) that can be repaid with a project's savings or various external sources in respect of a project's cash flows. Those projects do not contain investment capital and therefore generate no return on investment. Hence, they diminish the role of the JESSICA initiative as a potentially effective instrument in overcoming existing market failures.

One of the key assumptions of the JESSICA initiative was to contribute to sustainable urban development through the regeneration of the deprived areas of European cities. To this end, projects granted by the JESSICA revolving mechanisms and the outcomes resulting from their implementation were assessed drawing on the original assessment model. This is based on five contexts of sustainable urban development and takes into account the specific requirements funded by the European funds. The five contexts – namely financial, economic, social, spatial and horizontal – stipulated the evaluation dimensions of the projects and their outcomes. The results revealed that not all dimensions were reasonably represented by the JESSICA projects. The best represented dimensions were the financial, economic and spatial dimensions. In turn, the social and horizontal dimensions primarily responsible for the projects delivering positive externalities to society were not satisfactorily addressed, thus indicating a relatively weak performance in terms of dealing with bottlenecks diagnosed in particular urban areas. More detailed evidence derived from the value of composite indicators points to a strong correlation between the capacity of the projects to generate revenues, and the overall objective represented by the assessment model (sustainable urban development). In general, the projects that generate revenue are the largest contributors to sustainable urban development. A similar dependency pertains to the composite indicator and the status of the project promoter, i.e. private entity. Furthermore, closer inspection of the cluster analysis results (applied to reveal natural groupings of projects in terms of the JESSICA support areas) showed that the projects that reflect the JESSICA priorities in the best way are those executed within two support areas, that is, heritage and culture, and the redevelopment of brownfield sites. Taken together, these results suggest that the projects of higher value, generating revenue, coordinated by private entities and related to the aforementioned support areas bring more results in terms of all five dimensions that are responsible for assuring the complexity of sustainable urban development. When combining these findings with the previous ones, the conclusion can be drawn that the projects of a relatively high value and implemented by private entities emerge to be the best performers, thus claiming the JESSICA-led intervention.

Further analysis focused on assessing the impact of JESSICA projects on territorial cohesion at the local level provided some very interesting insights. It was found that economically demanding projects, as JESSICA projects seem to be, succeeded in dealing with the structural problems of less-favoured urban areas. Indeed, this outcome clearly demonstrates that repayable supportive instruments can be effectively applied to overcome market failures in urban areas. The most significant finding to emerge from the results is that the greatest territorial impacts are generated by those projects that best respond to the specific needs of particular deprived areas of the city. The more multiple and complex JESSICA projects are in relation to an individual urban area, the more they contribute to improvement of the territorial cohesion of urban areas. This means that projects fulfilling the requirements of territorial (integrated) perspectives of urban development, to the maximum possible extent, make the most efficient use of JESSICA funding. In general, it may be concluded that the results about the impacts of JESSICA projects on urban areas point to their positive contribution to improving the urban cohesion of a city.

Another finding from the study revealed that, despite some existing differentiations and dissimilarities between JESSICA regions in the implementation of the projects on account of their operational scopes, support areas or the achieved effects, the location of a project understood in terms of its capital city/non-capital city relation appeared to be statistically insignificant. This could indicate that JESSICA financial support was relatively equally distributed within particular JESSICA regions. In order to overcome the limitation of this analysis relying on the fact that location was understood in dichotomous terms, an in-depth examination was carried out to look closer at the spatial allocations of JESSICA funding across Polish cities within particular JESSICA regions, also having regard to the size of the cities. The analysis showed that the repayable assistance provided by JESSICA was transferred to many cities of different sizes, and nearly half of these funds were used to implement projects in small and medium-sized cities. This clearly suggests that, contrary to expectations, smaller cities have also considerably benefited from this instrument. Moreover, the spatial factor was not likely to be of great significance in absorbing JESSICA funds in relation to the repayment capacity of the JESSICA projects. This means that the projects best matching the assumptions of the JESSICA initiative were implemented in various cities, irrespective of their size and location. Furthermore, the examination covered also the dependencies in the context of the inside versus outside project location with regard to metropolitan areas of the capital cities of the particular regions (MA). The findings revealed that the bulk of JESSICA funding was addressed to investments undertaken, admittedly, in different cities regardless of their size but most of them were located within MA. This may confirm a more complex nature of the capacities in terms of the repayable assistance which accrues to project implementers in the functionally linked cities. This field of interest for policy-makers turns out to be relevant in order to build a more territorially targeted framework of EU financial instruments – more funds in the form of a repayable aid allocated to MA, whereas non-repayable grants channelled to the outlying cities.

In summary, as illustrated, the repayable assistance furnished by the JESSICA initiative provided an important incentive for triggering urban investments in both more and less dynamic urban areas, so as to contribute to increasing cohesion and growth across whole regions. However, not all JESSICA projects turned out to be sufficiently multiple and complex to meet the demanding requirements and targets of the revolving support mechanism.

6 Overall assessment and policy recommendations

6.1 Added value and challenges

The findings provided by this study add to the understanding of how the CP financial engineering instruments (demonstrated by the example of JESSICA) work in practice to support structural changes in urban areas. The analysis was carried out from the perspective of the implementation of the JESSICA projects and the effects they induced in particular Polish cities. In addition to that, the analysis was conducted in the context of the integrated approach to urban regeneration in order to compare the implementation process of the JESSICA projects with a theoretical model underpinning a proper approach to public interventions deployed to tackle urban deterioration. It can be stated that the overall assessment of JESSICA in confronting urban challenges is positive, albeit with some caveats. First, this instrument contributed to filling a finance gap for investment in deprived urban areas, enabling the realisation of investments, most of which would not have happened without financial support available at that time. A repayment assistance scheme resulted also in an increase in awareness among the beneficiaries of the European funds of a necessity to place greater focus on the financial and economic viability of the projects in the long run. Moreover, the projects are expected to be implemented in accordance with any applicable requirements in order to ensure efficiency and economic balance not only in the duration of their implementation but also throughout the whole reference period. This requires the project operations should be better matched to actual market conditions. Such an approach to the commercial viability of the undertakings over time, observed in many of the pursued projects, represents a crucial factor in ensuring affective and tailor-made actions aimed at addressing market failures.

Good examples of JESSICA projects that offered a variety of commercial products or services, while providing some facilities or services designed for the benefit and around the needs of residents, show clear signs of having a positive effect on broadly defined public interventions in urban areas. First, JESSICA triggered a change in the so-called grant-culture in favour of non-grant assistance, proving that public intervention targeted at cities based on repayable financial resources can be both effective and successful. Second, the JESSICA re-

---

Piotr Idczak

https://doi.org/10.1515/9783110762198-010

volving mechanism gave rise to the phasing out of dependence on EU grants and laid the foundations for the future reduction of non-reimbursable grants from CP. Next, the beneficiaries of CP funds at the regional and local levels gained new experience and expertise on dealing with the implementation of urban projects under a new supportive system based on multi-level and cross-sectoral cooperation. Finally, JESSICA changed the approach of financial institutions (formally UDFs but practically banks) to the issue of financing relatively risky investments in urban areas. By way of illustration, one of the interviewees said: *it was the first time when for the bank the environmental issues and project's social impacts were just as important as the assumption of business plan, internal rate of return and collateral for a loan.*[39] In addition, a few beneficiaries clearly stated that they could not apply for EU grants due to the non-eligibility of some of the costs associated with the operations they intended to implement. Thanks to the flexibility of JESSICA, it turned out to be possible. As one interviewee even put it: *implementation of the project under JESSICA funding was not so complicated in bureaucratic terms compared to grant-based funding.*[40] There are no bank charges and commissions for a loan granted by a UDF, and the interests are cheaper compared to credit products available in the market. Among the positive points one more needs to be mentioned, namely, the repayable funding provided by JESSICA beneficiaries and the interests paid by them. The managing authority could set up a regional fund from the resulting legacy resources making it possible to reuse them.

Conversely, in the course of this study, it appeared that there are some shortcomings in both the implementation level and the regulatory framework. Broadly, most of these shortcomings arise from the necessity of launching the "new philosophy" of financial management into a field which was primarily the domain of clear non-repayable grant-based intervention from European funds. The novelty of the JESSICA initiative and its revolving mechanism was not matched by the parallel creation of an effective set of legal regulations. As mentioned in section 3.4, the legal regulations related to FEIs were rather general. In the absence of clear provisions, the managing authorities had to apply the rules laid down under the relevant European funds regulations. This led to some interpretation problems and confusion because these regulations failed to take account of the specificities of the repayable instrument. Talking about this issue an interviewee said: *we always had more questions than answers, as a result, JESSICA became a challenging instrument, although, in accordance with the assump-*

---

[39] Interview with a beneficiary, 15 November 2018.
[40] Interview with a beneficiary, 14 November 2018.

*tions, it was not so.*⁴¹ The guidelines and recommendations prepared by COCOF provided guidance and clarifications on some issues regarding the setting up and implementation of FEIs. It should be added here that all interviewees on the implementation side highlighted a good cooperation between managing authorities (including the national one), EIB and UDFs.

Many beneficiaries and applicants reported problems with providing a proper guarantee with a view to ensuring the repayment of the JESSICA loan. Although there was a relatively wide variety of different forms of security for the loan repayment, the provision of many of them entailed often considerable additional costs that the beneficiaries had to incur. Consequently, these extra costs caused a real increase in the total cost of servicing the loan, making it unattractive to potential project promoters. JESSICA support became not much more attractive in comparison to the available market products. Savings of even a few percentage points did not encourage beneficiaries enough to take out a loan and then grapple with the red tape rules and documentations related to the EU funds. This effectively discouraged investors from involvement in applying for the "preferential" product that JESSICA represented. In this context, a further problem emerged regarding the risk of double financing. For instance, the guarantee funds that received financial support within the framework of the particular regional operational programme were not allowed to grant guarantees for other initiatives supported under that programme, which led to further loss of interest in this instrument.

A further problem identified, which could significantly result in low interest in JESSICA support and insufficient knowledge of the potential benefits and of how it functions, was a relatively weak communication policy. The observed shortage of information on JESSICA, in view of its seemingly more complex and challenging institutional framework, not only could have had a negative impact on the interest of potential investors but also could have limited the number of potential projects which at the appraisal stage could have been better assessed as providing a greater impact on local communities. By way of illustration, one of the interviewees, when asked how they found out about the JESSICA initiative, said: *accidentally, I was applying for credit at a bank and the bank informed me that my project perfectly met the requirements of JESSICA. I was glad because it was cheaper.*⁴² This is not a complaint to managing authorities or UDFs since the promotion of JESSICA did take place, which was confirmed dur-

---

41 Interview with the Marshal Office, 16 November 2018.
42 Interview with a beneficiary, 15 November 2018.

ing the collection of data for this study. However, information must not have been targeted properly and its range was insufficient.

A further challenge that was diagnosed, especially with respect to the theoretical achievements of this study, was linked to the final decision regarding the award of a loan. As is known, the JESSICA loan is granted by a UDF which, at the same time, takes full responsibility for the process of the appraisal of projects, their selection and making the decision on the award. Many interviewees argued that the UDF (i.e. a bank), in its decisions, is consistently geared towards the objectives which may differ from those of the managing authorities and city authorities.[43] To put it simply, commenting on this issue, some interviewees said that UDF pays considerably more attention to such aspects as: soundness of the financial business plan (feasibility study), level of the internal rate of return, guarantee of a loan, etc.[44] Managing authorities in turn wish in particular to highlight the social and environmental impacts of the projects on urban areas, thus displaying consistency with their commitment to achieving the operational programmes' and CP's objectives. As a result, some projects, characterised by a complex range of operations aimed at addressing many urban problems but simultaneously bearing a high level of investment risk, could be assessed lower by the UDF than those projects which are more uniform and ensure acceptable and safe levels of operating risk. In practice, the task of JESSICA to provide incentives for the private sector to enter into new and rather risky markets of urban areas generally appeared to be very challenging. As the findings from the Chapter 5 suggest, there were many projects in which the social and environmental issues were not treated as high priorities, while primarily an investment component was clearly visible. Since all of them were located in deprived urban areas delineated by the concentration of negative socio-economic phenomena, they appeared not to have been fully tailored to the specific needs of particular areas.

Turning now to the role of cities, it can be said that they, in principle, became "passive beneficiaries" of CP and, especially, of JESSICA. This decreased the importance of the intention to achieve greater added value by implementing integrated policy bundles, in a wider perspective, and IPSUDs, in a narrower perspective, by cities. With respect to JESSICA, one interviewee commented: *JESSICA funding system ignored the main decision-maker in terms of urban policy – the city authorities. Their role was limited to confirmation as to whether a particular proj-*

---

[43] For example: interviews with beneficiaries, 14 November 2018, 15 November 2018. Interviews with experts, 23 May 2016, 17 March 2017, 7 September 2018.
[44] For example: interviews with the Marshal Offices, 16 November 2017, 16 November 2018. Interviews with experts, 23 May 2016, 17 March 2017, 7 September 2018.

ect is located within the deprived area designated in the local regeneration programme (local name for IPSUD).[45] Cities and their subordinate entities had to apply for JESSICA funds in the same way as all beneficiaries and did not have any assurance regarding obtaining funding for their projects. This was not in itself seen, arguably, as a main obstacle because it ensured a competitive process for the selection of the urban projects. The greatest problem of JESSICA from the city point of view, though, lay elsewhere. As one interviewee put it: *decisions on what urban projects are fit for JESSICA support were made by UDF.*[46] The city authority played no role at all in the system as provided for in this initiative, although it was directly responsible for implementing the IPSUD. Inclusion of a project in an IPSUD did not prejudge its final scope of operations. The city authority could not formally provide any arguments in favour of one or another project in order to contribute more to achieving the objectives set out in an IPSUD according to the adopted timetable. The rationale for cities having a more active role in the JESSICA system stems from the fact that the JEESICA financial resources should not be viewed in isolation or just as a simple financial package. The participation of cities could considerably ensure a more holistic approach needed to optimise public interventions in urban areas.

All the aforementioned merits and caveats of the JESSICA initiative flow from the overall analysis in the previous chapters and information acquired during collection of the data for this study. They correspond to some extent with other findings indicating shortcomings of JESSICA which were documented in several studies (Dąbrowski, 2019; ECA, 2016; European Commission, 2012a; Kłos, 2018; Schneidewind et al., 2013; Wishlade & Michie, 2016, 2018). But they also make an original contribution to knowledge of the functioning of JESSICA.

6.2 Policy recommendations

Based on the findings obtained in the empirical analysis, the conclusions reached and a comprehensive overview of JESSICA during the period considered, this study provides recommendations for urban policy and policy practice. It focuses on a project perspective and, in this sense, the insights gained from this study fill a gap in the existing body of research on the JESSICA initiative.

---

[45] Interview with a high-level official of a city hall, 17 March 2017.
[46] Interview with an expert, 23 May 2016.

To begin with, JESSICA was set up to provide a more sustainable and efficient response to the needs of urban areas, as compared to non-repayable grants. This clearly means that this type of EU funding was involved in support of sustainable urban development/urban regeneration initiatives. In order to implement successfully economic regeneration initiatives, both the supply-side and demand-side factors need to be addressed. The demand side is shaped by the city's ability to mobilise local expenditure and to attract more financial resources from outside with the aim to enhance market opportunity, that is, demand. This may take the form of demand for particular industrial production or for the output of some service sectors. In other words, a demand-side policy approach relies on boosting demand and on motivating suppliers to meet expressed user needs. It has to lead to reducing existing barriers to development and to stimulating the emergence or the redesign of markets (OECD, 2011). The demand-driven measures should be implemented in a certain way providing opportunities, flexibility and the ability to allow market players (including residents) to gradually adapt, with individual preferences and available resources, to the market needs. Examples of demand-side urban policies include: subsidised loans and grants for business, career ladder initiatives for people, tax breaks and incentives, city economic development strategies, planning policy, city marketing campaigns, enhancement of amenities and services (Pike, Lee, Mackinnon, Kempton, & Iddawela, 2016).

In turn, supply-push theories stress the role of population growth, capital investment and technical progress. This kind of policy seeks to develop infrastructure including the building of new roads or improving the existing ones. Special attention is paid to the redevelopment of land and infrastructure accompanying business activities, matching it to market demand. Furthermore, policy-makers support links between education and research institutions which result in the better operation of science, technology and business activities. Last but not least, there must be investments in human capital through adequate training and cooperation with enterprises (Noon, Smith-Canham, & Eagland, 2000). The effects of the supply-driven factors, such as the formation of human capital (government-sponsored) and public investment in broadly understood infrastructure, take the form of new or renewed assets or values which will translate into more companies, jobs, sales, income and growth, thus accelerating development of run-down urban areas.

The active use of the policy instruments, which allows urban authorities to perform effective regeneration, needs to address both the supply-side and demand-side components. On the one hand, it would be ineffective and inefficient to provide major new infrastructure without sufficient demand to maintain its operation and sustain its use. On the other hand, however, city promotional campaigns to encourage people and investors to take some initiative for the city in the absence of appropriate infrastructure and facilities would be inevitably doomed to failure, making all the efforts unproductive (Noon, Smith-Canham, & Eagland, 2000). Decision-makers must assess carefully all the options considered for addressing the problems identified in the deprived areas, with a view to achieving a balance between different instruments provided by both side-forces or to adjusting them accordingly.

JESSICA seems to combine the measures of both sides. On the one hand, it encouraged investors by providing repayable financial resources for investment in projects forming part of an IPSUD, while on the other, its objectives were targeted specifically at projects such as urban infrastructure, cultural and specialised facilities, business spaces and energy efficiency improvements. Bearing in mind the specific requirements related to the complexity of the projects and the necessity to match appropriately their operation scopes, taking into consideration the specificity and needs of the particular urban areas, JESSICA should have been an excellent instrument for promoting and boosting sustainable economic growth in cities. The results of this study tend to confirm this suggestion. However, this does not undermine the fact that JESSICA has not been used on a large scale (only four regions used it in 2014–2020) and it has not attracted wide interest among potential investors. JESSICA *has proved to be difficult*, as one interviewee commented.[47] There are two main reasons for this. First, regulatory requirements which, indeed, have the potential to undermine the effectiveness of every financial instrument. When dealing with the European funds, there is a natural tendency to disburse the funds on time in order to avoid a loss of allocated money. As a result, priority is given to those projects which are "safe" rather than risky and more challenging, as many of the urban investments are. Therefore, the fund managers often have the incentive to support "easy" projects rather than insist on granting those which presumably are promising but had been rejected by a lender available in the market (Wishlade et al., 2019). In addition, the administrative requirements that are strictly necessary for FEIs often represent a disincentive to apply for repayable assistance. Notwithstanding these difficulties, FEIs, as JESSICA is, can effectively support urban regeneration as it was reported by this study. In the meantime many relevant amendments have been introduced to the regulations that were in force in the 2007–2013 period, but also the new legislative framework for the 2014–2020 period has provided provisions aimed at increasing flexibility in the financial management of FEIs, while taking into account some sectoral, regional and national

---

47 Interview with an expert, 7 September 2018.

specificities. The amendments and new conditions ensuring the more effective use of FEIs were documented and discussed in detail in other studies (Bode, 2016; Gloazzo, 2018; Michie, Mendez, & Gal, 2018; Schneidewind et al., 2013; Wishlade, 2018; Wishlade et al., 2019), and will not be rehearsed here.

The second reason, which is far more important in implementing JESSICA from this study's point of view, is related to the adopted operating philosophy of FEIs (i.e. JESSICA) towards urban areas. What is meant by this is that the rules governing JESSICA at the operating level do not differ, in practical terms, with respect to the essential rules of FEIs targeted at enterprises. Indeed, JESSICA includes the urban component and is targeted at urban areas. However, the urban component was incorporated solely at the level of the objectives to be achieved but not at the level of the implementation. JESSICA is a loan which through its objectives is directed towards urban needs. In practice, it is a loan which can be claimed by anyone (both private and public entities) who submits a project proposal responding to the specific needs of an individual urban area. Generally speaking, the main difference between JESSICA and other FEIs and commercial financial products is the urban component (objective) imposed by the priorities of an operational programme and rules managing the European funds. This significantly impedes the functioning of JESSICA as compared to other FEIs. A potential beneficiary wants to perform first of all its own goals, but in this case it needs to additionally contribute to achieving specific goals of an urban area. It is better when the goals are compatible with each other, however, this does not have to happen often. Given the obstacles related to JESSICA, as aforementioned, nothing prevents a potential investor from taking a loan/credit available in the market.

The change in the operating philosophy proposed in this study relies on incorporating the cities into the institutional system of JESSICA. Cities have still been seen equally as potential investors, although JESSICA should contribute to the benefit of their prosperity. If follows that if cities take full responsibility for implementing an IPSUD, and if JESSICA aims to financially support the projects included in an IPSUD through the funds managed by a UDF, it would be highly desirable to empower cities by giving them a more privileged position in the JESSICA institutional system. Based on the theoretical and conceptual underpinning of the integrated urban regeneration as well as taking advantage of the model of the integrated approach to urban regeneration in which city authorities play a central and decisive role in driving forward an IPSUD in keeping with multi-level and multi-sectoral governance, it is concluded that such an assertion is all the more justified (Chapter 2). Since regions are directly involved in implementing the operational programmes and have competences from preparing the programme itself, through the selection of projects for co-financing under the

European funds, to assessing the level of achievement of relevant objectives, there is no reason to make city authorities more active participants in CP. Indeed, such a possibility was provided for in, for example, the Community strategic guidelines on cohesion in 2007–2013 (Council, 2006a). This is not just in order to provide cities directly with the competences of the managing authorities, but to involve them throughout the whole process of project appraisal and selection of projects for co-financing, thus incorporating them into the institutional framework of the JESSICA system.

To be more precise, by participating in JESSICA's decision-making system, a city could be referred to as the "implementing body". The place of cities in the functional structure of the JESSICA institutional system is presented in Figure 35. Each city that expressed a wish to join the JESSICA institutional system, would have at its disposal a portion of JESSICA funding. Not all cities would be entitled to participate in the system. The response to the question of which cities would be allowed to take part in the system is delivered by the analysis of the spatial distribution of the JESSICA funding with regard to the metropolitan areas of the regional capital cities (MAs) – see section 5.4. The results demonstrate that nearly 70% of the total JESSICA funding was directed towards urban projects implemented in cities located within MAs. A possible explanation for these results can be mutual interactions between cities within the economic and functional extent covered by MAs. In a sense, this explanation can be underpinned especially by reference to the spatial hierarchy of the urban system (section 1.3). This means, then, that there are some cities located closer to the regional capital city which possess the essential minimum of capabilities to offer goods and services that satisfy the existing desire of inhabitants. These cities can benefit more from the cumulative processes induced by means of agglomeration economies that occur for the sake of a greater economic density. The JESSICA projects should provide a complex scope of operations. Therefore, presumably, the greater possibilities to implement complex projects financed from a repayable instrument will arise in cities with an appropriate and diverse demand, i.e. those situated within MAs. Accordingly, these cities should be favoured with the possibility of making use of the JESSICA financial support at the expense of the cities located outside MAs. The latter could benefit more from grant-based financial resources provided by the European funds, while the former would be excluded from this kind of support or such support would be limited accordingly. Such a configuration would certainly add to shaping the territorial context of FEIs, as noted by Wishlade and colleagues (2019), and help to promote territorial cohesion, as proposed by Medeiros and Rauhut (2020) and Nyikos (2016). The additional criteria of the selection of the cities (located within MAs) entitled to a portion of the JESSICA support would derive from, for example, the needs diagnosed in an IPSUD or other conditions set out by the managing authority.

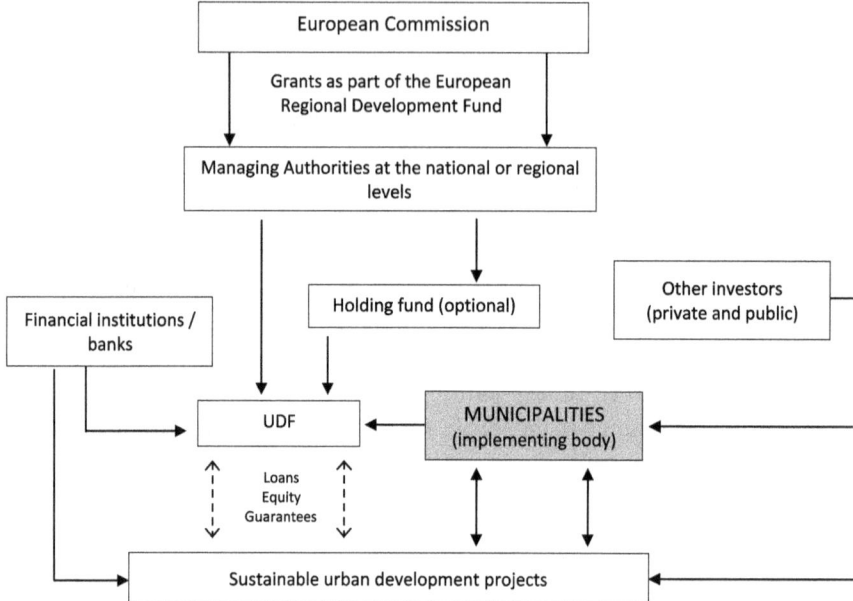

Figure 35: Proposal for a new JESSICA institutional system
Source: the authors' own elaboration

Cities involved in the implementation of an IPSUD would have an a extra package of incentives. They could encourage private investors to join the fulfilment of an IPSUD by providing them with the JESSICA loan. Cities would be responsible for the substantive assessment of the projects and the verification of the compliance of the project operations with the fundamental assumptions and objectives of the IPSUD. If cities find that a given project is suitable enough, they forward it to a UDF. At the next stage, the UDF appraises the proposed project's compliance with financial rules laid down for the EU funds. Finally, the UDF also makes a decision on the submitted project financing, and takes responsibility for provisioning and servicing the JESSICA loan. In addition to that, cities could assume a large portion of the responsibilities and formalities related to the provision of the loan as they were reported by aforementioned studies as the most challenging factor. Moreover, cities could also contribute to building many partnerships oriented to improving the living conditions in deprived areas. But, most importantly, in this way the JESSICA initiative would actually provide repayable financial resources for investments in projects forming part of an IPSUD and reinforce the sustainable funding of urban development.

Turning now to the types of project to be financed from the JESSICA instrument, it is clear that not all urban investments are suitable enough for support from repayable resources. Projects have to provide for a desired scale of long-term viability. However, finding a balance between the need for profitability to repay a loan, and for achieving positive impacts on sustainable urban development often represents a major challenge. The results of this study found that there are some projects characterised by clear opportunities for ensuring fair return on their investment as well as social and economic impacts. These are mostly large projects with a high investment value which possess all necessary capacities to generate profits and ensure the repayment of the loan, but also they can give rise to positive externalities for the local communities in compliance with an IPSUD. To highlight more the overall socio-economic impacts of a project, it is recommended to place greater emphasis on the economic efficiency of urban projects, which includes the estimated values of urban ecosystem services that can arise along with implementing particular urban projects. By doing so, it is possible to determine the total project performance obtained without isolation from the environmental and social context. The inclusion of these values into the project's cash flows will affect the economic performance indicators that may serve, at the appraisal stage of the regeneration projects, as a baseline for prioritising investments (projects) in deprived urban areas by informing their overall contribution towards the creation of wealth and growth (Idczak, Musiałkowska, & Mrozik, 2019a). Such investments are able to achieve or sustain profitability or positive cash flow from their operating activities, and also to enhance the leverage effects, thus making JESSICA more important as a powerful instrument focused on overcoming market failures. Hence, cities should select such projects as described, while ensuring complementarity of activities under an IPSUD. Therefore, the investments should be implemented in a tactical way and accordingly complemented by a wider range of social and participatory interventions which, being coherent and adjusted to the needs of the urban area of interest, result in a wider ranging impact on cities.

Conclusions

Cities have always been providers of a wide range of functions. Not surprisingly, they are subject to the influence of systemic changes, and because urbanisation is very rapid by its nature, they are in a state of continuous transformation. In fact, cities grapple with a variety of interrelated challenges like changing industrial structure and labour market needs, pollution, poverty and inequality, ageing infrastructure and climate change. The process of urban change can be an opportunity for cities if they are capable of embracing it positively and with a certain flexibility, but some urban areas, mostly inner-city ones, which fail to adapt face stagnation or even deprivation. Urban change processes are unparalleled and may affect particular spheres of urban life differently. Therefore, this study analysed in the first section the processes that decide how cities grow and evolve, while also serving the liveability of their inhabitants. Knowledge of the basic motives and factors leading forcibly to urbanisation is essential to the understanding of urbanisation, beyond the standard perception of a dichotomous division between city and countryside where the former always wins and the latter always loses.

People and firms often seek spatial proximity because, for plenty of economic and social reasons, they want to interact. Most of the decisions they make relate to the fulfilment of needs, which is conditioned by the availability and allocation of limited resources. This calls for constantly striving to achieve the highest possible level of economic efficiency, which triggers the operation of economic forces capable of, through market mechanisms, providing the most efficient economic outcomes. Hence, economic forces are commonly perceived as the most powerful of urbanising forces that reinforce the tendency for both people and firms to prefer urban concentration. Since urban systems, because of their distributive and balance-oriented properties, are driven mainly by economic forces, cities should be understood as economic organisations. Therefore, natural (geographical) factors may help to explain where cities are located but do not provide an understanding of why they exist and how they grow. This tends to remain the domain of market forces.

People and firms have always been in the habit of agglomerating in certain locations because they have been attracted by the benefits that come from locating near one another. These location-specific economies of scale, known as agglomeration economies, contribute to increased productivity and economic growth. Spatial clustering provides a variety of external benefits such as supplies

---

Piotr Idczak

https://doi.org/10.1515/9783110762198-011

of skilled labour, a large home market, sharing of suppliers, and specialisation etc. Theoretically, in a nutshell, if external benefits clearly outweigh the costs of higher rents, wages, and transport costs that are generated by agglomeration, spatial clustering will occur. If the cumulative benefits do not exceed the costs, people and firms will disperse to places with lower costs or higher benefits. As a result, the continuous cumulative processes of adaptation sparked by agglomeration economies can result in the formation of spatial core–periphery structures even in the absence of some natural advantages, thus underpinning the spatially hierarchical organisation of the urban system.

However, the same market forces that operate for the benefit of agglomerations may also lead to the optimum scale of operation being exceeded, causing the emergence of negative externalities that discourage agglomeration and repel economic activities. While market forces may bring about equilibrium in the long run, it is doubtful whether this can happen in reference to a spatial-economic configuration. The existence of agglomeration diseconomies seems to be particularly important in urban areas more than elsewhere because, due to high density, they can generate plenty of undesirable impacts (traffic congestion, pollution, devaluation of property, environmental decay, social exclusion and polarisation, crime, urban sprawl etc.). In addition, due to the complex interplay of many factors and functions, the market mechanism does not work smoothly in urban areas to allocate efficiently resources and income with a view to achieving an improvement in the quality of life. If this is the case, public authorities should act to compensate market failures and thereby addressing the problems of negative effects and social costs. Market failures are among the main reasons (in particular urban sprawl and economic discrimination are seen as triggers) responsible for the processes of deterioration of inner-city areas. The inefficiency of a city to tailor itself adequately to continuously changing demand and supply conditions brings about socio-spatial inequalities as result of which some inner-city areas become not only physically marginalised and suffer degradation but also lose well-educated people because of job shortages or unattractive living and working conditions. Urban deterioration is undeniably a diseconomy of urban growth, therefore city authorities are obliged to establish anticipated strategies and effective local policies aimed at counteracting adverse economic tendencies and concerns.

Responses to the social and economic decay that occurs in urban areas and societies include a wide range of significant interventions involving coordinated actions carried out under the auspices of urban authorities, commonly referred to as urban regeneration. This process is focused on improving the quality of deprived areas and creating favourable conditions for sustainable and inclusive growth. Urban regeneration combines architectural and urban dynamics with economic development, social inclusion, spatial order and environmental protection. All these causes mean that urban regeneration is a comprehensive process that requires an integration of actions from different sectors and multi-agency governance as well as a collaborative style of planning and implementation. Therefore, the first specific objective of this study was to define initiatives embracing spatial, economic, social, environmental and governance aspects that, in light of an integrated approach, support urban regeneration. Based on the extensive literature review (theories, concepts and previous research findings), a comprehensive set of the initiatives was elaborated (Table 2). This set specifies various activities that under broad public–private consensus should restore the functioning of market mechanisms and reverse the deprivation of inner-city areas. The activities should be carried out by relevant agencies in a "joined-up" holistic approach to solving the interrelated problems of unemployment, crime, low educational attainment, poor health, housing and the local physical environment etc. Consequently, the first specific objective was achieved.

Notwithstanding, regeneration actions should be neither limited to the deprived areas nor counteract only the consequences of urban sprawl. Urban regeneration requires a comprehensive approach in which area-based and target-oriented actions (favouring the most deprived inner-city areas and/or socially excluded residents) are accompanied by measures taking into account morphological, social and economic issues evident across the whole city. This means that the framework of urban regenerating policies must be based on a holistic approach integrating spheres and actors. Because of this, the second specific objective set out in this study relied on identifying regeneration measures applied in various European cities which proved to be successful, and drawing on that, building a model of integrated urban regeneration applicable at the European level. Making use of the systemic approach, the urban regeneration themes were discussed which provided a background for constructing a model. The background was collected using theoretical considerations, good experiences and information from reports including vital insights on the effects of regeneration. This background laid down a solid basis for the framework for conceptualising the integrated approach to urban regeneration. As a result, the model of the integrated approach to urban regeneration applicable at the European level was constructed (Figure 5). The model presents an integrated framework of practices that decision-makers should consider when implementing urban regeneration in cities, and in broader urban policy. In many aspects, it is compatible with the key features of the Pact of Amsterdam which launched the Urban Agenda for the EU (2016) and the *New Leipzig Charter* (2020) which advocate an integrated approach in addressing urban problems. At the core of the model is a triad of determinants: (1) urban authorities (or an authorised body) should perform a decisive role in urban regeneration on the basis of multi-level and multi-sectoral governance; (2) an integrated urban regeneration programme (IURP) that encompass all actions and projects designed to address the problems of deprived urban areas should be rooted in the integrated approach and favour the concentration of resources; (3) all regeneration actions should be focused on a deprived area (or areas) designated within a city. Thus, the second specific objective was achieved.

Any urban area cannot be considered in isolation as it is an inherent part of an all-embracing system. The economic performance of each urban area, as well as its future development, will reflect what share of the regional and national total output it produces relative to that of other urban areas (Goodall, 1972). Economic prosperity as well as socio-economic decline in any urban area are affected by those in other urban areas in the region and finally associated with the national economy. Hence, in order to avoid failures that can be attributed to the lack of taking greater account of wider impacts of socio-economic processes occurring in a geographical scale, what had to be determined was the position of urban regeneration in view of the so-called integrated approach aimed at achieving territorial cohesion, as stated in the third specific objective. Following the literature survey and previous research findings, it was found that urban regeneration actions should be fully integrated into the common framework of territorially coordinated policies, which are not implemented as isolated actions but constitute a part of general development policy. Because of this, city authorities should incorporate the priorities of territorial integration into IURP, so as to ensure that IURP's objectives and goals, actions and tools are integrated within a context of the wider geographical realities. Moreover, they have also to be consistent with the targets, and underpin the implementation of supra-local strategies and the general development policy of the state. This aspect was illustrated in the model of integrated urban regeneration (Figure 5) and broadly discussed in section 2.3, enabling achievement of the third specific objective.

JESSICA, as a new financial instrument designed to support sustainable urban development, turned out to be a very ambitious initiative. JESSICA required specific knowledge, skills and legislation other than those applied in traditional grant schemes. The lack of clarity in terms of regulations and rules made JESSICA a difficult instrument to support urban development. Managing authorities showed a wider conservatism and attachment to a traditional approach to distributing JESSICA funds by not including cities in the JESSICA institutional system. Indeed, cities did not become a powerful partner in the decision-making process on integrated urban development supported by JESSICA. This, however, lies at the core of the model of integrated urban regeneration which puts cities first in the decision-making on urban development (Chapters 3 and 4, and partly also Chapter 6). As a result, specific objective number four was achieved which aimed to assess the rules and institutional system of JESSICA and compare them to the model approach to integrated urban regeneration.

In the further part of the study (Chapter 5), research works were carried out focused on dealing with the fifth specific objective and its operational objectives. The basic assumption underlying the JESSICA initiative was to provide an alternative approach to traditional grants consisting in the use of financial engineering instruments aimed at the implementation of more effective and efficient municipal projects. These instruments were intended to support investments that would include actions promoting sustainable urban development, but also provide tangible incentives that would reduce the risk of investments being undertaken under higher risk conditions and, consequently, overcome existing market failures. By doing so, JESSICA was seen to provide an important contribution to building up sustainable funding, i.e. a funding mechanism which involves public and private institutions investing in sustainable economic activities and projects, while taking into account social and governance aspects, and providing funds in the long run. Thus, the general aim was to check to what extent these assumptions were met by JESSICA projects implemented in Poland. This study has found that generally two out of three JESSICA projects implemented mostly by private entities generated revenues and gave rise to positive market effects. As far as the remainder of the projects is concerned – that is, those that did not provide any of the similar effects – they were pursued mainly by public entities. Just over half of the projects contributed to creating positive social impacts. Among projects characterised by a lack of the desired stimulus for local communities were those executed largely within two support areas: energy efficiency and urban infrastructure. The research has also shown that the most impactful factors in achieving the results expected by the projects were the legal status of the beneficiary and the value of the JESSICA project – the effects were higher if the projects were implemented by companies and were of a high value (total cost of a project). Those projects, by reason of a complex range of services or goods provided, were not only able, by nature, to generate profits and ensure repayment of the JESSICA loan by their own means, but also triggered positive externalities for local communities as set out in the IPSUDs. Those projects, thanks to capital back-flows, raised the role of JESSICA as a powerful instrument aimed at addressing existing market failures. Moreover, by employing the original assessment model that allowed analysis of the impact of the projects on sustainable urban development, this study provided further interesting insights, supporting to a large extent the earlier findings. It was found that the projects characterised by a relatively high value and pursued by private entities proved to be the best performers not only in meeting the JESSICA assumptions, but also in delivering outcomes that are responsible for assuring the complexity of sustainable urban development, thus justifying the possibility of applying the JESSICA-led interventions in disadvantaged urban areas. Furthermore, the second major findings related to the projects' impact on territorial cohesion showed that the greatest territorial impacts were generated by those projects that were best tailored to the specific needs of particular deprived areas of the city. This also revealed that repayable supportive instruments, as JESSICA is, can be effectively applied to overcome the market failures in urban areas. Finally, when analysing the spatial distribution of the JESSICA funding, the study revealed that the repayable assistance provided by JESSICA was directed to support the projects implemented in various cities, irrespective of their size and location. However, most of the cities that benefited from JESSICA were located within MAs. This has important policy implications because it points to the possibility of a more territorially targeted framework of EU financial instruments – more repayable aid for cities inside MAs, while non-repayable for cities outside MAs.

In the final chapter an effort was made to draw lessons for decision-makers (the last specific objective) and by doing so to contribute to diminishing the shortcomings of JESSICA reported in other studies. Taken all together, the assessment of JESSICA in relation to urban challenges is positive, albeit with some caveats. While the positive assessment is connected with the new culture in which public intervention is based on repayable financial resources, providing a more powerful catalytic effect than grant assistance, the caveats stemmed mainly from the lack of appropriate implementing readiness. JESSICA turned out to be new and both regulatory rules and beneficiaries were not well enough prepared. Therefore, in order to make JESSICA more effective and easier at the implementation level, this study made two strong recommendations for policy practice. First, cities should be incorporated into the JESSICA institutional system, and, as implementing bodies, they should assume a large portion of the responsibilities and formalities related to the provision of the loan (Figure 35), thus ensuring more coherence in the projects with the IPSUD. Second, JESSICA assistance should be addressed to mostly large projects with a high investment value but which should be implemented in cities located within MAs. These recommendations should result in unlocking the potential of the JESSICA initiative and strengthen its impact in overcoming existing market failures and promoting sustainable urban development.

To sum up, this study makes a few theoretical and practical contributions to the literature on financial engineering instruments used for the purpose of public intervention and on EU cohesion policy. First, it emphasises the role of market forces as the most powerful of urbanising forces responsible for the functioning of cities, and strongly stresses that they cannot be ignored even in urban regeneration. Second, it presents urban regeneration through the lens of five dimensions and specifies the set of activities to be taken into consideration in each of them. Third, it proposes a new model of integrated approach to urban regeneration applicable at the European level, which constitutes an original contribution of this work. Fourth, based on a personally compiled database it explores the JESSICA initiative from the perspective of the implementation of the projects and the effects they generated, thus providing for the first time (to the best of our knowledge) relevant evidence on JESSICA in Poland. Finally, it offers theoretically rooted and research-based policy recommendations for EU cohesion policy, including the proposal of the new JESSICA institutional system.

References

Aalbers, M. B., & van Beckhoven, E. (2010). The integrated approach in neighbourhood renewal: More than just a philosophy? *Tijdschrift Voor Economische En Sociale Geografie (Journal of Economic & Social Geography)*, *101*(4), 449–461. https://doi.org/10.1111/j.1467-9663.2009.00574.x

Acierno, A. (2013). Urban regeneration and market-led planning during the Thatcher years. *Territorio Della Ricerca Su Insediamenti e Ambiente*, *6*(10), 263–268. https://doi.org/10.6092/2281-4574/1734

Acierno, A. (2017). Integrated urban development and culture-led regeneration in the EU. *Territorio Della Ricerca Su Insediamenti e Ambiente*, *10*(1), 7–14. https://doi.org/10.6092/2281-4574/5324

Adams, D., & Tiesdell, S. (2010). Planners as market actors: Rethinking state–market relations in land and property. *Planning Theory & Practice*, *11*(2). https://doi.org/10.1080/14649351003759631

Almeida, J., Condessa, B., Pinto, P., & Ferreira, J. A. (2013). Municipal urbanization tax and land-use management: The case of Tomar, Portugal. *Land Use Policy*, *31*, 336–346. https://doi.org/10.1016/J.LANDUSEPOL.2012.07.017

André, I., Carmo, A., Abreu, A., Estevens, A., & Malheiros, J. (2012). Learning for and from the city: The role of education in urban social cohesion. *Belgeo*, (4), 0–19. https://doi.org/10.4000/belgeo.8587

Arup. (2009). *JESSICA Evaluation Study – West Poland. Final Report.* Retrieved from http://www.eib.org/attachments/jessica-poland-west_en.pdf

Atkinson, R. (1999). Discourses of partnership and empowerment in contemporary British urban regeneration. *Urban Studies*, *36*(1), 59–72. https://doi.org/10.1080/0042098993736

Atkinson, R. (2015). The urban dimension in cohesion policy: Past developments and future prospects. *European Structural and Investment Funds Journal*, *3*(1), 21–31.

Badach, J., & Dymnicka, M. (2017). Concept of "good urban governance" and its application in sustainable urban planning. *IOP Conference Series: Materials Science and Engineering*, *245*(8). https://doi.org/10.1088/1757-899X/245/8/082017

Barca, F. (2009). *An Agenda for a Reformed Cohesion Policy: A Place-Based Approach to Meeting European Union Challenges and Expectations.* Brussels: European Commission. Retrieved from https://ec.europa.eu/migrant-integration/sites/default/files/2010-12/docl_17396_240404999.pdf

Barca, F., McCann, P., & Rodríguez-Pose, A. (2012). The case for regional development intervention: Place-based versus place-neutral approaches. *Journal of Regional Science*, *52*(1), 134–152. https://doi.org/10.1111/j.1467-9787.2011.00756.x

Bartocci, L., & Picciaia, F. (2020). Looking for new paths to realize cross-sector collaboration for urban regeneration: The case of Castel del Giudice (Italy). *Sustainability*, *12*(1), 1–15. https://doi.org/10.3390/su12010292

Billert, A. (2008). Sens i funkcja ustawy rewitalizacyjnej (Meaning and function of an act on urban regeneration). In J. J. Parysek & A. Tölle (Eds.), *Wybrane problemy rozwoju i rewitalizacji miast: Aspekty poznawcze i praktyczne* (Some problems of urban development and regeneration: Cognitive and practical issues) (pp. 13–19). Poznań: Bogucki Wydawnictwo Naukowe.

Billert, A. (2019). Rewitalizacja miast jako program publiczny na przykładzie Niemiec w latach 1971–2000 (Urban regeneration as a public scheme based on the example of Germany in the years 1971–2000). *Rocznik Lubuski*, *45*(2), 37–50. https://doi.org/10.34768/rl.2019.v452.03

Bode, M. (2015). Financial instruments in cohesion policy. *European Structural and Investment Funds Journal*, *3*(3), 173–186.

Bode, M. (2016). Making better use of the EU budget through financial instruments: A reality check. *European Structural and Investment Funds Journal*, *4*(4), 179–203.

Böhme, K., Doucet, P., Komornicki, T., Zaucha, J., & Swiatek, D. (2011). *How to Strengthen the Territorial Dimension of "Europe 2020" and the EU Cohesion Policy*. Warsaw: Ministry of Regional Development.

Bollen, K. A., Glanville, J. L., & Stecklov, G. (2007). Socio-economic status, permanent income, and fertility: A latent-variable approach. *Population Studies*, *61*(1), 15–34. https://doi.org/10.1080/00324720601103866

Borck, R. (2005). *Social Agglomeration Externalities* (DIW Discussion Papers No. 505). Berlin: Deutsches Institut für Wirtschaftsforschung. Retrieved from http://hdl.handle.net/10419/18356

Bradley, J., & Zaucha, J. (Eds.). (2017). *Territorial Cohesion: A Missing Link between Economic Growth and Welfare. Lessons from the Baltic Tiger*. Gdańsk: Uniwersytet Gdański Katedra Makroekonomii. Retrieved from https://rcin.org.pl/dlibra/publication/83805/edition/64988

Breuer, W., & Brueser, D. (2013). Failures in urban capital markets and consequences for project funding. *SSRN Electronic Journal*, 1–43. https://doi.org/10.2139/ssrn.2343489

Brewer, A. (2011). The concept of an agricultural surplus, from Petty to Smith. *Journal of the History of Economic Thought*, *33*(4), 487–505. https://doi.org/10.1017/S1053837211000290

Brown, G., Sanders, S., & Reed, P. (2018). Using public participatory mapping to inform general land use planning and zoning. *Landscape and Urban Planning*, *177*, 64–74. https://doi.org/10.1016/j.landurbplan.2018.04.011

Brueckner, J. K. (2000). Urban sprawl: Diagnosis and remedies. *International Regional Science Review*, *23*(2), 160–171. https://doi.org/10.1177/016001700761012710

Brueckner, J. K. (2001). Urban sprawl: Lessons from urban economics. *Brookings-Wharton Papers on Urban Affairs*, *2001*(1), 65–97. https://doi.org/10.1353/urb.2001.0003

Brueckner, J. K., & Helsley, R. W. (2011). Sprawl and blight. *Journal of Urban Economics*, *69*(2), 205–213. https://doi.org/10.1016/j.jue.2010.09.003

Brülhart, M., & Sbergami, F. (2009). Agglomeration and growth: Cross-country evidence. *Journal of Urban Economics*, *65*(1), 48–63. https://doi.org/10.1016/j.jue.2008.08.003

Budde, R., Ehlert, C., Neumann, U., Peistrup, M., Grabow, B., Hollbach-Grömig, B., ... Bergs, R. (2010). *Second State of European Cities Report*. Essen: Rheinisch-Westfälisches Institut für Wirtschaftsforschung. Retrieved from https://ec.europa.eu/regional_policy/sources/docgener/studies/pdf/urban/stateofcities_2010.pdf

Button, K. J. (1976). *Urban Economics: Theory and Policy*. London: Palgrave Macmillan. https://doi.org/10.1007/978-1-349-15661-0

Cadell, C., Falk, N., & King, F. (2008). *Regeneration in European Cities: Making Connections*. York: Joseph Rowntree Foundation. Retrieved from https://www.jrf.org.uk/file/37373/download?token=lFKPUT0n&filetype=full-report

Capello, R. (2001). Agglomeration economies and urban productivity: Urbanisation vs. localisation economies in the metropolitan area of Milan. *Jahrbuch Für Regionalwissenschaft*, *21*, 1–23. Retrieved from http://www-sre.wu-wien.ac.at/ersa/ersaconfs/ersa99/Papers/a354.pdf

Capello, R., & Faggian, A. (2002). An economic-ecological model of urban growth and urban externalities: Empirical evidence from Italy. *Ecological Economics*, *40*(2), 181–198. https://doi.org/10.1016/S0921-8009(01)00252-X

Carley, M., Chapman, M., Hastings, A., Kirk, K., & Young, R. (2000). *Urban Regeneration through Partnership: A Study in Nine Urban Regions in England, Scotland and Wales*. Bristol: The Policy Press. Retrieved from https://citeseerx.ist.psu.edu/viewdoc/download?doi=10.1.1.472.5610&rep=rep1&type=pdf

Castells-Quintana, D., & Royuela, V. (2014). Agglomeration, inequality and economic growth. *The Annals of Regional Science*, *52*(2), 343–366. https://doi.org/10.1007/s00168-014-0589-1

Cavaleri, S. A. (1992). System dynamics: A form of the integrative system approach. In J. A. Vennix, J. Faber, W. J. Scheper, & C. A. Takkenberg (Eds.), *System Dynamics 1992: Proceedings of the International System Dynamics Conference* (pp. 89–98). Boston: System Dynamics Society. Retrieved from https://proceedings.systemdynamics.org/1992/proceed/pdfs/caval089.pdf

Cervelló-Royo, R., Garrido-Yserte, R., & Segura-García del Río, B. (2012). An urban regeneration model in heritage areas in search of sustainable urban development and internal cohesion. *Journal of Cultural Heritage Management and Sustainable Development*, *2*(1), 44–61. https://doi.org/10.1108/20441261211223261

Chen, H. T. (2012). Theory-driven evaluation: Conceptual framework, application and advancement. In R. Strobl, O. Lobermeier, & W. Heitmeyer (Eds.), *Evaluation von Programmen und Projekten für eine demokratische Kultur* (pp. 17–40). Wiesbaden: Springer Fachmedien Wiesbaden. https://doi.org/10.1007/978-3-531-19009-9

Christopoulos, D. C. (2009). *Towards Representative Expert Surveys: Legitimizing the Collection of Expert Data. Eurostat Conference for New Techniques and Technologies for Statistics*. Brussels. Retrieved from http://eprints.uwe.ac.uk/12085

Churski, P., Borowczak, A., & Perdał, R. (2015). Struktura inwestycji finansowanych ze środków unijnych a czynniki rozwoju w obszarach wzrostu w Polsce (The structure of investments funded by the European funds towards development factors in the areas of growth in Poland). In E. Małuszyńska, G. Mazur, & I. Musiałkowska (Eds.), *Polska – 10 lat członkostwa w Unii Europejskiej* (Poland – 10 years of membership in the European Union) (pp. 183–199). Poznań: Wydawnictwo Uniwersytetu Ekonomicznego w Poznaniu.

Churski, P., & Perdał, R. (2016). Where do cohesion policy funds flow and do they have any impact? The Polish lesson. *Barometr Regionalny* (Regional Barometer), *14*(3), 7–24. Retrieved from http://br.wszia.edu.pl/zeszyty/pdfs/br45_01churski.pdf

Ciesiółka, P. (2018). Urban regeneration as a new trend in the development policy in Poland. *Quaestiones Geographicae*, *37*(2), 109–123. https://doi.org/10.2478/quageo-2018-0015

Ciesiółka, P., & Rogatka, K. (2015). Rola miejscowych planów zagospodarowania przestrzennego w procesie rewitalizacji miast na przykładzie metropolii Poznań (Role of local spatial development plans in the process of urban revitalisation: The case of the Poznań metropolis). *Problemy Rozwoju Miast* (Urban Development Issues), *12*(4), 27–36.

Cinyabuguma, M., & McConnell, V. (2013). Urban growth externalities and neighborhood incentives: Another cause of urban sprawl? *Journal of Regional Science*, *53*(2), 332–348. https://doi.org/10.1111/jors.12008

Clark, W. A. V., & Rushton, G. (1970). Models of intra-urban consumer behavior and their implications for central place theory. *Economic Geography*, *46*(3), 486. https://doi.org/10.2307/143384

CNSP. (2012). Koncepcja Przestrzennego Zagospodarowania Kraju 2030 (Concept of the National Spatial Development 2030), Pub. L. No. 252. Poland: Monitor Polski.

Colantonio, A., & Dixon, T. (2011). *Urban Regeneration and Social Sustainability: Best Practice from European Cities*. Oxford: Wiley-Blackwell.

Colini, L., Czischke, D., Güntner, S., Tosics, I., & Ramsden, P. (2013). *Against Divided Cities in Europe*. Saint-Denis: Urbact. Retrieved from https://urbact.eu/sites/default/files/import/general_library/19765_Urbact_WS4_DIVIDED_low_FINAL.pdf

Collier, P., Glaeser, E. L., Venables, T., & Manwaring, P. (2020). *Urban Land Use Planning for Economic Growth* (IGC Policy Framing Paper). International Growth Centre. Retrieved from https://www.theigc.org/wp-content/uploads/2020/10/Urban-land-use-planning-21-august-low-res.pdf

Committee of the Regions. (2010). Opinion of the Committee of the Regions on "The role of urban regeneration in the future of urban development in Europe". Retrieved from https://eur-lex.europa.eu/legal-content/EN/TXT/?uri=uriserv:OJ.C_.2010.267.01.0025.01.ENG

Corcoran, M. P. (2006). The challenge of urban regeneration in deprived European neighbourhoods: A partnership approach. *Economic and Social Review*, *37*(3), 399–422. Retrieved from http://hdl.handle.net/2262/61747

Cornelius, N., & Wallace, J. (2010). Cross-sector partnerships: City regeneration and social justice. *Journal of Business Ethics*, *94*, 71–84. https://doi.org/10.1007/s10551-011-0780-6

Couch, C., Fraser, C., & Percy, S. (Eds.). (2003). *Urban Regeneration in Europe*. Oxford, UK: Blackwell Science. https://doi.org/10.1002/9780470690604

Couch, C., Sykes, O., & Börstinghaus, W. (2011). Thirty years of urban regeneration in Britain, Germany and France: The importance of context and path dependency. *Progress in Planning*, *75*(1), 1–52. https://doi.org/10.1016/j.progress.2010.12.001

Council. (2006a). Council Decision of 6 October 2006 on Community strategic guidelines on cohesion. Retrieved from https://eur-lex.europa.eu/legal-content/EN/TXT/PDF/?uri=CELEX:32006D0702&from=EN

Council. (2006b). Council Regulation (EC) No 1083/2006 of 11 July 2006 laying down general provisions on the European Regional Development Fund, the European Social Fund and the Cohesion Fund and repealing Regulation (EC) No 1260/1999. Retrieved from https://eur-lex.europa.eu/legal-content/EN/TXT/PDF/?uri=CELEX:32006R1083&from=EN

Czischke, D., Moloney, C., & Turcu, C. (2015). Raising the game in environmentally sustainable urban regeneration. *Sustainable Regeneration in Urban Areas, URBACT II Capitalisation*, 6–14.

Dąbrowski, M. (2014). Engineering multilevel governance? Joint European Support for Sustainable Investment in City Areas (JESSICA) and the involvement of private and financial actors in urban development policy. *Regional Studies*, *48*(12), 2006–2019. https://doi.org/10.1080/00343404.2014.914625

Dąbrowski, M. (2015). "Doing more with less" or "doing less with less"? Assessing EU cohesion policy's financial instruments for urban development. *Regional Studies, Regional Science, 2*(1), 73–96. https://doi.org/10.1080/21681376.2014.999107

Dąbrowski, M. (2019). *Financial Instruments and Territorial Cohesion. Case Study Report.* Luxembourg: ESPON. Retrieved from https://www.espon.eu/sites/default/files/attachments/Wielkopolskie_case study.pdf

Dannefer, D. (2020). Systemic and reflexive: Foundations of cumulative dis/advantage and life-course processes. *The Journals of Gerontology: Series B, 75*(6), 1249–1263. https://doi.org/10.1093/geronb/gby118

Dawley, S., Conway, C., & Charles, D. (2005). *The Dynamics of Learning and Knowledge within Community-Led Urban Regeneration: The Lower Ouseburn Valley as a "Community of Practice"?* (Centre for Urban and Regional Development Studies Working Paper). University of Newcastle upon Tyne. Retrieved from https://www.dime-eu.org/working-papers/wp12/dynamics-of-learning-and-knowledge#attachments

De Gregorio Hurtado, S. (2015). The implementation of the URBAN community initiative: A transformative driver towards collaborative urban regeneration? Answers from Spain. *European Journal of American Studies, 10*(3), 2.4. https://doi.org/10.4000/ejas.11354

De Gregorio Hurtado, S. (2017). 25 years of urban regeneration in the EU. *Territorio Della Ricerca Su Insediamenti e Ambiente, 10*(1), 15–19. https://doi.org/10.6092/2281-4574/5318

De Gregorio Hurtado, S. (2018). The EU urban policy in the period 2007–13: Lessons from the Spanish experience. *Regional Studies, Regional Science, 5*(1), 212–230. https://doi.org/10.1080/21681376.2018.1480903

de Magalhães, C. (2015). Urban regeneration. In *International Encyclopedia of the Social & Behavioral Sciences* (pp. 919–925). Amsterdam: Elsevier. https://doi.org/10.1016/B978-0-08-097086-8.74031-1

De Medici, S., Riganti, P., & Viola, S. (2018). Circular economy and the role of universities in urban regeneration: The case of Ortigia, Syracuse. *Sustainability, 10*(11), 4305. https://doi.org/10.3390/su10114305

Degen, M., & García, M. (2012). The transformation of the "Barcelona Model": An analysis of culture, urban regeneration and governance. *International Journal of Urban and Regional Research, 36*(5), 1022–1038. https://doi.org/10.1111/j.1468-2427.2012.01152.x

DLA Piper. (2010). *Use of ERDF Funding in JESSICA Funds* (Issue Paper on the Legal Environment). Luxembourg.

Dorussen, H., Lenz, H., & Blavoukos, S. (2005). Assessing the reliability and validity of expert interviews. *European Union Politics, 6*(3), 315–337. https://doi.org/10.1177/1465116505054835

Dotti, N. F. (2013). The unbearable instability of structural funds' distribution. *European Planning Studies, 21*(4), 596–614. https://doi.org/10.1080/09654313.2012.722956

Duranton, G. (2009). Are cities engines of growth and prosperity for developing countries? In M. Spence, P. C. Annez, & R. M. Buckley (Eds.), *Urbanization and Growth* (pp. 67–113). Washington, D.C.: World Bank.

Duranton, G., & Kerr, W. (2018). The logic of agglomeration. In G. L. Clark, M. P. Feldman, M. S. Gertler, & D. Wójcik (Eds.), *The New Oxford Handbook of Economic Geography*. New York: Oxford University Press. https://doi.org/10.1093/oxfordhb/9780198755609.013.14

Duranton, G., & Puga, D. (2004). Micro-foundations of urban agglomeration economies. In J. V. Henderson & J.-F. Thisse (Eds.), *Handbook of Regional and Urban Economics* (pp. 2063–2117). Amsterdam: Elsevier.

Dziembała, M. (2019). Smart city as a steering center of the region's sustainable development and competitiveness. In A. Visvizi & M. Lytras (Eds.), *Smart Cities: Issues and Challenges* (pp. 149–169). Amsterdam: Elsevier. https://doi.org/10.1016/B978-0-12-816639-0.00009-0

ECA. (2016). *Implementing the EU Budget through Financial Instruments: Lessons to Be Learnt from the 2007–2013 Programme Period.* Luxembourg. https://doi.org/10.2865/98596

Edwards, M. E. (2007). *Regional and Urban Economics and Economic Development: Theory and Methods.* New York: Auerbach Publications.

EIB. (2008). *JESSICA – A New Way of Using EU Funding to Promote Sustainable Investments and Growth in Urban Areas.* Luxembourg. Retrieved from http://www.eib.org/attachments/thematic/jessica_2008_en.pdf

EIB. (2012a). *JESSICA. UDF Handbook. Horizontal Study. Final Report.* Luxembourg. Retrieved from https://ec.europa.eu/regional_policy/sources/thefunds/instruments/doc/jessica/jessica_udf_handbook_final_report_120712_en.pdf

EIB. (2012b). *JESSICA for Smart and Sustainable Cities. Horizontal Study.* Luxembourg. Retrieved from https://www.eib.org/attachments/documents/jessica_horizontal_study_smart_and_sustainable_cities_en.pdf

ESPON. (2012). *Territorial Impact Assessment of Policies and EU Directives.* Luxembourg.

European Commission. (2006a). Commission Regulation (EC) No 1828/2006 of 8 December 2006 setting out rules for the implementation of Council Regulation (EC) No 1083/2006 laying down general provisions on the European Regional Development Fund, the European Social Fund and the Cohesion. *Official Journal of the European Union.* Retrieved from https://eur-lex.europa.eu/legal-content/EN/ALL/?uri=CELEX%3A32006R1828

European Commission. (2006b). Communication from the Commission to the Council and Parliament – Cohesion policy and cities: The urban contribution to growth and jobs in the regions, Pub. L. No. 385, 13. Retrieved from https://eur-lex.europa.eu/legal-content/EN/TXT/PDF/?uri=CELEX:52006DC0385&from=EN

European Commission. (2007). Note of the Commission services on financial engineering in the 2007–13 programming period, Pub. L. No. COCOF/07/0018/01-EN, 7. Retrieved from https://ec.europa.eu/regional_policy/sources/docoffic/cocof/2007/cocof_07_0018_01_en.pdf

European Commission. (2008a). Green paper on territorial cohesion. Turning territorial diversity into strength, Pub. L. No. COM(2008) 616, COM(2008) 616. Brussels.

European Commission. (2008b). Guidance note on financial engineering. Brussels. Retrieved from https://ec.europa.eu/regional_policy/sources/docoffic/cocof/2008/cocof_08_0002_03_en.pdf

European Commission. (2009). *Promoting Sustainable Urban Development in Europe: Achievements and Opportunities.* Brussels. https://doi.org/10.2776/85168

European Commission. (2010). Guidance note on eligibility of energy efficiency and renewable energies interventions under the ERDF and the Cohesion Fund (2007–2013) in the building sector including housing, Pub. L. No. COCOF 08/0034/04-EN, 11.

Retrieved from https://ec.europa.eu/regional_policy/sources/docoffic/cocof/2008/ cocof_08_0034_04_en.pdf

European Commission. (2011a). *Cities of Tomorrow: Challenges, Visions, Ways Forward.* Luxembourg: Publications Office of the European Union. https://doi.org/10.2776/41803

European Commission. (2011b). JESSICA implementation in the EU Member States. State of play. European Commission. Retrieved from https://ec.europa.eu/regional_policy/ sources/thefunds/doc/instruments/jessica/20111019_jessica _state_of_play.pdf

European Commission. (2012a). Financial instruments in cohesion policy. Brussels. Retrieved from https://ec.europa.eu/regional_policy/sources/docoffic/official/communic/financial/ financial_instruments_2012_en.pdf

European Commission. (2012b). Revised guidance note on financial engineering instruments under Article 44 of Council Regulation (EC) No 1083/2006. Brussels. Retrieved from https://ec.europa.eu/regional_policy/sources/docoffic/cocof/2010/ cocof_10_0014_05_en.pdf

European Commission. (2013). JESSICA: Joint European Support for Sustainable Investment in City Areas. Retrieved from https://ec.europa.eu/regional_policy/archive/thefunds/ instruments/jessica_en.cfm

European Parliament and Council. (2006). Regulation (EC) No 1080/2006 of the European Parliament and of the Council of 5 July 2006 on the European Regional Development Fund and repealing Regulation (EC) No 1783/1999. Retrieved from https://eur-lex.europa.eu/legal-content/EN/TXT/PDF/?uri=CELEX:32006R1080&from=en

Evans, A. W. (1985). *Urban Economics: An Introduction.* Oxford: Basil Blackwell.

Evans, G. (2005). Measure for measure: Evaluating the evidence of culture's contribution to regeneration. *Urban Studies, 42*(5–6), 959–983. https://doi.org/10.1080/ 00420980500107102

Evans, G., & Shaw, P. (2004). *The Contribution of Culture to Regeneration in the UK: A Review of Evidence. A Report to DCMS.* London: London Metropolitan University. Retrieved from http://repository.londonmet.ac.uk/6109/

Evans, J., & Jones, P. (2008). Rethinking sustainable urban regeneration: Ambiguity, creativity, and the shared territory. *Environment and Planning A: Economy and Space, 40*(6), 1416–1434. https://doi.org/10.1068/a39293

Fainstein, S., & Fainstein, N. (2018). The spatial dimension of poverty. In A. Andreotti, D. Benassi, & Y. Kazepov (Eds.), *Western Capitalism in Transition: Global Processes, Local Challenges* (pp. 239–255). Manchester: Manchester University Press.

Faludi, A. (2009). *Territorial Cohesion under the looking glass. Synthesis Paper about the History of the Concept and Policy Background to Territorial Cohesion.* Retrieved from https://ec.europa.eu/regional_policy/archive/consultation/terco/pdf/lookingglass.pdf

Ferilli, G., Sacco, P. L., Tavano Blessi, G., & Forbici, S. (2017). Power to the people: When culture works as a social catalyst in urban regeneration processes (and when it does not). *European Planning Studies, 25*(2), 241–258. https://doi.org/10.1080/ 09654313.2016.1259397

Ferry, M. (2013). *The Achievements of Cohesion Policy: Evidence and Methodological Challenges from an EU10 Perspective* (GRINCOH Working Paper Series No. 8.01). Glasgow: European Policies Research Centre, University of Strathclyde. Retrieved from http://www.grincoh.eu/media/serie_8__cohesion_and_its_dimensions/ grincoh_wp8.01_ferry.pdf

Fischer, K. (2011). Central places: The theories of von Thünen, Christaller, and Lösch. In H. A. Eiselt & V. Marianov (Eds.), *Foundations of Location Analysis* (pp. 471–505). New York: Springer. https://doi.org/10.1007/978-1-4419-7572-0_20

Florida, R. (2002). *The Rise of the Creative Class: And How It's Transforming Work, Leisure, Community and Everyday Life*. New York: Basic Books.

Fotino, F. (2014). The JESSICA action in Italy 2007–2013: Bottlenecks, opportunities, and directions for the future. *European Structural and Investment Funds Journal, 2*(3), 245–255. Retrieved from https://estif.lexxion.eu/article/ESTIF/2014/3/9

FUAW. (2018). Uchwała nr 22/18 Sejmiku Województwa Mazowieckiego z dnia 19 grudnia 2018 r. w sprawie Planu zagospodarowania przestrzennego województwa mazowieckiego (Resolution No. 22/18 of the Council of the Mazowieckie Region regarding the spatial development plan of the Mazowieckie Region). Retrieved from https://www.mazovia.pl/wojewodztwo/plan-zagospodarowania-wojewodztwa-mazowieckiego/

Fujita, M., & Krugman, P. (1995). When is the economy monocentric?: Von Thünen and Chamberlin unified. *Regional Science and Urban Economics, 25*(4), 505–528. https://doi.org/10.1016/0166-0462(95)02098-F

Fujita, M., & Krugman, P. (2004). The new economic geography: Past, present and the future. *Papers in Regional Science, 83*(1), 139–164. https://doi.org/10.1007/s10110-003-0180-0

Fujita, M., Krugman, P., & Mori, T. (1999). On the evolution of hierarchical urban systems. *European Economic Review, 43*(2), 209–251. https://doi.org/10.1016/S0014-2921(98)00066-X

Gagolewski, M., Bartoszuk, M., & Cena, A. (2016). Genie: A new, fast, and outlier-resistant hierarchical clustering algorithm. *Information Sciences, 363*, 8–23. https://doi.org/10.1016/j.ins.2016.05.003

Gagolewski, M., Cena, A., & Bartoszuk, M. (2016). Hierarchical clustering via penalty-based aggregation and the Genie approach. In T. Vicenç, N. Yasuo, N.-A. Guillermo, & Y. Cristina (Eds.), *Modeling Decisions for Artificial Intelligence* (pp. 191–202). Cham: Springer. https://doi.org/10.1007/978-3-319-45656-0_16

Garbolino, E., Chéry, J.-P., & Guarnieri, F. (2019). The systemic approach: Concepts, method and tools. In F. Guarnieri & E. Garbolino (Eds.), *Safety Dynamics: Evaluating Risk in Complex Industrial Systems* (pp. 1–30). Cham: Springer. https://doi.org/10.1007/978-3-319-96259-7_1

García, B. (2004). Cultural policy and urban regeneration in western European cities: Lessons from experience, prospects for the future. *Local Economy, 19*(4), 312–326. https://doi.org/10.1080/0269094042000286828

Giuliano, G., Kang, S., & Yuan, Q. (2019). Agglomeration economies and evolving urban form. *The Annals of Regional Science, 63*(3), 377–398. https://doi.org/10.1007/s00168-019-00957-4

Glaeser, E. L. (Ed.) (2010). *Agglomeration Economics*. Chicago: University of Chicago Press.

Glaeser, E. L. (2011). *Triumph of the City: How Our Greatest Invention Makes Us Richer, Smarter, Greener, Healthier, and Happier*. New York: Penguin Press.

Glaeser, E. L. (2014). A world of cities: The causes and consequences of urbanization in poorer countries. *Journal of the European Economic Association, 12*(5), 1154–1199. https://doi.org/10.1111/jeea.12100

Glaeser, E. L., Kahn, M. E., & Rappaport, J. (2008). Why do the poor live in cities? The role of public transportation. *Journal of Urban Economics*, *63*(1), 1–24. https://doi.org/10.1016/j.jue.2006.12.004

Glaeser, E. L., Kolko, J., & Saiz, A. (2001). Consumer city. *Journal of Economic Geography*, *1*(1), 27–50. https://doi.org/10.1093/jeg/1.1.27

Gloazzo, C. (2018). The financial accountability of financial instruments in cohesion policy: Distinctive features? *European Structural and Investment Funds Journal*, *6*(2), 100–110.

Goetz, E. G., Lewis, B., Damiano, A., & Calhoun, M. (2019). *The Diversity of Gentrification: Multiple Forms of Gentrification in Minneapolis and St. Paul*. Minnesota: Center for Urban and Regional Affairs (CURa), University of Minnesota. Retrieved from http://gentrification.dl.umn.edu/sites/gentrification.dl.umn.edu/files/media/diversity-of-gentrification-012519.pdf

Goodall, B. (1972). *The Economics of Urban Areas*. Oxford: Pergamon Press.

Górniak, J., & Mazur, S. (2012). *Zarządzanie strategiczne rozwojem* (Strategic management of development). Warszawa: Ministry of Regional Development. Retrieved from http://www.euroreg.uw.edu.pl/dane/web_euroreg_publications_files/1206/zarzadzanie_strategiczne_rozwojem.pdf

Graebner, C. (2018). How to relate models to reality? An epistemological framework for the validation and verification of computational models. *Journal of Artificial Societies and Social Simulation*, *21*(3). https://doi.org/10.18564/jasss.3772

Guarino, N., & Giaretta, P. (1995). Ontologies and knowledge bases: Towards a terminological clarification. In N. J. Mars (Ed.), *Towards Very Large Knowledge Bases: Knowledge Building & Knowledge Sharing* (pp. 25–32). Amsterdam: IOS Press.

Hausner, J. (2008). *Zarządzanie publiczne* (Public Management). Warsaw: Wydawnictwo Naukowe Scholar.

Heffner, K. (2016). Proces suburbanizacji a polityka miejska w Polsce (Suburbanisation towards urban policy in Poland). In *Miasto – region – gospodarka w badaniach geograficznych. W stulecie urodzin Profesora Ludwika Straszewicza* (City – region – economy in geographical reserach. Celebrating the 100th anniversary of the birth of Professor Ludwik Straszewicz (pp. 75–110). Łódź: Wydawnictwo Uniwersytetu Łódzkiego. https://doi.org/10.18778/8088-005-4.05

Henderson, J. V., Shalizi, Z., & Venables, A. J. (2001). Geography and development. *Journal of Economic Geography*, *1*(1), 81–105. Retrieved from https://www.jstor.org/stable/26160401

Henderson, S., Bowlby, S., & Raco, M. (2007). Refashioning local government and inner-city regeneration: The Salford experience. *Urban Studies*, *44*(8), 1441–1463. https://doi.org/10.1080/00420980701373495

Henderson, V. (2003). The urbanization process and economic growth: The so-what question. *Journal of Economic Growth*, *8*(1), 47–71. https://doi.org/10.1023/A:1022860800744

Henderson, W. L., & Ledebur, L. C. (1972). *Urban Economics: Processes and Problems*. New York: John Wiley & Sons.

Hieronymi, A. (2013). Understanding systems science: A visual and integrative approach. *Systems Research and Behavioral Science*, *30*(5), 580–595. https://doi.org/10.1002/sres.2215

Hirschman, A. O. (1958). *The Strategy of Economic Development*. New Haven and London: Yale University Press.

Hołuj, A. (2018). Ekonomiczne i ekologiczne efekty zewnętrzne w planowaniu przestrzennym (Economic and ecological externalities in spatial planning). *Acta Universitatis Lodziensis. Folia Oeconomica, 4*(336), 137–155. https://doi.org/10.18778/0208-6018.336.09

Hübner, D. (2008). Financial Engineering in EU Cohesion Policy. Speech delivered on 10 December 2008 at the event of the European Association of Public Banks, "The Gate to the Latest Development in Financial Europe".

Idczak, P. (2020). JESSICA_projects_TIA. Mendeley Data. V1. https://doi.org/10.17632/rysmc2pmhs.1

Idczak, P., & Mrozik, K. (2021). The territorial impacts of JESSICA projects in municipalities: Evidence from the city of Poznań. *Ruch Prawniczy, Ekonomiczny i Socjologiczny* (Journal of Law, Economics and Sociology), *83*(1), 293–307. https://doi.org/10.14746/rpeis.2021.83.1.21

Idczak, P., Mrozik, K., & Musiałkowska, I. (2021). Spatial distribution of JESSICA funding across Polish municipalities: Perspective of territorial dimension of EU cohesion policy. *Studia Regionalne i Lokalne* (Regional and Local Studies), *85*(3), 7–20. https://doi.org/10.7366/1509499538501

Idczak, P., & Musiałkowska, I. (2019). The capacity of JESSICA projects to repay loans based on own revenues. *Entrepreneurial Business and Economics Review, 7*(2), 141–157. https://doi.org/10.15678/EBER.2019.070208

Idczak, P., & Musiałkowska, I. (2021). Urban regeneration as a specific type of public policy response to urban decline: The case of Poland. *Open Political Science, 4*(1), 204–218. https://doi.org/10.1515/openps-2021-0019

Idczak, P., Musiałkowska, I., & Mrozik, K. (2019a). Ecosystem services in the appraisal of the economic performance of urban regeneration projects exemplified by the JESSICA initiative. *Ekonomia i Środowisko* (Economics and Environment), *70*(3), 114–129. https://doi.org/10.34659/2019/3/38

Idczak, P., Musiałkowska, I., & Mrozik, K. (2019b). Zdolność projektów JESSICA do oddziaływania na procesy rynkowe w miastach (The ability of JESSICA projects to influence the market processes in cities). *Biuletyn KPZK PAN* (Journal of the Committee for Spatial Economy and Regional Planning, Polish Academy of Sciences), *273/274*, 202–222.

Jackson, W. A. (2002). Functional explanation in economics: A qualified defence. *Journal of Economic Methodology, 9*(2), 169–189. https://doi.org/10.1080/13501780110078981

Jacquier, C., Bienvenue, S., & Schlappa, H. (2007). *Regenera: Urban regeneration of deprived neighbourhoods across Europe*. Lyon: Urbact. Retrieved from https://urbact.eu/sites/default/files/import/general_library/070212rapport_GB.pdf

Jadach-Sepioło, A. (2017). Local development factors in urban regeneration: Theoretical approach. *Studia Regionalia, 46*, 73–87. https://doi.org/10.12657/studreg-46-05

Jadach-Sepioło, A. (2021). *Model rewitalizacji miast polskich na tle doświadczeń niemieckich* (Model of urban regeneration based on German experiences). Warsaw–Kraków: Instytut Rozwoju Miast i Regionów.

Janas, K., Jarczewski, W., & Wańkowicz, W. (2010). *Model rewitalizacji miast* (Model of urban regeneration). Kraków: Instytut Rozwoju Miast.

Jarczewski, W., & Ziobrowski, Z. (Eds.). (2010). *Rewitalizacja miast polskich – diagnoza* (Urban regeneration of Polish cities – diagnosis). Kraków: Instytut Rozwoju Miast.

Jolliffe, I. T. (2002). *Principal Component Analysis* (Second edition). New York: Springer. https://doi.org/10.1007/b98835

Kaczmarek, M. (2016). Zastosowanie analizy głównych składowych w ewaluacji skali pomiaru użyteczności serwisu internetowego (The application of principal component analysis in evaluating the scale of the web usability measurement). *Studia Oeconomica Posnaniensia*, 4(1), 128–141. https://doi.org/10.18559/SOEP.2016.1.9

Kaczmarek, S. (2001). *Rewitalizacja terenów poprzemysłowych: nowy wymiar w rozwoju miast* (Regeneration of post-industrial areas: New dimension in the development of cities). Łódź: Wydawnictwo Uniwersytetu Łódzkiego.

Kim, J. (2016). Vehicle fuel-efficiency choices, emission externalities, and urban sprawl. *Economics of Transportation*, 5, 24–36. https://doi.org/10.1016/j.ecotra.2015.10.001

Kłos, A. (2018). Barriers to the implementation of financial instruments under cohesion policy. *Yearbook of the Institute of East-Central Europe*, 16(3), 93–115.

Kolenikov, S., & Angeles, G. (2009). Socioeconomic status measurement with discrete proxy variables: Is principal component analysis a reliable answer? *Review of Income and Wealth*, 55(1), 128–165. https://doi.org/10.1111/j.1475-4991.2008.00309.x

Krugman, P. (1991). Increasing returns and economic geography. *Journal of Political Economy*, 99(3), 483–499. https://doi.org/10.1086/261763

Krugman, P. (1998). What's new about the new economic geography? *Oxford Review of Economic Policy*, 14(2), 7–17. https://doi.org/10.1093/oxrep/14.2.7

Krugman, P., & Wells, R. (2012). *Mikroekonomia* (Microeconomics). Warsaw: Wydawnictwo Naukowe PWN.

Kuźnik, F. (2015). Miejskie obszary funkcjonalne a polityka miejska (Functional urban areas in regional urban policy perspective). *Studia Ekonomiczne* (Economic Studies), 250(250), 7–24.

Lang, T. (2005). *Insights in the British Debate about Urban Decline and Urban Regeneration* (IRS Working Papers No. 32). Erkner: Leibniz-Institut für Regionalentwicklung und Strukturplanung. Retrieved from http://hdl.handle.net/10419/228562

Larsen, J. N., & Engberg, L. A. (2011). Organisational change and knowledge management in urban regeneration planning. *Tidsskrift for Kortlægning Og Arealforvaltning* (Danish Journal of Geoinformatics and Land Managemen), 46(1), 114–126. https://doi.org/10.5278/ojs.tka.v119i46.596

Leipzig Charter. (2007). Leipzig Charter on Sustainable European Cities. Leipzig: European Commission. Retrieved from https://ec.europa.eu/regional_policy/archive/themes/urban/leipzig_charter.pdf

Lepore, D., Sgobbo, A., & Vingelli, F. (2017). The strategic approach in urban regeneration: The Hamburg model. *Journal of Urban Planning, Landscape & Environmental Design*, 2(3), 185–218. https://doi.org/10.6092/2531-9906/5415

Lever, J., Krzywinski, M., & Altman, N. (2016). Logistic regression. *Nature Methods*, 13(7), 541–542. https://doi.org/https://doi.org/10.1038/nmeth.3904

Lorens, P., & Martyniuk-Pęczek, J. (2009). *Wybrane zagadnienia rewitalizacji miast* (Some issues of urban regeneration). Gdańsk: Wydawnictwo Urbanista.

Mak, A., & Stouten, P. (2014). Urban regeneration in Rotterdam: Economic and social values. *European Spatial Research and Policy*, 21(1), 101–122. https://doi.org/10.2478/esrp-2014-0008

Markowski, T. (2011). *Terytorialny wymiar zintegrowanej polityki rozwoju – oczekiwania i wyzwania wobec planowania i systemu instytucjonalnego* (Territorial dimension of integrated development policy – expectations and challenges towards planning and the institutional system). Warsaw: KPZG. Retrieved from http://www.lodzkie.pl/wps/wcm/connect/228f458048511957a85bac91f205df23/T_Markowski_Terytorialny_wymiar_zint_polityki_rozwoju_13092011.pdf?MOD=AJPERES

Markowski, T. (2018). Polityka urbanistyczna państwa – koncepcja, zakres i struktura instytucjonalna w systemie zintegrowanego zarządzania rozwojem (State Urban Policy – concept, institutional scope and structure in integrative management of the development). *Studia KPZK PAN* (Studies of the Committee for Spatial Economy and Regional Planning, Polish Academy of Sciences), *183*, 89–101. Retrieved from https://journals.pan.pl/dlibra/publication/123575/edition/107788/content

Marra, G., Barosio, M., Eynard, E., Marietta, C., Tabasso, M., & Melis, G. (2016). From urban renewal to urban regeneration: Classification criteria for urban interventions. Turin 1995–2015: Evolution of planning tools and approaches. *Journal of Urban Regeneration and Renewal*, *9*(4), 367–380.

McCann, P. (2001). *Urban and Regional Economics*. Oxford: Oxford University Press.

McCann, P., & van Oort, F. (2019). Theories of agglomeration and regional economic growth: A historical review. In P. Nijkamp & R. Capello (Eds.), *Handbook of Regional Growth and Development Theories* (pp. 6–23). Cheltenham: Edward Elgar Publishing. https://doi.org/10.4337/9781788970020.00007

McCarthy, J. (2000). Cultural strategies and urban regeneration: The case of Dundee. *European Spatial Research and Policy*, *7*(1), 23–36. Retrieved from http://esrap.geo.uni.lodz.pl/uploads/publications/articles/v7n1/John McCARTHY.pdf

McDonald, J. F. (1997). *Fundamentals of Urban Economics*. Upper Saddle River, NJ: Prentice Hall.

Medda, F. R., Caschili, S., & Modelewska, M. (2012). Financial mechanisms for historic city core regeneration and brownfield redevelopment. In G. Licciardi & R. Amirtahmasebi (Eds.), *The Economics of Uniqueness: Investing in Historic City Cores and Cultural Heritage Assets for Sustainable Development* (pp. 213–243). Washington, D.C.: World Bank.

Medeiros, E. (2014). *Territorial Impact Assessment (TIA): The Process, Methods, Techniques* (ZOE | Dinâmicas e Políticas Regionais e Urbanas). Lisbon: Centro de Estudos Geográficos.

Medeiros, E. (2016). Territorial cohesion: An EU concept. *European Journal of Spatial Development*, *60*, 1–30. Retrieved from https://archive.nordregio.se/Global/EJSD/Refereed articles/refereed60.pdf

Medeiros, E. (2019). Debating the urban dimension of territorial cohesion. In E. Medeiros (Ed.), *Territorial Cohesion: The Urban Book Series* (pp. 3–22). Cham: Springer. https://doi.org/10.1007/978-3-030-03386-6_1

Medeiros, E., & Rauhut, D. (2020). Territorial cohesion cities: A policy recipe for achieving territorial cohesion? *Regional Studies*, *54*(1), 120–128. https://doi.org/10.1080/00343404.2018.1548764

Memorandum of Understanding. (2006). Memorandum of Understanding in Respect of a Coordinated Approach to the Financing of Urban Renewal and Development for Programming Period 2007–2013 of the Community Structural Funds between the

European Commission, the European Investment Bank and the Council of Europe Development Bank. Retrieved from http://ec.europa.eu/regional_policy/archive/funds/2007/jjj/doc/pdf/urban_mou_signed.pdf

Mendez, C. (2011). The Lisbonization of EU cohesion policy: A successful case of experimentalist governance? *European Planning Studies*, *19*(3), 519–537. https://doi.org/10.1080/09654313.2011.548368

Michie, R., Mendez, C., & Gal, F. (2018). *Results, Review and Reform: Delivering Programme Objectives While Preparing for the Post-2020 Cohesion Policy* (IQ-Net Review Paper No. 43(1)). Delft: European Policies Research Centre Delft. Retrieved from https://eprc-strath.org/wp-content/uploads/2021/10/IQ-Net_Review_Paper_431-2018A.pdf

Mikrut-Majeranek, M. (2015). Miasto miejscem nieustannego eksperymentu (City a place of continuous experimentation). *Anthropos?*, *24*, 121–134.

Miller, H. (2014). *What Are the Features of Urbanisation and Cities that Promote Productivity, Employment and Salaries?*. London: EPS-PEAKS. Retrieved from https://assets.publishing.service.gov.uk/media/57a089efe5274a27b200032b/What_are_the_features_of_urbanisation_and_cities_that_promote_productivity_employment_and_salaries.pdf

Moretti, E. (2014). *Cities and Growth* (IGC Evidence Paper). London: International Growth Centre. Retrieved from https://www.theigc.org/wp-content/uploads/2014/09/IGCEvidencePaperCities.pdf

Mori, Y., Tanaka, Y., & Tarumi, T. (1998). Principal component analysis based on a subset of variables for qualitative data. In C. Hayashi, K. Yajima, H.-H. Bock, N. Ohsumi, Y. Tanaka, & Y. Baba (Eds.), *Data Science, Classification, and Related Methods* (pp. 547–554). Tokyo: Springer Japan.

Mulligan, G. F., Partridge, M. D., & Carruthers, J. I. (2012). Central place theory and its reemergence in regional science. *The Annals of Regional Science*, *48*(2), 405–431. https://doi.org/10.1007/s00168-011-0496-7

Murzyn, D. (2018). Urban development under EU cohesion policy: An example of major cities in Poland. *Urban Development Issues*, *53*(1), 27–35. https://doi.org/10.1515/udi-2017-0003

Musiałkowska, I., & Idczak, P. (2016). The use of repayable financial instruments in the process of regeneration of degraded urban areas on the example of the JESSICA initiative. In *Changes and Challenges in the Modern World Economy* (vol. 1, pp. 115–136). Poznań: PUEB Press. Retrieved from https://depot.ceon.pl/handle/123456789/12083

Musiałkowska, I., & Idczak, P. (2018). Is the JESSICA initiative truly repayable instrument? The Polish case study. *Prace Naukowe Uniwersytetu Ekonomicznego We Wrocławiu* (Research Papers of Wroclaw University of Economics and Business), *536*, 143–151. https://doi.org/10.15611/pn.2018.536.13

Musiałkowska, I., & Idczak, P. (2020). JESSICA initiative to support sustainable urban development projects in Poland. In I. Musiałkowska, P. Idczak, & O. Potluka (Eds.), *EU Cohesion Policy in Eastern and Southern Europe: Taking Stock and Drawing Lessons for the Future* (pp. 169–200). Berlin: De Gruyter. https://doi.org/10.1515/9788395720451-009

Musterd, S., Marcińczak, S., van Ham, M., & Tammaru, T. (2017). Socioeconomic segregation in European capital cities: Increasing separation between poor and rich. *Urban Geography*, *38*(7), 1062–1083. https://doi.org/10.1080/02723638.2016.1228371

MUSV. (2017). Rozporządzenie Rady Ministrów z dnia 26 czerwca 2017 r. w sprawie utworzenia w województwie śląskim związku metropolitalnego pod nazwą "Górnośląsko-Zagłębiowska Metropolia" (Cabinet of Ministers ordinance of 26 June 2017 on the creation of the Metropolis of the Upper Silesian Union in the Śląskie region). Retrieved from http://isap.sejm.gov.pl/isap.nsf/download.xsp/WDU20170001290/O/D20171290.pdf

Myrdal, G. (1957). *Economic Theory and Under-Developed Regions*. London: G. Duckworth.

Nadler, M., & Nadler, C. (2018). Promoting investment in sustainable urban development with JESSICA: Outcomes of a new EU policy initiative. *Urban Studies*, *55*(9), 1839–1858. https://doi.org/10.1177/0042098017702815

Neto, P., & Serrano, M. M. (2011). *Governance and City Regeneration: A New Methodological Approach for Design and Evaluation*. European Regional Science Association (ERSA). Retrieved from http://hdl.handle.net/10419/120035

New Leipzig Charter. (2020). *The New Leipzig Charter: The Transformative Power of Cities for the Common Good*. European Commission. Retrieved from https://ec.europa.eu/regional_policy/sources/docgener/brochure/new_leipzig_charter/new_leipzig_charter_en.pdf

Noon, D., Smith-Canham, J., & Eagland, M. (2000). Economic regeneration and funding. In P. Roberts & H. Sykes (Eds.), *Urban Regeneration: A Handbook* (First, pp. 61–85). London: SAGE Publications Ltd.

Noworól, A. (2010). Rewitalizacja jako wyzwanie polityki rozwoju (Urban regeneration as a challenge of the development policy). In K. Skalski (Ed.), *O budowie metod rewitalizacji w Polsce – aspekty wybrane* (Developing methods for urban regeneration in Poland – selected aspects) (pp. 29–46). Kraków: Instytut Spraw Publicznych UJ.

Noworól, A., & Noworól, K. (2017). Rewitalizacja obszarów miejskich jako wehikuł rozwoju lokalnego (Revitalization of urban areas as a vehicle of local development). *Studia KPZK PAN (Studies of the Committee for Spatial Economy and Regional Planning, Polish Academy of Sciences*, *177*, 129–144. https://doi.org/10.24425/118589

Nussbaumer, J., & Moulaert, F. (2004). Integrated area development and social innovation in European cities. *City*, *8*(2), 249–257. https://doi.org/10.1080/1360481042000242201

Nyikos, G. (2016). *Financial Instruments in the 2014–20 Programming Period: First Experiences of Member States*. Brussels: European Parliament. https://doi.org/10.2861/279642

OECD. (2008). *Handbook on Constructing Composite Indicators: Methodology and User Guide* (OECD Statistics Working Papers). OECD Publications. https://doi.org/10.1787/533411815016

OECD. (2011). *OECD Urban Policy Reviews, Poland 2011*. Paris: OECD. https://doi.org/10.1787/9789264097834-en

OECD. (2018). *Divided Cities: Understanding Intra-urban Inequalities*. Paris: OECD Publishing. https://doi.org/10.1787/9789264300385-en

Olejniczak, K. (2008). *Mechanizmy wykorzystania ewaluacji: Studium ewaluacji średniookresowych INTERREG III* (Mechanism for use of evaluation: INTERREG III study of the mid-term evaluations). Warsaw: Scholar.

Olsson, U. (1979). Maximun likelihood estimation of the polychoric correlation. *Psychometrika*, *44*(4), 443–460.
Palazzo, A. L. (2017). Culture-led regeneration in Rome: From the factory city to the knowledge city. *International Studies. Interdisciplinary Political and Cultural Journal*, *19*(1), 13–27. https://doi.org/10.1515/ipcj-2017-0002
Paradowska, M. (2006). Unijne metody internalizacji kosztów zewnętrznych transportu a sytuacja w Polsce (EU methods of transport external costs internalization and the situation in Poland). *Logistics and Transport*, *2*, 43–54.
Parkinson, M. (2014). *Integrated urban regeneration in 2014: Anything new under the sun and so what for Spain?* European Institute for Urban Affairs. Retrieved from https://www.diba.cat/documents/228621/31438172/Integrated+Urban+Regeneration+in+2014+-+Anything+new+under+the+sun+and+so+what+for+Spain+-+M.+Parkinson+2014.pdf/88e241ad-0a6d-4466-b6ea-e22e44ad2de8
Pastak, I., & Kährik, A. (2016). The impacts of culture-led flagship projects on local communities in the context of post-socialist Tallinn. *Czech Sociological Review*, *52*(6), 963–990. https://doi.org/10.13060/00380288.2016.52.6.292
Pawson, R., & Tilley, N. (1997). *Realistic Evaluation*. London: Sage.
Pawson, R., & Tilley, N. (2001). Realistic evaluation bloodlines. *The American Journal of Evaluation*, *22*(3), 317–324. https://doi.org/10.1016/S1098-2140(01)00141-2
Pfeiffer, D., & Niehaves, B. (2005). Evaluation of conceptual models: A structuralist approach. In *ECIS 2005 Proceedings 43*. Atlanta: European Conference on Information Systems. Retrieved from https://aisel.aisnet.org/ecis2005/43/
Pike, A., Lee, N., Mackinnon, D., Kempton, L., & Iddawela, Y. (2016). Cities and demand-side policies for inclusive growth. Submission for the RSA Inclusive Growth Commission in January 2016. Retrieved from http://www.ncl.ac.uk/media/wwwnclacuk/curds/files/RSA IGC Submission – Cities and Demand-side Policies for Inclusive Growth.pdf
Ploegmakers, H., & Beckers, P. (2015). Evaluating urban regeneration: An assessment of the effectiveness of physical regeneration initiatives on run-down industrial sites in the Netherlands. *Urban Studies*, *52*(12), 2151–2169. https://doi.org/10.1177/0042098014542134
PMA. (2019). Uchwała Nr V/70/19 Sejmiku Województwa Wielkopolskiego z dnia 25 marca 2019 r. w sprawie uchwalenia Planu zagospodarowania przestrzennego województwa wielkopolskiego wraz z Planem zagospodarowania przestrzennego miejskiego obszaru funkcjonalnego Poznania (Resolution No. V/70/19 of the Council of the Wielkopolskie Region of 25 March 2019 on the adoption of the spatial development plan of the Wielkopolskie Region including the spatial development plan of the urban functional area of the city of Poznań). Retrieved from http://www.wbpp.poznan.pl/index.php?option=com_content&task=view&id=198&Itemid=1%0A
Pratt, A. C. (2009). Urban regeneration: From the arts "feel good" factor to the cultural economy. A case study of Hoxton, London. *Urban Studies*, *46*(5–6), 1041–1061. https://doi.org/10.1177/0042098009103854
Proost, S., & Thisse, J.-F. (2019). What can be learned from spatial economics? *Journal of Economic Literature*, *57*(3), 575–643. https://doi.org/10.1257/jel.20181414
R Core Team. (2018). R: A language and environment for statistical computing. R Foundation for Statistical Computing. Retrieved from https://www.r-project.org/

Ramsden, P. (2011). *Cities and Disadvantaged Neighbourhoods*. Retrieved from https://urbact.eu/sites/default/files/import/general_library/Rapport_Urbact_II.pdf

Regnier, C., & Legras, S. (2018). Urban structure and environmental externalities. *Environmental and Resource Economics*, *70*(1), 31–52. https://doi.org/10.1007/s10640-016-0109-0

Richardson, H. W. (1995). Economies and diseconomies of agglomeration. In H. Giersch (Ed.), *Urban Agglomeration and Economic Growth* (pp. 123–155). Heidelberg: Springer. https://doi.org/https://doi.org/10.1007/978-3-642-79397-4_6

Roberts, P. (2008). The evolution, definition and purpose of urban regeneration. In P. Roberts & H. Sykes (Eds.), *Urban Regeneration: A Handbook* (pp. 9–36). London: Sage. https://doi.org/10.4135/9781446219980

Robinson, F., Shaw, K., & Davidson, G. (2005). "On the side of the Angels": Community involvement in the governance of neighbourhood renewal. *Local Economy*, *20*(1), 13–26. https://doi.org/10.1080/0269094042000313584

Robinson, W., & Schutjer, W. (1982). The agricultural surplus as a factor in development. *Journal of Rural Development*, *5*(1), 73–90. https://doi.org/10.22004/ag.econ.287377

Rode, P. (2018). *Governing Compact Cities: How to Connect Planning, Design and Transport*. Cheltenham: Edward Elgar Publishing. https://doi.org/10.4337/9781788111362

Rodrigue, J.-P. (2020). *The Geography of Transport Systems* (Fifth edition). Abingdon, Oxon: Routledge. https://doi.org/10.4324/9780429346323

Runge, A. (2012). Metodologiczne problemy badania miast średnich w Polsce (Methodological problems associated with research on midsize towns in Poland). *Prace Geograficzne (Geographical Studies)*, (129), 83–101. https://doi.org/10.4467/20833113PG.12.015.0523

Schmutzler, A. (1999). The new economic geography. *Journal of Economic Surveys*, *13*(4), 355–379. https://doi.org/10.1111/1467-6419.00087

Schneidewind, P., Radzyner, A., Hahn, M., Gaspari, E., Michie, R., & Wishlade, F. (2013). *Financial Engineering Instruments in Cohesion Policy*. Brussels: European Parliament's Committee on Regional Development. https://doi.org/10.2861/28814

Schuurmans, A., Dyrbøl, S., & Guay, F. (2019). Buildings in urban regeneration. In A. Almusaed (Ed.), *Sustainable Cities: Authenticity, Ambition and Dream* (pp. 1–20). London: IntechOpen. https://doi.org/10.5772/intechopen.81803

Skalski, K. (2016). Wprowadzenie do problematyki rewitalizacji na lata 2015–2020 (An introduction to urban regeneration issues for the period 2015–2020). Paper presented at the 4th Congress of Revitalisation in Wałbrzych, 19–21 September 2016.

Śleszyński, P. (2013). Delimitacja Miejskich Obszarów Funkcjonalnych stolic województw (Delimitation of the Functional Urban Areas around Poland's voivodship capital cities). *Przegląd Geograficzny (Polish Geographical Review)*, *85*(2), 173–197. https://doi.org/10.7163/PrzG.2013.2.2

SMA. (2020). Uchwała nr XVII/214/20 Sejmiku Województwa Zachodniopomorskiego z dnia 24 czerwca 2020 r. zmieniająca uchwałę w sprawie uchwalenia Planu Zagospodarowania Przestrzennego Województwa Zachodniopomorskiego (Resolution No. XVII/214/20 of the Council of the Zachodniopomorskie Region of 24 June 2020 amending the resolution on the adoption of the spatial development plan of the Zachodniopomorskie Region). Retrieved from http://rbgp.pl/pzpwz-2020/

Smętkowski, M. (2011). Wpływ polityki spójności na dyfuzję procesów rozwojowych w otoczeniu dużych polskich miast (The impact of EU Cohesion Policy on diffusion of development processes in the regional surroundings of large Polish cities). *Studia Regionalne i Lokalne* (Regional and Local Studies), (5), 123–154.

Smętkowski, M., Jałowiecki, B., & Gorzelak, G. (2009). Obszary metropolitalne w Polsce – diagnoza i rekomendacje (Metropolitan areas of Poland: Assessment and recommendations). *Studia Regionalne i Lokalne* (Regional and Local Studies), *35*(1), 52–73.

Stiglitz, J. E. (2013). *Ekonomia sektora publicznego* (Economics of the public sector). Warsaw: Wydawnictwo Naukowe PWN.

Stouten, P. (2011). Changing contexts in urban regeneration. *Atlantis: Magazine for Urbanism and Landscape Architecture*, *22*(1), 4–7. Retrieved from https://issuu.com/atlantismagazine/docs/atlantis_22.1_urban_society

Stouten, P. (2016). Urban design and the changing context of urban regeneration in the Netherlands. *European Spatial Research and Policy*, *23*(1), 111–126. https://doi.org/10.1515/esrp-2016-0006

Stryjakiewicz, T., Ciesiółka, P., & Jaroszewska, E. (2012). Urban shrinkage and the post-socialist transformation: The case of Poland. *Built Environment*, *38*(2), 196–213. https://doi.org/10.2148/benv.38.2.196

Szlachta, J., & Zaucha, J. (2010). *A New Paradigm of the EU Regional Development in the Context of the Poland's National Spatial Development Concept* (No. 1/2010). Sopot: Institute for Development. Retrieved from https://instytut-rozwoju.org/WP/IR_WP_1.pdf

Tallon, A. (2013). *Urban Regeneration in the UK* (Second edition). London: Routledge. https://doi.org/10.4324/9780203802847

Taylor, M. A. P. (2021). *Climate Change Adaptation for Transportation Systems*. Amsterdam: Elsevier. https://doi.org/10.1016/C2018-0-00205-4

TCMA. (2016). Uchwała Nr 318/XXX/16 Sejmiku Województwa Pomorskiego z dnia 29 grudnia 2016 r. w sprawie uchwalenia nowego planu zagospodarowania przestrzennego województwa pomorskiego oraz stanowiącego jego część planu zagospodarowania przestrzennego obszaru metropolitalnego Trójmiasta (Resolution No. 318/XXX/16 of the Council of the Pomorskie Region of 29 December 2016 on the adoption of the new spatial development plan of the Pomorskie Region including, as its integral part, the spatial development plan of the Tricity metropolitan area). Retrieved from http://edziennik.gdansk.uw.gov.pl/eli/POL_WOJ_PM/2017/603/ogl/pol/pdf%0A

Thorns, D. C. (2002). *The Transformation of Cities: Urban Theory and Urban Life*. London: Palgrave Macmillan. https://doi.org/10.1007/978-1-4039-9031-0

Toledo Declaration. (2010). Toledo Informal Ministerial Meeting on Urban Development Declaration. Toledo: European Commission. Retrieved from https://ec.europa.eu/regional_policy/archive/newsroom/pdf/201006_toledo_declaration_en.pdf

Tosics, I. (2011). Dilemmas of integrated area-based urban renewal. *Problemy Rozwoju Miast* (Urban Development Issues), *8*(3–4), 31–37.

Tosics, I. (2015). *Integrated Regeneration of Deprived Areas and the New Cohesion Policy Approach*. Retrieved from https://urbact.eu/sites/default/files/20150909_urbact_deprived-areas_gb_md_1.pdf

Trillo, C. (2014). Urban Regeneration and New Partnerships among Public Institutions, Local Entrepreneurs and Communities. *Advanced Engineering Forum*, *11*, 303–313. https://doi.org/10.4028/www.scientific.net/AEF.11.303

Turcu, C. (2012a). Local experiences of urban sustainability: Researching housing market renewal interventions in three English neighbourhoods. *Progress in Planning*, *78*(3), 101–150. https://doi.org/10.1016/j.progress.2012.04.002

Turcu, C. (2012b). Local experiences of urban sustainability: Researching housing market renewal interventions in three English neighbourhoods. *Progress in Planning*, *78*(3), 101–150. https://doi.org/10.1016/j.progress.2012.04.002

Tyler, P., Warnock, C., Provins, A., & Lanz, B. (2013). Valuing the benefits of urban regeneration. *Urban Studies*, *50*(1), 169–190. https://doi.org/10.1177/0042098012452321

Uebersax, J. S. (2015). Introduction to the tetrachoric and polychoric correlation coefficients. Retrieved from http://www.john-uebersax.com/stat/tetra.htm

UNHABITAT. (2007). *Inclusive and Sustainable Urban Planning: A Guide for Municipalities. Analysis* (vol. 1). UNON Publishing Service Section.

Urbact. (2013). URBACT Markets. Town Centre Regeneration. Thematic Guidelines. Retrieved from https://urbact.eu/urbact-markets-guidelines-offers-cities-new-route-map-development

Urban Agenda. (2016). Urban Agenda for the EU. Pact of Amsterdam. European Commission. Retrieved from https://ec.europa.eu/futurium/en/system/files/ged/pact-of-amsterdam_en.pdf

URPofP. (2013). *Urban Regeneration Programme for the City of Poznań* (Third edition). Retrieved from https://www.poznan.pl/mim/public/main/attachments.att?co=show&instance=1017&parent=81623&lang=pl&id=238308

van den Bergh, J. C. J. M. (2010). Externality or sustainability economics? *Ecological Economics*, *69*(11), 2047–2052. https://doi.org/10.1016/j.ecolecon.2010.02.009

van der Pennen, T., & van Bortel, G. (2016). Exemplary urban practitioners in neighbourhood renewal: Survival of the fittest … and the fitting. *Voluntas*, *27*, 1323–1342. https://doi.org/10.1007/s11266-015-9600-4

van der Zwet, A., Bachtler, J., Ferry, M., McMaster, I., & Miller, S. (2017). *Integrated Territorial and Urban Strategies: How Are ESIF Adding Value in 2014–2020?* Brussels: European Commission. https://doi.org/10.2776/50425

van Kempen, R., Wassenberg, F., & van Meer, A. (2007). Upgrading the physical environment in deprived urban areas: Lessons from integrated policies. *Informationen Zur Raumentwicklung* (Information on Spatial Development), *7/8*, 487–497.

van Meerkerk, I., Boonstra, B., & Edelenbos, J. (2013). Self-organization in urban regeneration: A two-case comparative research. *European Planning Studies*, *21*(10), 1630–1652. https://doi.org/10.1080/09654313.2012.722963

van Meeteren, M., & Poorthuis, A. (2018). Christaller and "big data": Recalibrating central place theory via the geoweb. *Urban Geography*, *39*(1), 122–148. https://doi.org/10.1080/02723638.2017.1298017

Venables, A. J. (2005). Spatial disparities in developing countries: Cities, regions, and international trade. *Journal of Economic Geography*, *5*(1), 3–21. https://doi.org/10.1093/jnlecg/lbh051

Verhoef, E., & Nijkamp, P. (2003). *Externalities in the Urban Economy* (Tinbergen Institute Discussion Paper, 2003–078/3), 1–24. https://doi.org/10.2139/ssrn.457580

Verhoef, E., & Nijkamp, P. (2008). Urban environmental externalities, agglomeration forces, and the technological "deus ex machina". *Environment and Planning A, 40*(4), 928–947. https://doi.org/10.1068/a38434

Vranken, J., de Decker, P., & van Nieuwenhuyze, I. (2003). *Social Inclusion, Urban Governance, and Sustainability: Towards a Conceptual Framework for the UGIS Research Project.* Antwerp: Garant.

Wachelke, J. (2013). Beyond social representations: The conceptual bases of the structural approach on social thinking. *Revista Interamericana de Psicología/Interamerican Journal of Psychology, 47*(1), 131–138.

Walesiak, M., & Bąk, A. (1997). Wykorzystanie analizy czynnikowej w badaniach marketingowych (The applications of factor analysis in marketing research). *Badania Operacyjne i Decyzje* (Operations research and decisions), *1*(1), 77–87.

Wang, B., Shi, W., & Miao, Z. (2015). Confidence analysis of standard deviational ellipse and its extension into higher dimensional euclidean space. *PLOS ONE, 10*(3), 1–17. https://doi.org/10.1371/journal.pone.0118537

Wassenberg, F., & van Dijken, K. (2011). *A Practitioner's View on Neighbourhood Regeneration: Issues, Approaches and Experiences in European Cities.* The Hague: Nicis Institute.

Wassenberg, F., van Meer, A., & van Kempen, R. (2007). *Strategies for Upgrading the Physical Environment in Deprived Urban Areas: Examples of Good Practice in Europe.* Retrieved from http://resolver.tudelft.nl/uuid:7ccaa37b-206e-4dc7-b0ed-7d2d01b5d79e

Wasserstein, R. L., & Lazar, N. A. (2016). The ASA's statement on p-values: Context, process, and purpose. *The American Statistician, 70*(2), 129–133. https://doi.org/10.1080/00031305.2016.1154108

Węcławowicz, G., Łotocka, M., & Baucz, A. (2010). *Rozwój miast w Polsce. Raport wprowadzający Ministerstwa Rozwoju Regionalnego opracowany na potrzeby przygotowania Przeglądu OECD krajowej polityki miejskiej w Polsce* (Development of the cities in Poland. The introductory report of the Ministry of Regional Development drawn up for the needs of the OECD Review of the National Urban Policy in Poland). Warsaw: Ministerstwo Rozwoju Regionalnego. Retrieved from http://eregion.wzp.pl/sites/default/files/rozwoj_miast_w_polsce_0.pdf

Weeber, R., Nothdorf, P., & Fischer, R. (2011). *CoNet's Guide to Social Cohesion: Integrated Approaches in Disadvantaged Neighbourhoods.* Berlin: Urbact. Retrieved from https://urbact.eu/sites/default/files/import/Projects/CoNet/outputs_media/CoNet_s_Guide_to_Social_Cohesion_01.pdf

Wishlade, F. (2018). Financial instruments in ESIF: Past, present and future conditional. *European Structural and Investment Funds Journal, 6*(2), 89–99.

Wishlade, F., & Michie, R. (2016). Financial instruments in ESI funds programmes: A look to the future with a view to the past. *European Structural and Investment Funds Journal, 4*(4), 204–213.

Wishlade, F., & Michie, R. (2018). *Financial Instruments in Practice: Uptake and Limitations.* OECD. Retrieved from https://www.oecd.org/cfe/regionaldevelopment/Wishlade_Michie_Financial-Instruments-in-Practice.pdf

Wishlade, F., Moodie, J., Penje, O., Norlen, G., Korthals Altes, W., Assirelli Pandolfi, C., & de la Fuente Abajo, A. (2019). *Financial Instruments and Territorial Cohesion. Final Report.*

Luxembourg: ESPON. Retrieved from https://www.espon.eu/sites/default/files/attachments/ESPON Financial Instruments_Main Report_Final.pdf

Wojnarowska, A., & Kozłowski, S. (2011). *Rewitalizacja zdegradowanych obszarów miejskich. Zagadnienia teoretyczne* (Regeneration of urban deprived areas. Theoretical issues). Łódź: Wydawnictwo Uniwersytetu Łódzkiego.

Worren, N. (2016). Functional analysis of organizational designs. *International Journal of Organizational Analysis*, *24*(5), 774–791. https://doi.org/10.1108/IJOA-03-2015-0846

Xie, F., Liu, G., & Zhuang, T. (2021). A comprehensive review of urban regeneration governance for developing appropriate governance arrangements. *Land*, *5*(10), 1–28. https://doi.org/10.3390/land10050545

Yang, X., & Grigorescu, A. (2017). Measuring economic spatial evolutional trend of Central and Eastern Europe by SDE method. *Contemporary Economics*, *11*(3), 253–266. https://doi.org/10.5709/ce.1897-9254.241

Yuill, R. S. (1971). The standard deviational ellipse: An updated tool for spatial description. *Geografiska Annaler. Series B, Human Geography*, *53*(1), 28. https://doi.org/10.2307/490885

Zaucha, J., Świątek, D., & Stańczuk-Olejnik, K. (2013). *Place-Based Territorially Sensitive and Integrated Approach*. Warsaw: Ministry of Regional Development.

Index

Aesthetic-design approach 75
Aesthetic mappings 8, 150, 152, 155
Agglomeration diseconomies 23f., 26, 33f., 36, 43, 56, 138f., 212
Agglomeration economies 1, 14, 18–20, 22f., 31, 41f., 72, 207, 211f.
Agglomerative hierarchical clustering 173f.
Agglomerative linkages 143, 186
Agricultural surplus 13–15
Amenities 11, 17, 19, 26, 38, 46, 49, 51, 65, 80, 85f., 97, 204
Anova analysis 8, 144, 162, 166, 167
Area-based regenerative actions 83
Azimuth 186f.
Azimuth angle 151

Backward linkages 22
Barycenter 152
Bi-directional linkages 22
Binary rating scale 143
Binary response variable 143f.
Binary variables 8, 157
Built-up area 13
Business environment 6, 11, 19, 81, 101, 129
Business plan 121, 123, 126, 200, 202

Capital back-flows 196, 215
Cash flows 168, 196, 209
Cash in-flows 142f.
Catalytic effect 4, 216
Central place theory 28
Centrifugal forces 21–23, 26
Centripetal forces 21, 23
Centroid 152
Christaller-type urban hierarchies 23, 30
Cluster analysis 148, 173, 175, 197
Co-financing 108, 120, 127, 206f.
Cognitive model 91
Collaborative governance 70
Commercial return 113, 135, 167
Common Strategic Framework 93
Community-based initiatives 64

Composite indicator 147, 170–178, 197
Congestion 23, 37–39, 50, 72
Consumer's utility functions 19
Convergence 100f., 122
Core–periphery model 21, 22f., 212
Cross-sectoral collaboration 62, 76, 94
Cumulative circular causation 44, 46

Decision-making process 57, 61, 72, 78, 92, 214
De-commitment 110
Demand-side policy 204
Density regulations 49f.
Deprived urban areas 3, 5–7, 46–48, 50, 57, 59, 70, 72, 80, 82, 89, 92, 94, 96, 101, 106, 167, 182f., 185, 196, 199, 202, 209, 214
Descriptive research 7f.
Devaluation 24, 212
Directional distribution method 8, 150
Disadvantaged urban areas 4, 130, 154, 216
Discontinuous leapfrog development 49
Diseconomy 25, 47, 56, 138, 212
Disintegration 65

Eccentricity 151f., 188f.
Economic agents 13, 26
Economic discrimination 44, 212
Economic efficiency 11, 61, 168, 170, 175, 196, 209, 211
Economic forces 11f., 15, 18, 211
Economic organisation 11, 211
Economic productivity 12, 45
Economies of scale 12–15, 18, 20, 22, 46, 56, 211
Efficient allocation of resources 18
Efficient utilisation 16
Eigenvalue 170
Eligibility 110, 116, 119, 122, 200
Eminent domain 50f., 78
Employability 62, 68, 83
Empowerment 71, 79, 94, 97

https://doi.org/10.1515/9783110762198-013

Environmental sustainability   55, 138
Epistemological reasoning   87
Equity   72, 113, 117, 121 f., 124 f., 129
Euclidian distance   148
European funds   92, 100 f., 108, 110, 129, 143, 146, 197, 199 f., 205–207
European Structural and Investment Funds   93
Exogenous interventions   53
Experts' judgements   8, 149
Extensive literature survey   8
External diseconomies   24, 34
External economies   14, 19 f., 25

Faceted scatterplot   152, 155
Factor loadings   147
Feasibility study   202
Field studies   7 f., 140
Financial efficiency   61
Financial engineering   4, 102, 106, 108, 116 f., 168, 171
Financial engineering instruments   4 f., 7, 109, 111 f., 116 f., 123 f., 135, 140, 174, 199, 215 f.
Financial engineering mechanism   6, 108
Financial revolving instruments   5, 136
Financial sustainability   168
Financial viability   62, 154
Forward linkages   22
Functional approach   52, 89
Functional hierarchy   30, 32
Functional urban system   33

General equilibrium   11, 16, 18, 23
General locational equilibrium   31
General theory of equilibrium   22
Generic model   73
Genie linkage   8, 148, 173 f.
Gentrification   46, 66, 84
Geocoding   8, 140
Geoms   153
Geoprocessing   139
GIS technique   185
Grant-culture   5, 136, 199
Green Paper   107
Guarantee funds   111, 121, 201

Holding fund   111 f., 116, 118 f., 121, 123, 126 f., 131 f.
Holistic approach   59, 63 f., 72 f., 203, 213
Holistic process   58
Holistic renewal   58
Horizontal collaboration   52, 54
Horizontal integration   55, 73, 78, 96
Hosmer-Lemeshow test   162
Housing communities   155, 178
Housing cooperatives   155, 178, 196

Implementing body   207
Increasing returns   14, 21 f., 40, 72
Increasing returns to scale   1, 14, 18, 23, 26
Information spill-overs   18, 22
Inner-city areas   1, 8, 39 f., 43 f., 46, 50, 57, 59 f., 64, 66, 71, 73, 91, 94, 96–98, 154, 212 f.
Integrated approach   4, 6, 53–55, 57, 60, 63 f., 68–70, 92–94, 97 f., 101–103, 106 f., 113, 138, 170, 213 f.
Integrated place-based approach   8, 53 f.
Integrated plan for sustainable urban development   103, 111, 113, 141, 174
Integrated urban development   91–93, 102, 105–107, 180, 196, 214
Integrated urban planning   4
Integrated urban regeneration   6, 70 f., 75, 87 f., 91–93, 95, 97 f., 104–106, 133, 199, 206, 213, 215, 217
Integrated urban regeneration programme   68, 70 f., 79, 94, 96, 214
Interlinked deprivations   2
Internal returns to scale   19 f.
Intervention mechanism   7
Intra-urban development patterns   42
Intra-urban disparities   2
Intra-urban inequalities   2

"Joined-up" holistic approach   63, 213

Kruskal-Wallis rank sum test   157, 172,

Labour market   2 f., 20, 24, 42, 44 f., 68, 83, 106, 154, 181, 211
Labour market adjustment mechanism   34

Labour productivity   14
Labour's marginal product   24 f.
Land rents   21 f., 33
Land use planning   49, 60, 62, 69
Latent variables   145, 147
Leipzig charter   92, 105
Leverage effect   5, 109, 136, 196, 209
Leveraging   4, 80, 83, 108
Liability relief   80
Lifelong operating costs   168
Living standards   2, 50, 80, 82
Loan funds   111, 125
Localisation economies   19 f.
localisation economies   20
Local skilled labour pool   18
Logical reasoning   8
Logistic regression   8, 143, 159 f., 162
Logit model   160
Long-run equilibrium   33 f.
Low work-intensity households   2

Managing authorities   109, 113, 118, 124, 129, 133, 135, 200–202, 207, 214
Marginal private cost   17
Marginal social cost   16
Market failures   4, 18, 26, 34 f., 37–39, 41, 49, 51, 63, 68 f., 72, 109, 154, 156, 167, 178, 181, 196 f., 199, 209, 212, 215 f.
Market forces   1, 8, 13 f., 18, 23, 29, 32, 35, 37, 51, 58, 64, 72, 75, 80, 97, 211 f., 216
Market incentives   62, 80
Market mechanisms   11, 49, 63, 109, 211, 213
Market rivalry   36
Market-size effects   21
Maximum likelihood   144, 147
Mezzanine capital   121
Modelling   8, 87–89
Model of integrated urban regeneration   6, 8, 90, 213 f.
Multi-agency governance   59, 71, 213
Multi-agency partnerships   73
Multi-level cooperation   62
Multi-level governance   4, 54 f., 78, 91 f., 96
Multi-level partnerships   54
Multiple deprivation   55
Multiplier effects   62

Multivariate analysis   145
Municipal authority   52

Nagelkerke pseudo-R^2 162
Natural monopolies   17
Negative externalities   1, 16, 23 f., 26, 36 f., 40, 72, 103, 212
Net social welfare loss   35
Net value added   195
New economic geography   21, 32
New Leipzig Charter   96, 98, 213
Non-parametric statistical hypothesis tests   8
Non-traded local inputs   18
Non-transferability   17

Observation participatory method   8
Odds ratio   144, 159, 160, 162
One-size-fits-all   53, 57, 73
Ontological approach   88
Operational programmes   93, 101–103, 107, 111, 115, 117 f., 121, 123, 126–129, 131, 206
Organic systems   11 f., 51
Out-of-pocket costs   36, 38

Participatory observation method   140
Participatory political institutions   54
Passive beneficiaries   202
Physical redesign   85
Physical upgrading   55, 82
Place-based approaches   92
Policy intensity   182
Pollution   1, 23 f., 36 f., 39, 50, 103, 211 f.
Polycentric urban system   55, 93, 138
Polychoric correlation   147
Population at risk of poverty   2
Positive externalities   1, 16 f., 72, 85, 124, 171 f., 180, 195, 197, 209, 215
Post-hoc Dunn's multiple comparison test   157
Potential impacts values   182
Price mechanism   16 f., 43
Price system   16
Principal component analysis   8, 147, 170
Private disutility   36

Profitability 40, 117, 127, 135, 139, 142, 153, 160, 168, 170, 177 f., 185, 195 f., 209
Progressive degradation 2
Property tax abatements 80
Public–private partnerships 5, 110 f., 128
Public procurement 111 f.
Public realm 86
Pull motives 12
Pure external diseconomies 21 f.
Pure external economies 21 f.

Quality of life 1 f., 12, 34 f., 57 f., 62, 71, 86, 88, 97 f., 103, 113, 168, 212

Realistic evaluation 8
Reclamation 59, 66
Reconstruction 59, 181, 184
Recovery 61, 85
Regeneration scheme 74, 76, 79, 81, 83, 85, 87
Regression model 144, 162
Regulatory relief 80
Rehabilitation 59, 102, 174, 177
Remediation tax credits 80
Renewable financial model 135
Renewal 55, 59 f., 65, 72, 113, 131, 181
Renovation 59, 180, 183
Repayability 139, 150, 152 f., 180, 185, 190 f., 195
Repayable financial instruments 8, 111
Repayable instruments 135 f.
Repayable model 4
Repayment assistance 199
Resilience 82
Restoration 37, 59–63, 84, 154
Restructuring, 59
Return flows 135
Return on investment 159 f., 177 f., 196
Revenue-generating project 142, 153, 172, 174–176, 194 f.
Revolving financing model 135
Revolving financing system 4
Revolving funding instrument 5
Revolving investment funds 4
Revolving mechanism 107, 141, 196, 200
Ring-fencing 94

Run-down urban areas 50, 56 f., 59, 68, 101, 104, 204

Scalar optimisation 143
Self-balancing market mechanism 16
Self-financing capacity 136, 175, 195
Self-reinforcing mechanism 14
Separate neighbourhoods 45
Set-aside urban zones 43
Settlement patterns 28, 33
Social disparities 2, 41 f.
Social overhead capital 21, 46
Social polarisation 44, 60, 84
Social sustainability 59
Social tensions 1, 103
Socio-economic transformation 6, 46, 72
Socio-spatial segregation 3, 44
Spatial economic general equilibrium 21
Spatial hierarchy 29, 207
Spatially hierarchical organisation 29 f., 212
Spatially uneven distribution 13
Spatial pattern 14, 21, 32, 34, 154, 186
Spatial polarisation 2
Spatial variations 2
Spill-over effects 62
Sprawl-generating market failures 40
Standard deviational ellipse 8, 150, 186
State-aid 121, 126, 128
Structural approach 88 f.
Suburbanisation 3
Supplementary industries 14
Supply-driven factors 204
Supply-push theories 204
Sustainable development 51 f., 58–60, 76, 96, 99 f., 107, 138
Sustainable funding 4, 209, 215
Sustainable integrated urban development 92, 105
Sustainable urban development 3 f., 6, 49, 59, 87, 91–93, 96, 101–104, 123, 133, 135, 137 f., 141, 144–146, 167, 170–172, 176, 180, 195–197, 204, 209, 214–216
Sustainable urban regeneration 5, 60, 67, 84, 94
Systemic approach 8, 87 f., 213
Systems thinking 87, 90 f.

Target-oriented tendency 64
TARGET_TIA 8, 148 f.
Territorial cohesion 6, 52, 54 f., 103, 107, 138 f., 181, 185, 197, 207, 214, 216
Territorial impact assessment 8, 141, 148
Territorial impacts indicator 181
Territorial integration 55, 73, 96, 138, 214
Thick labour markets 21
Toledo Declaration 91, 106
Top-down approach 53, 76
Trading "nodes" 15
Traffic congestion 1, 22–24, 36, 39, 103, 212
Triangulation 140
Tri-city 143, 186

Unemployment 2, 41, 45 f., 63, 82, 97, 180 f., 213
Unpriced agglomeration diseconomies 26
Upper Silesian conurbation 143, 186
URBACT network 104
Urban Acquis 92, 105
Urban Agenda 64, 98, 213
URBAN Community Initiative 101
Urban concentration 11, 23, 42, 211
Urban consumption opportunities 19
Urban decay 43, 47, 55, 65, 73, 88, 91, 93, 104, 139
Urban decline 40 f., 56, 58, 65, 74, 80
Urban deprivation 2, 77, 180 f.
Urban deterioration 46 f., 51, 56, 199, 212
Urban development funds 7, 106, 111, 117 f., 121, 123 f., 126 f., 140, 159
Urban economics 8, 11, 13, 18, 21
Urban economies 18, 82
Urban economy 13, 16 f., 41
Urban hierarchy 29, 31, 33 f., 65

Urbanisation 11–14, 16, 24–26, 31 f., 35, 37, 47, 51 f., 55, 63, 65, 72, 144, 211
Urbanisation economies 19 f., 28
Urban planning 53, 71, 106, 146, 149
Urban policy 6, 8, 49, 51–53, 56, 69 f., 72, 74, 84, 91, 93, 98 f., 103–107, 116, 133, 138, 184, 202 f., 213
Urban regeneration 4, 6, 8, 51, 56–64, 66, 68–81, 83–91, 93 f., 96–98, 101, 104–106, 125, 130 f., 133, 138, 149, 180, 184, 204 f., 212–214, 217
Urban sensibility 182
Urban settlements 1 f.
Urban space 2 f., 58, 60, 69
Urban spatial master plans 49, 62
Urban sprawl 1, 24, 37, 39 f., 43, 49 f., 55, 64, 102 f., 139, 212 f.
Urban strategic planning 52
Urban system 11 f., 28–31, 34, 36, 40, 47, 61, 65, 207, 211 f.
Urban transformation 49 f., 56 f., 64, 75, 81, 94
Urban transition 3

Value-weight ratio 27
Venture capital fund 111
Vertical collaboration 52, 54
Vertical integration 55, 73, 96
Viability 61, 71, 80, 110, 153, 167, 199, 209

Waivers of development fees 80
Weighting 147
Well-being 3, 6, 14, 36, 68, 85, 99, 103
Wilcoxon rank sum test 143, 157 f.

Zoning 34, 50, 62